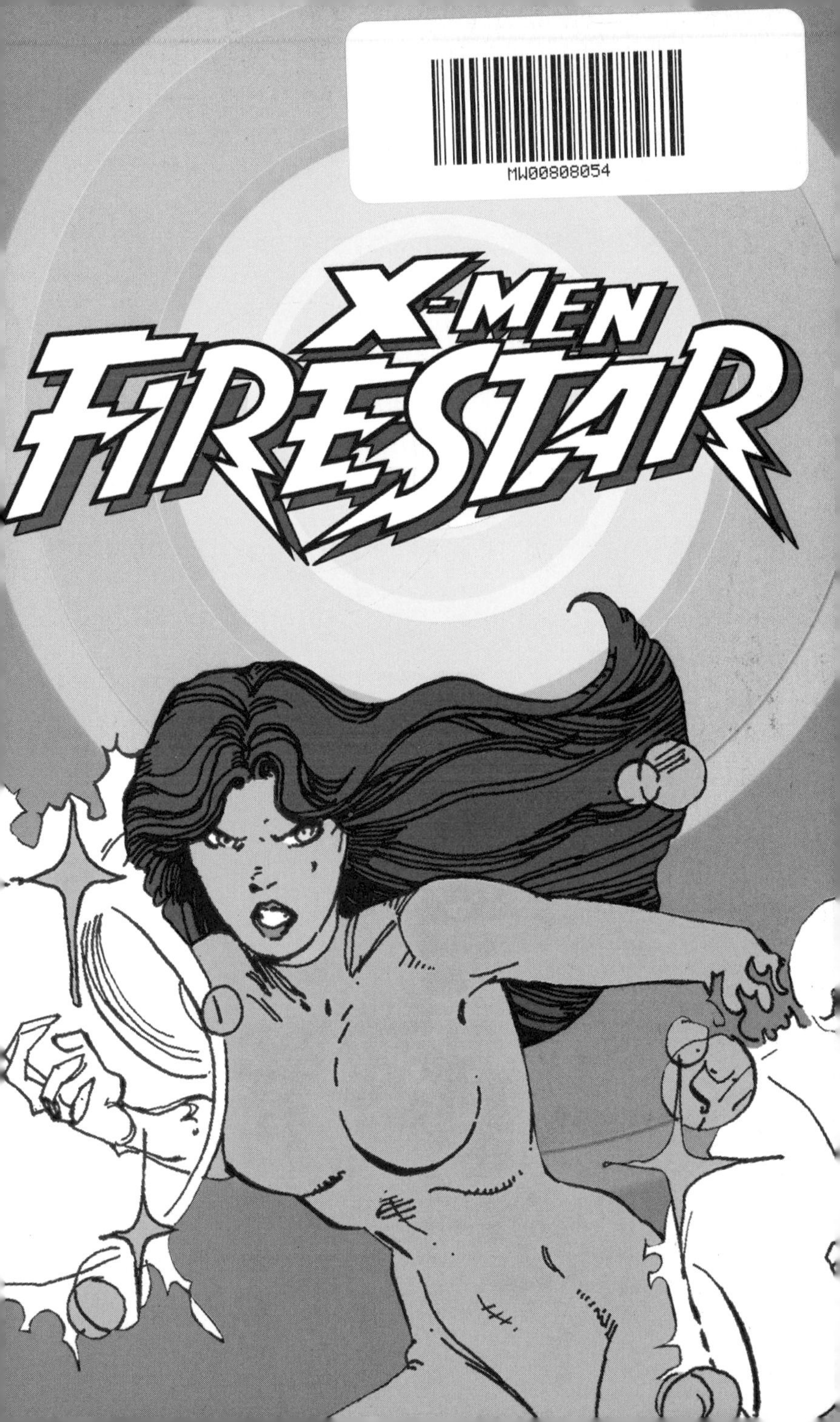
X-MEN
FIRESTAR

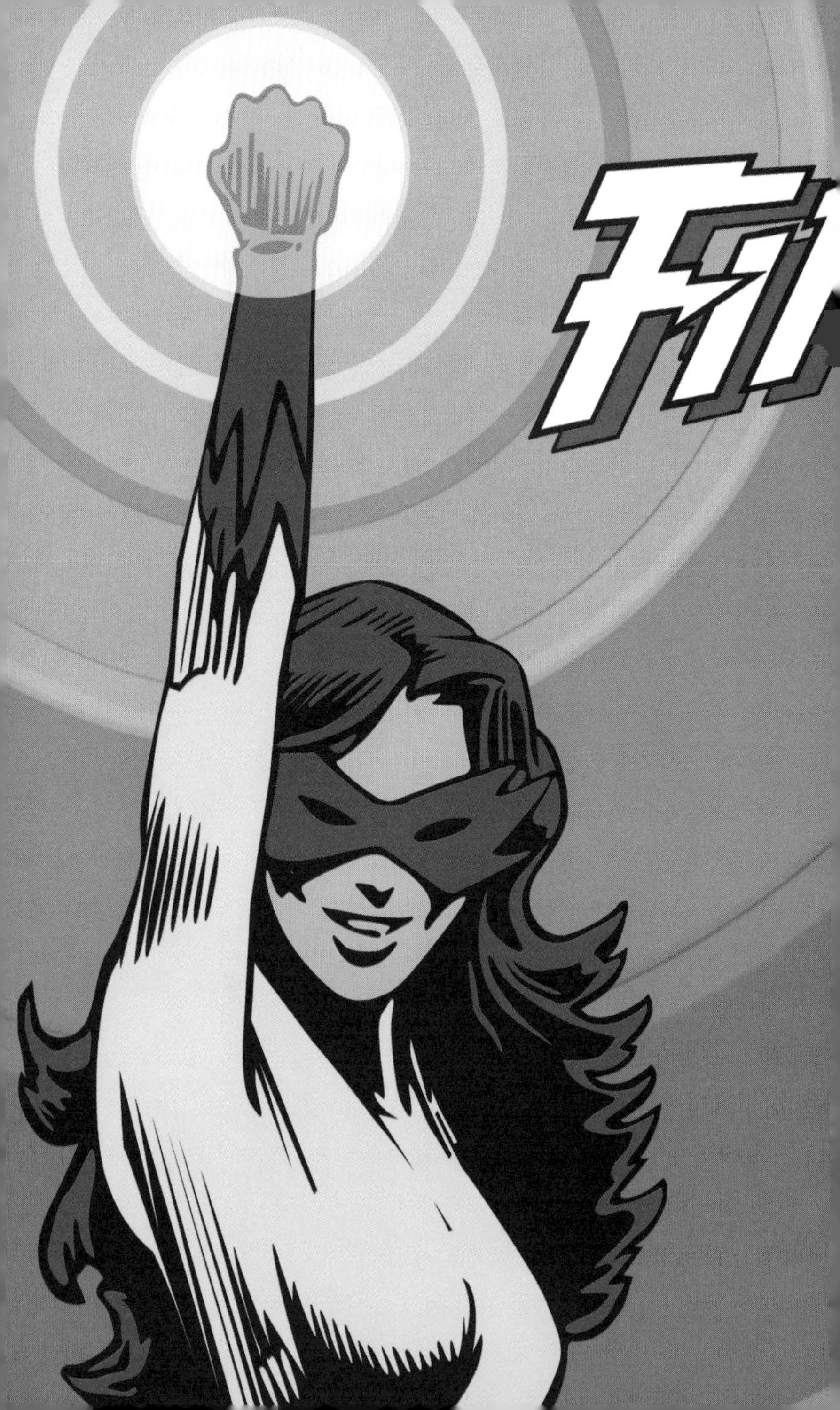

Writer: **Tom DeFalco**
Penciler: **Mary Wilshire**
Inkers: **Steve Leiloha & Bob Wiacek**
Colors: **Daina Graziunis**
Letters: **Tom Orzechowski & L. Lois Buhalis**
Editor: **Ann Nocenti**

Front Cover Art: **Barry Windsor-Smith**
Front Cover Colors: **Tom Smith**
Back Cover Art: **Mary Wilshire**

Collection Editor: **Mark D. Beazley**
Assistant Editor: **Michael Short**
Associate Editor: **Jennifer Grünwald**
Senior Editor, Special Projects: **Jeff Youngquist**
Vice President of Sales: **David Gabriel**
Production & Color Reconstruction: **Jerron Quality Color**
Book Designer: **Jhonson Eteng**
Vice President of Creative: **Tom Marvelli**

Editor-in-Chief: **Joe Quesada**
Publisher: **Dan Buckley**

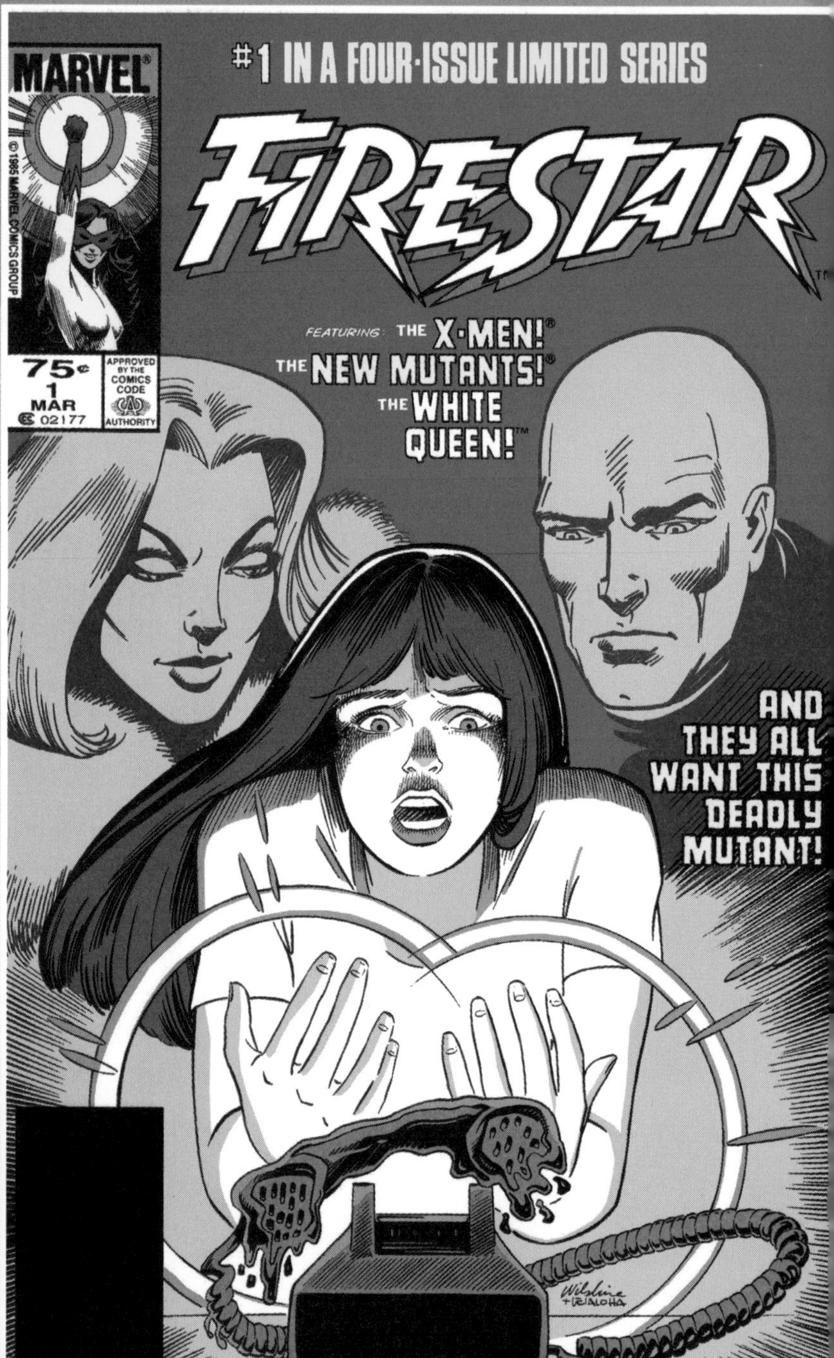
MARVEL
© 1985 MARVEL COMICS GROUP
75¢
1
MAR
02177
APPROVED BY THE COMICS CODE AUTHORITY
#1 IN A FOUR-ISSUE LIMITED SERIES
FIRESTAR
FEATURING: THE X-MEN!
THE NEW MUTANTS!
THE WHITE QUEEN!
AND THEY ALL WANT THIS DEADLY MUTANT!

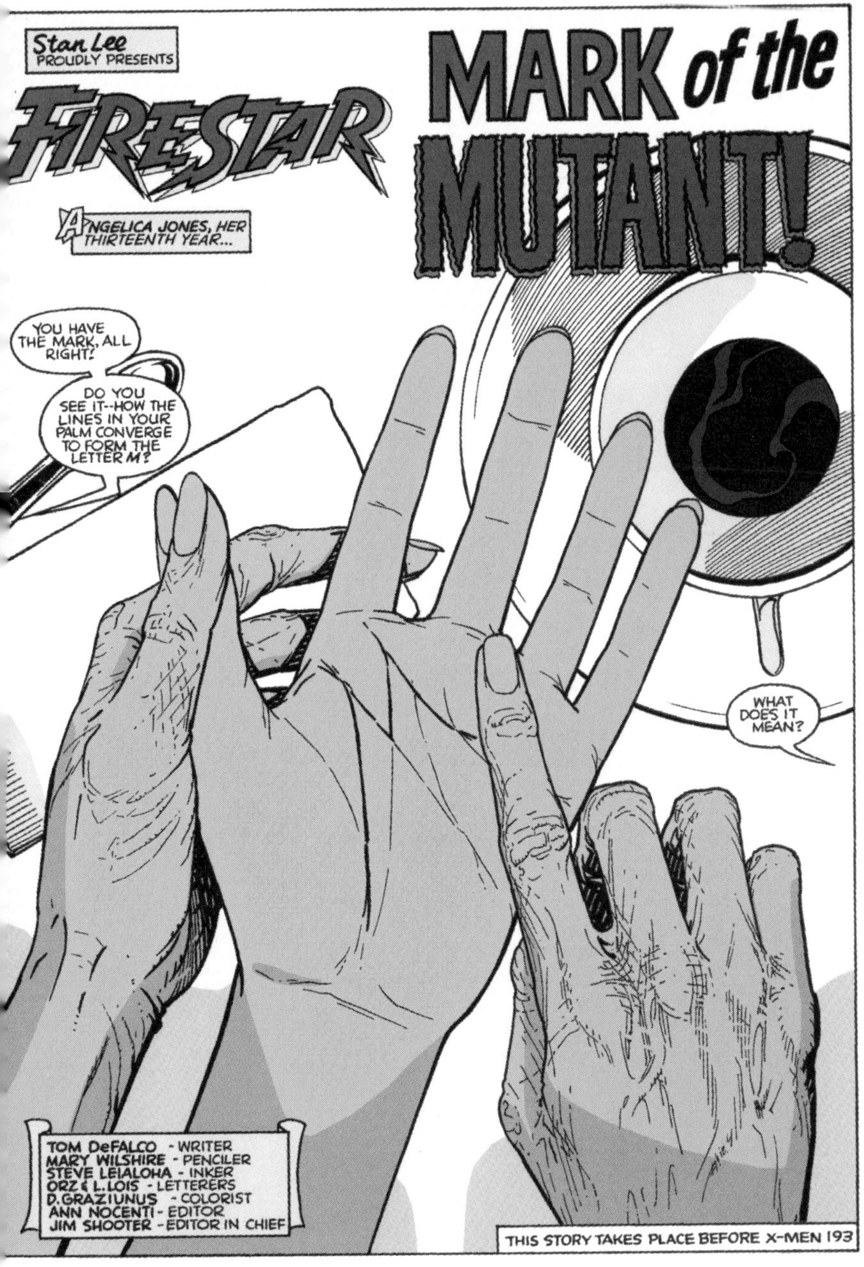
Stan Lee PROUDLY PRESENTS
FIRESTAR
MARK of the MUTANT!
ANGELICA JONES, HER THIRTEENTH YEAR...
YOU HAVE THE MARK, ALL RIGHT!
DO YOU SEE IT--HOW THE LINES IN YOUR PALM CONVERGE TO FORM THE LETTER M?
WHAT DOES IT MEAN?
TOM DeFALCO - WRITER
MARY WILSHIRE - PENCILER
STEVE LEIALOHA - INKER
ORZ & L. LOIS - LETTERERS
D. GRAZIUNUS - COLORIST
ANN NOCENTI - EDITOR
JIM SHOOTER - EDITOR IN CHIEF
THIS STORY TAKES PLACE BEFORE X-MEN 193

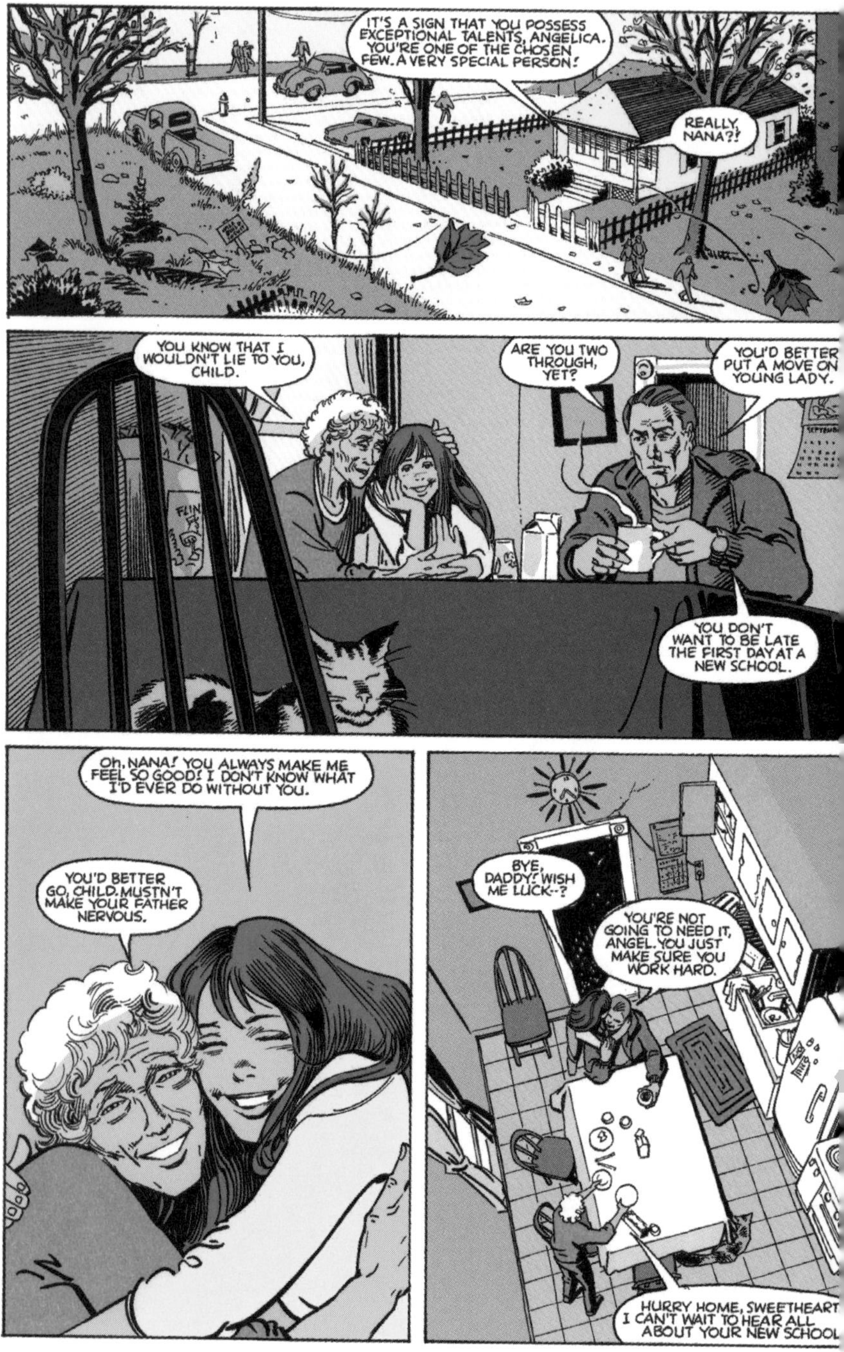
IT'S A SIGN THAT YOU POSSESS EXCEPTIONAL TALENTS, ANGELICA. YOU'RE ONE OF THE CHOSEN FEW. A VERY SPECIAL PERSON!
REALLY, NANA?!
YOU KNOW THAT I WOULDN'T LIE TO YOU, CHILD.
ARE YOU TWO THROUGH, YET?
YOU'D BETTER PUT A MOVE ON YOUNG LADY.
YOU DON'T WANT TO BE LATE THE FIRST DAY AT A NEW SCHOOL.
Oh, NANA! YOU ALWAYS MAKE ME FEEL SO GOOD! I DON'T KNOW WHAT I'D EVER DO WITHOUT YOU.
YOU'D BETTER GO, CHILD. MUSTN'T MAKE YOUR FATHER NERVOUS.
BYE, DADDY! WISH ME LUCK--?
YOU'RE NOT GOING TO NEED IT, ANGEL. YOU JUST MAKE SURE YOU WORK HARD.
HURRY HOME, SWEETHEART I CAN'T WAIT TO HEAR ALL ABOUT YOUR NEW SCHOOL

SLAM

Y'KNOW, MA, I REALLY WISH YOU WOULDN'T MAKE SUCH A FUSS OVER ANGELICA. IT ISN'T RIGHT TO TELL HER SHE'S SO SPECIAL--WHEN SHE'S ONLY AN AVERAGE STUDENT.

WHY NOT? WHAT'S THE HARM IN IT?

THE CHILD COULD USE SOME ENCOURAGEMENT. SHE'S VERY INTELLIGENT-- AND IT ISN'T HER FAULT THAT SHE LOST HER MOTHER--OR THAT SHE'S CONSTANTLY MOVING FROM SCHOOL TO SCHOOL BECAUSE OF YOUR JOB!

GET OFF MY BACK, MA! YOU KNOW HOW MUCH I HATE TO KEEP UPROOTING THE FAMILY, BUT I'VE GOT TO GO WHERE THERE'S WORK...

KNOW, SON, AND DON'T MEAN TO CRITICIZE. IT'S JUST THAT A SENSITIVE GIRL LIKE ANGELICA NEEDS...

UNN

MA--!

I--I'M ALL RIGHT, BARTHOLOMEW!

JUST GIVE ME A SECOND TO CATCH MY BREATH...

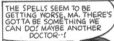

THE SPELLS SEEM TO BE GETTING WORSE, MA. THERE'S GOTTA BE SOMETHING WE CAN DO! MAYBE ANOTHER DOCTOR--!

NO, SON! WE'VE ALREADY WASTED ENOUGH MONEY ON DOCTORS.

THERE ISN'T ANYTHING THEY CAN DO FOR ME. I'M JUST AN OLD WOMAN WHO'S STARTING TO WEAR OUT.

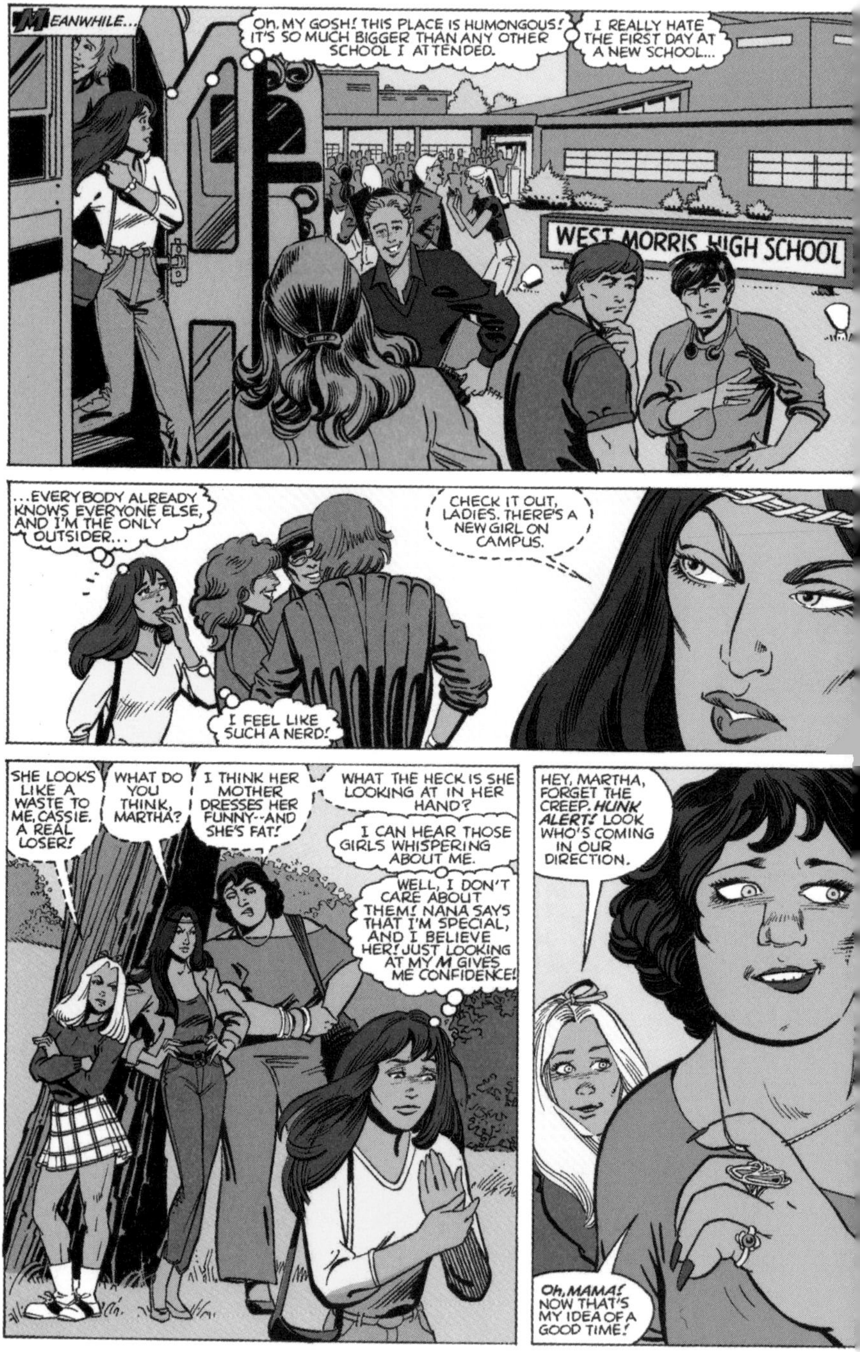
MEANWHILE...
Oh, MY GOSH! THIS PLACE IS HUMONGOUS! IT'S SO MUCH BIGGER THAN ANY OTHER SCHOOL I ATTENDED.
I REALLY HATE THE FIRST DAY AT A NEW SCHOOL...
WEST MORRIS HIGH SCHOOL
...EVERYBODY ALREADY KNOWS EVERYONE ELSE, AND I'M THE ONLY OUTSIDER...
CHECK IT OUT, LADIES. THERE'S A NEW GIRL ON CAMPUS.
I FEEL LIKE SUCH A NERD!
SHE LOOKS LIKE A WASTE TO ME, CASSIE. A REAL LOSER!
WHAT DO YOU THINK, MARTHA?
I THINK HER MOTHER DRESSES HER FUNNY--AND SHE'S FAT!
WHAT THE HECK IS SHE LOOKING AT IN HER HAND?
I CAN HEAR THOSE GIRLS WHISPERING ABOUT ME.
WELL, I DON'T CARE ABOUT THEM! NANA SAYS THAT I'M SPECIAL, AND I BELIEVE HER! JUST LOOKING AT MY M GIVES ME CONFIDENCE!
HEY, MARTHA, FORGET THE CREEP. HUNK ALERT! LOOK WHO'S COMING IN OUR DIRECTION.
Oh, MAMA! NOW THAT'S MY IDEA OF A GOOD TIME!

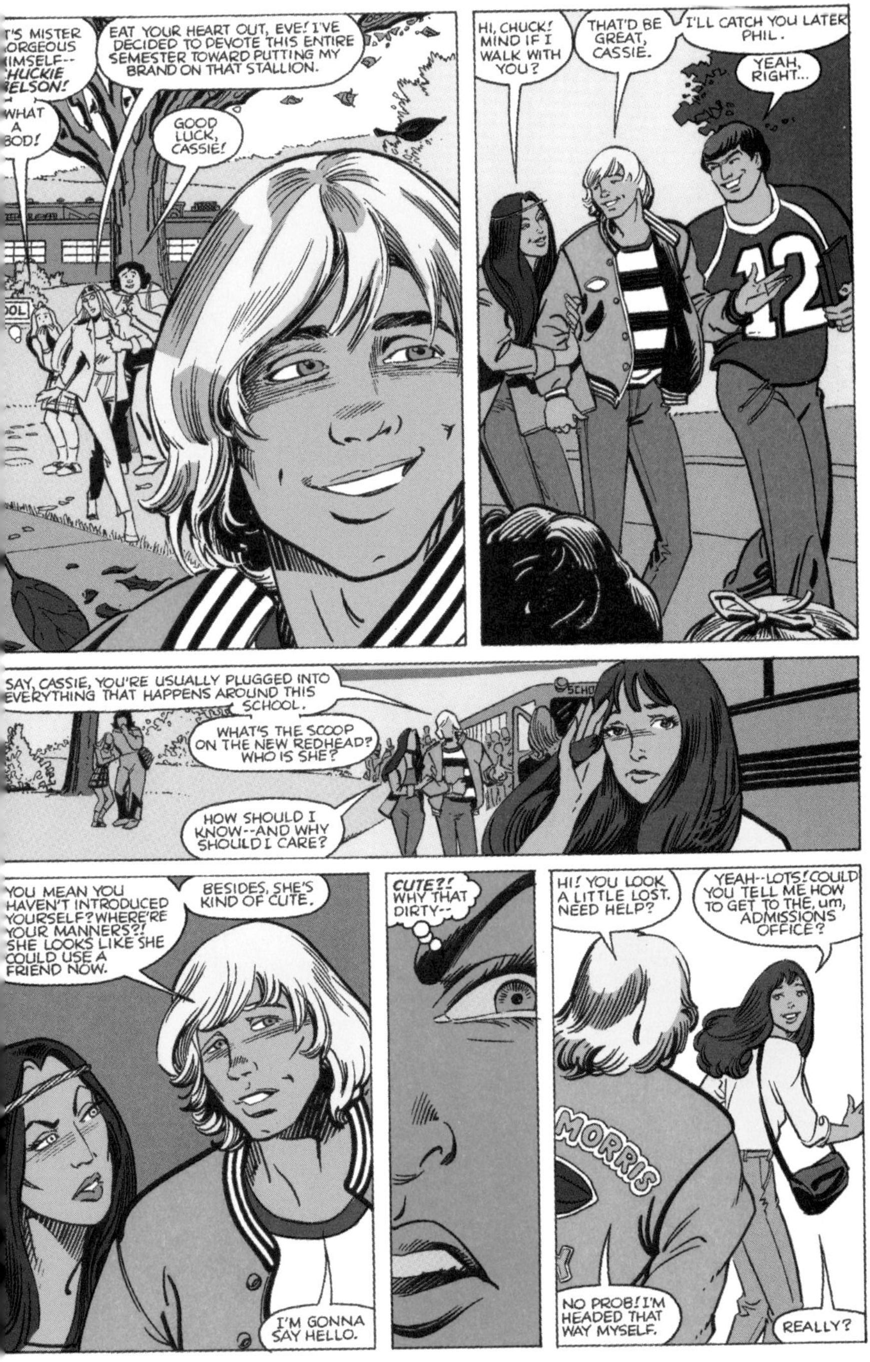

T'S MISTER ORGEOUS IMSELF-- HUCKIE ELSON!
WHAT A BOD!
EAT YOUR HEART OUT, EVE! I'VE DECIDED TO DEVOTE THIS ENTIRE SEMESTER TOWARD PUTTING MY BRAND ON THAT STALLION.
GOOD LUCK, CASSIE!
HI, CHUCK! MIND IF I WALK WITH YOU?
THAT'D BE GREAT, CASSIE.
I'LL CATCH YOU LATER PHIL.
YEAH, RIGHT...
12
SAY, CASSIE, YOU'RE USUALLY PLUGGED INTO EVERYTHING THAT HAPPENS AROUND THIS SCHOOL.
WHAT'S THE SCOOP ON THE NEW REDHEAD? WHO IS SHE?
HOW SHOULD I KNOW--AND WHY SHOULD I CARE?
YOU MEAN YOU HAVEN'T INTRODUCED YOURSELF? WHERE'RE YOUR MANNERS?! SHE LOOKS LIKE SHE COULD USE A FRIEND NOW.
BESIDES, SHE'S KIND OF CUTE.
I'M GONNA SAY HELLO.
CUTE?! WHY THAT DIRTY--
HI! YOU LOOK A LITTLE LOST. NEED HELP?
YEAH--LOTS! COULD YOU TELL ME HOW TO GET TO THE, um, ADMISSIONS OFFICE?
MORRIS
NO PROB! I'M HEADED THAT WAY MYSELF.
REALLY?

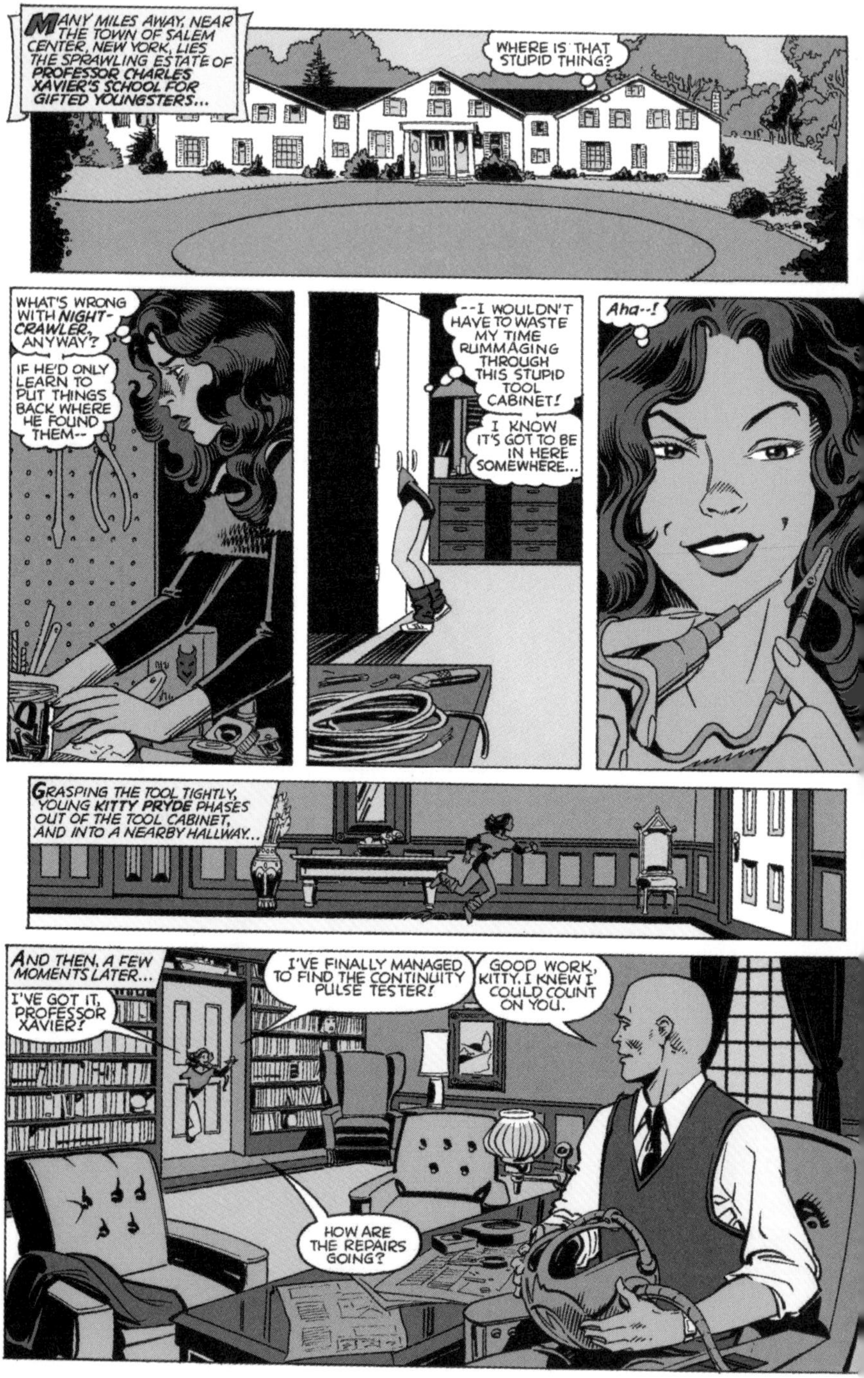
MANY MILES AWAY, NEAR THE TOWN OF SALEM CENTER, NEW YORK, LIES THE SPRAWLING ESTATE OF PROFESSOR CHARLES XAVIER'S SCHOOL FOR GIFTED YOUNGSTERS...
WHERE IS THAT STUPID THING?
WHAT'S WRONG WITH NIGHT-CRAWLER, ANYWAY?
IF HE'D ONLY LEARN TO PUT THINGS BACK WHERE HE FOUND THEM--
--I WOULDN'T HAVE TO WASTE MY TIME RUMMAGING THROUGH THIS STUPID TOOL CABINET!
I KNOW IT'S GOT TO BE IN HERE SOMEWHERE...
Aha--!
GRASPING THE TOOL TIGHTLY, YOUNG KITTY PRYDE PHASES OUT OF THE TOOL CABINET, AND INTO A NEARBY HALLWAY...
AND THEN, A FEW MOMENTS LATER...
I'VE GOT IT, PROFESSOR XAVIER!
I'VE FINALLY MANAGED TO FIND THE CONTINUITY PULSE TESTER!
GOOD WORK, KITTY. I KNEW I COULD COUNT ON YOU.
HOW ARE THE REPAIRS GOING?

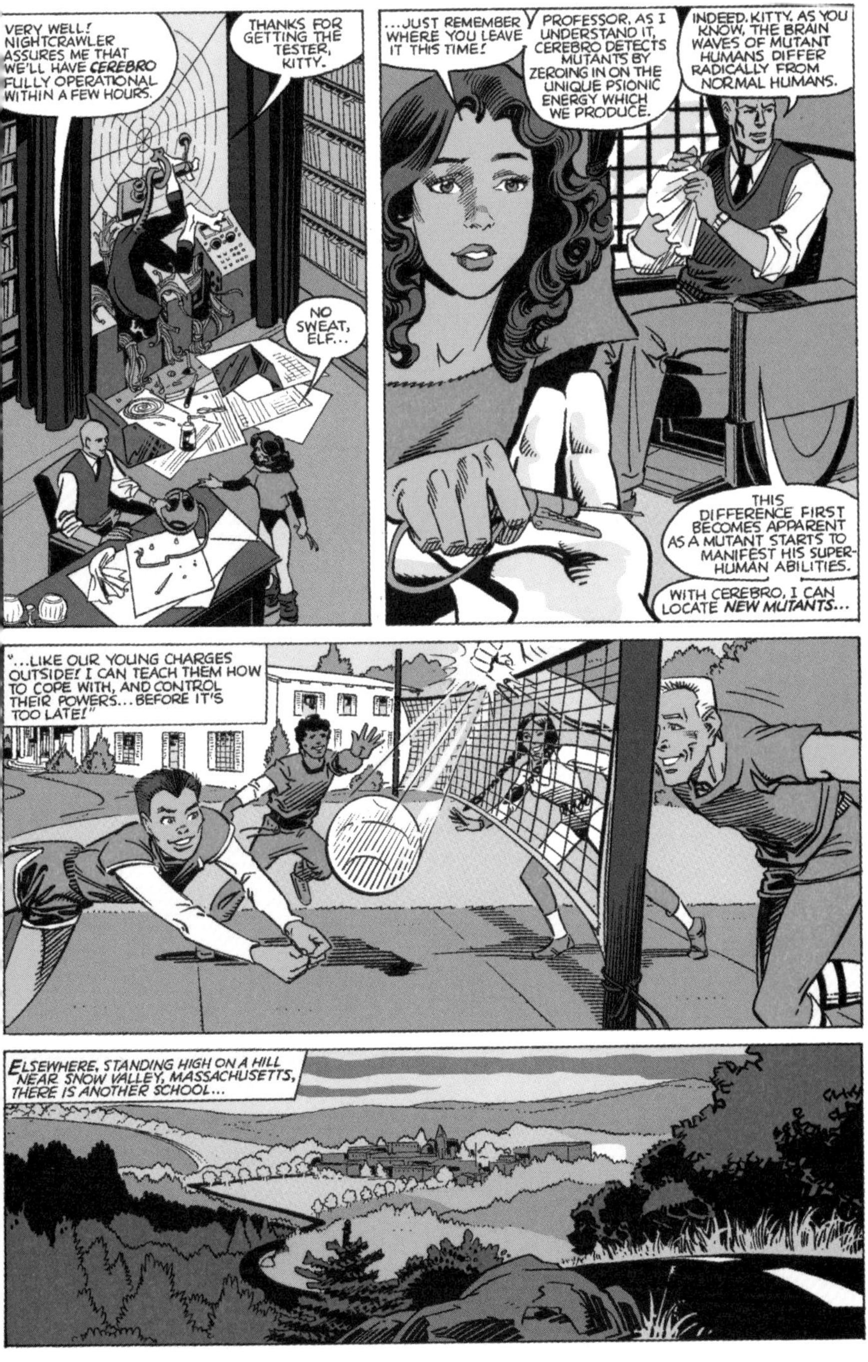
VERY WELL! NIGHTCRAWLER ASSURES ME THAT WE'LL HAVE CEREBRO FULLY OPERATIONAL WITHIN A FEW HOURS.
THANKS FOR GETTING THE TESTER, KITTY.
NO SWEAT, ELF...
...JUST REMEMBER WHERE YOU LEAVE IT THIS TIME!
PROFESSOR, AS I UNDERSTAND IT, CEREBRO DETECTS MUTANTS BY ZEROING IN ON THE UNIQUE PSIONIC ENERGY WHICH WE PRODUCE.
INDEED, KITTY. AS YOU KNOW, THE BRAIN WAVES OF MUTANT HUMANS DIFFER RADICALLY FROM NORMAL HUMANS.
THIS DIFFERENCE FIRST BECOMES APPARENT AS A MUTANT STARTS TO MANIFEST HIS SUPER-HUMAN ABILITIES.
WITH CEREBRO, I CAN LOCATE NEW MUTANTS...
"...LIKE OUR YOUNG CHARGES OUTSIDE! I CAN TEACH THEM HOW TO COPE WITH, AND CONTROL THEIR POWERS... BEFORE IT'S TOO LATE!"
ELSEWHERE, STANDING HIGH ON A HILL NEAR SNOW VALLEY, MASSACHUSETTS, THERE IS ANOTHER SCHOOL...

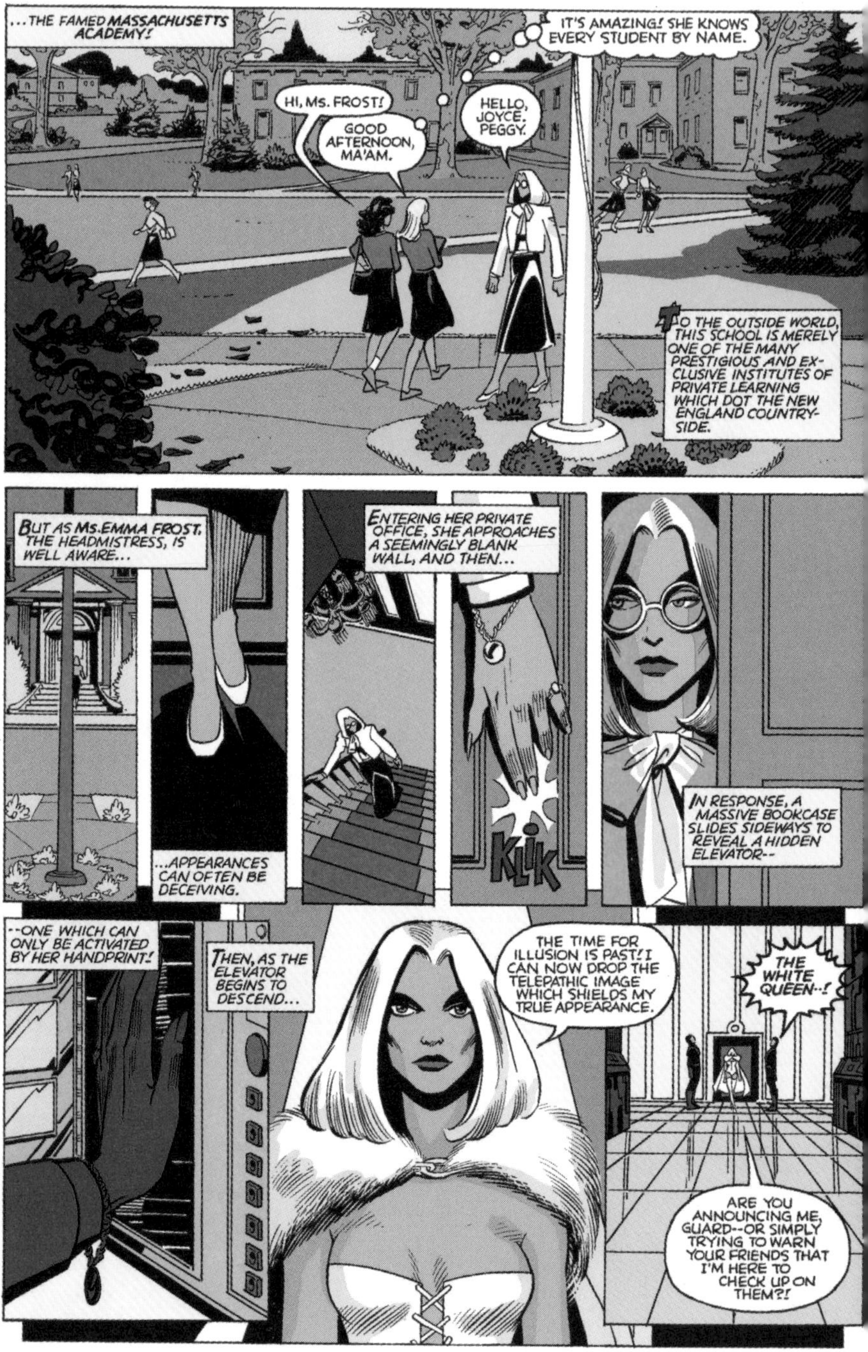
...THE FAMED MASSACHUSETTS ACADEMY!
IT'S AMAZING! SHE KNOWS EVERY STUDENT BY NAME.
HI, Ms. FROST!
GOOD AFTERNOON, MA'AM.
HELLO, JOYCE. PEGGY.
TO THE OUTSIDE WORLD, THIS SCHOOL IS MERELY ONE OF THE MANY PRESTIGIOUS AND EXCLUSIVE INSTITUTES OF PRIVATE LEARNING WHICH DOT THE NEW ENGLAND COUNTRYSIDE.
BUT AS Ms. EMMA FROST, THE HEADMISTRESS, IS WELL AWARE...
...APPEARANCES CAN OFTEN BE DECEIVING.
ENTERING HER PRIVATE OFFICE, SHE APPROACHES A SEEMINGLY BLANK WALL, AND THEN...
KLIK
IN RESPONSE, A MASSIVE BOOKCASE SLIDES SIDEWAYS TO REVEAL A HIDDEN ELEVATOR--
--ONE WHICH CAN ONLY BE ACTIVATED BY HER HANDPRINT!
THEN, AS THE ELEVATOR BEGINS TO DESCEND...
THE TIME FOR ILLUSION IS PAST! I CAN NOW DROP THE TELEPATHIC IMAGE WHICH SHIELDS MY TRUE APPEARANCE.
THE WHITE QUEEN--!
ARE YOU ANNOUNCING ME, GUARD--OR SIMPLY TRYING TO WARN YOUR FRIENDS THAT I'M HERE TO CHECK UP ON THEM?!

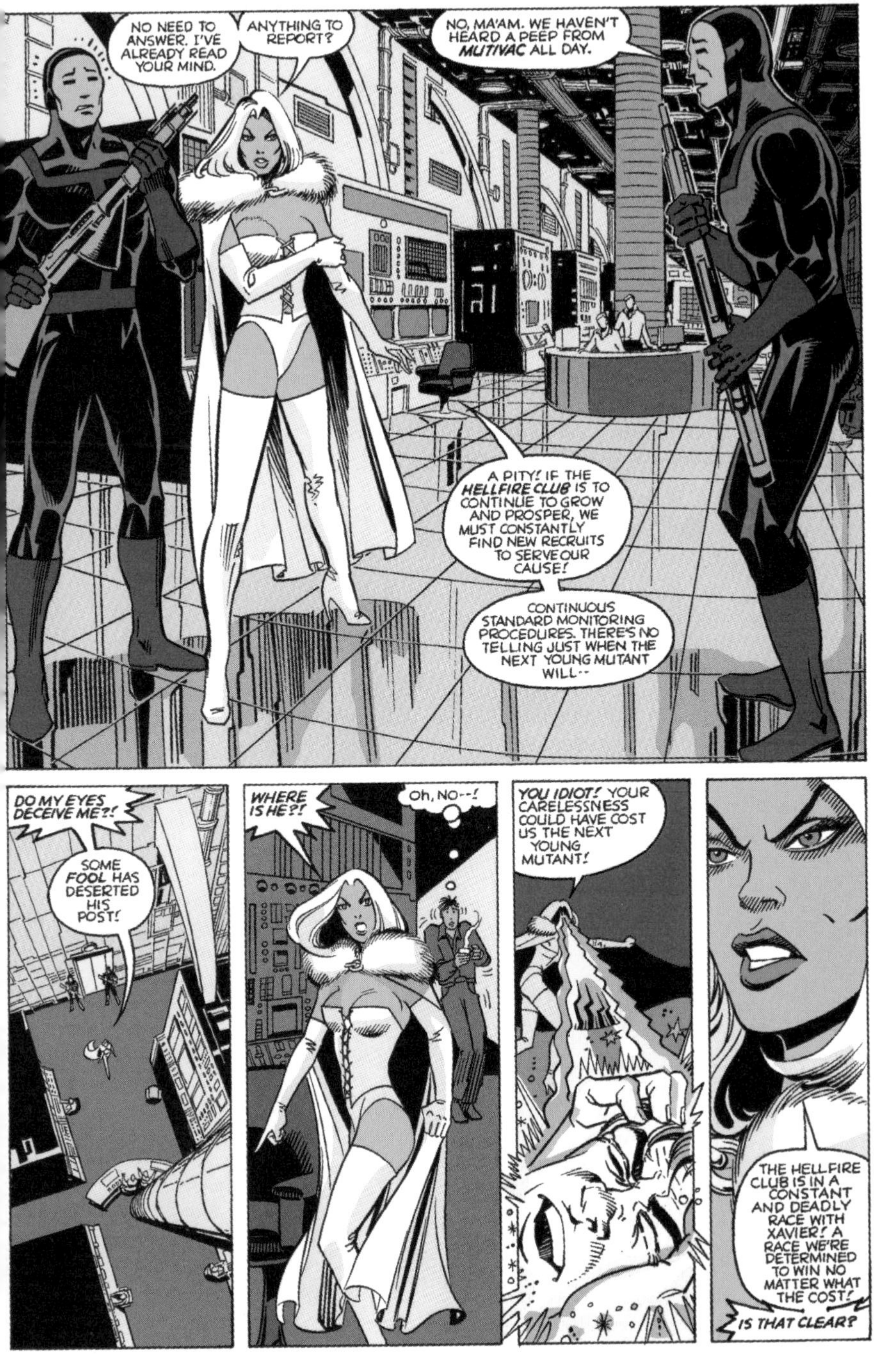
ANYTHING TO REPORT?
NO NEED TO ANSWER. I'VE ALREADY READ YOUR MIND.
NO, MA'AM. WE HAVEN'T HEARD A PEEP FROM MUTIVAC ALL DAY.
A PITY! IF THE HELLFIRE CLUB IS TO CONTINUE TO GROW AND PROSPER, WE MUST CONSTANTLY FIND NEW RECRUITS TO SERVE OUR CAUSE!
CONTINUOUS STANDARD MONITORING PROCEDURES. THERE'S NO TELLING JUST WHEN THE NEXT YOUNG MUTANT WILL--
DO MY EYES DECEIVE ME?!
SOME FOOL HAS DESERTED HIS POST!
WHERE IS HE?!
Oh, NO--!
YOU IDIOT! YOUR CARELESSNESS COULD HAVE COST US THE NEXT YOUNG MUTANT!
THE HELLFIRE CLUB IS IN A CONSTANT AND DEADLY RACE WITH XAVIER! A RACE WE'RE DETERMINED TO WIN NO MATTER WHAT THE COST!
IS THAT CLEAR?

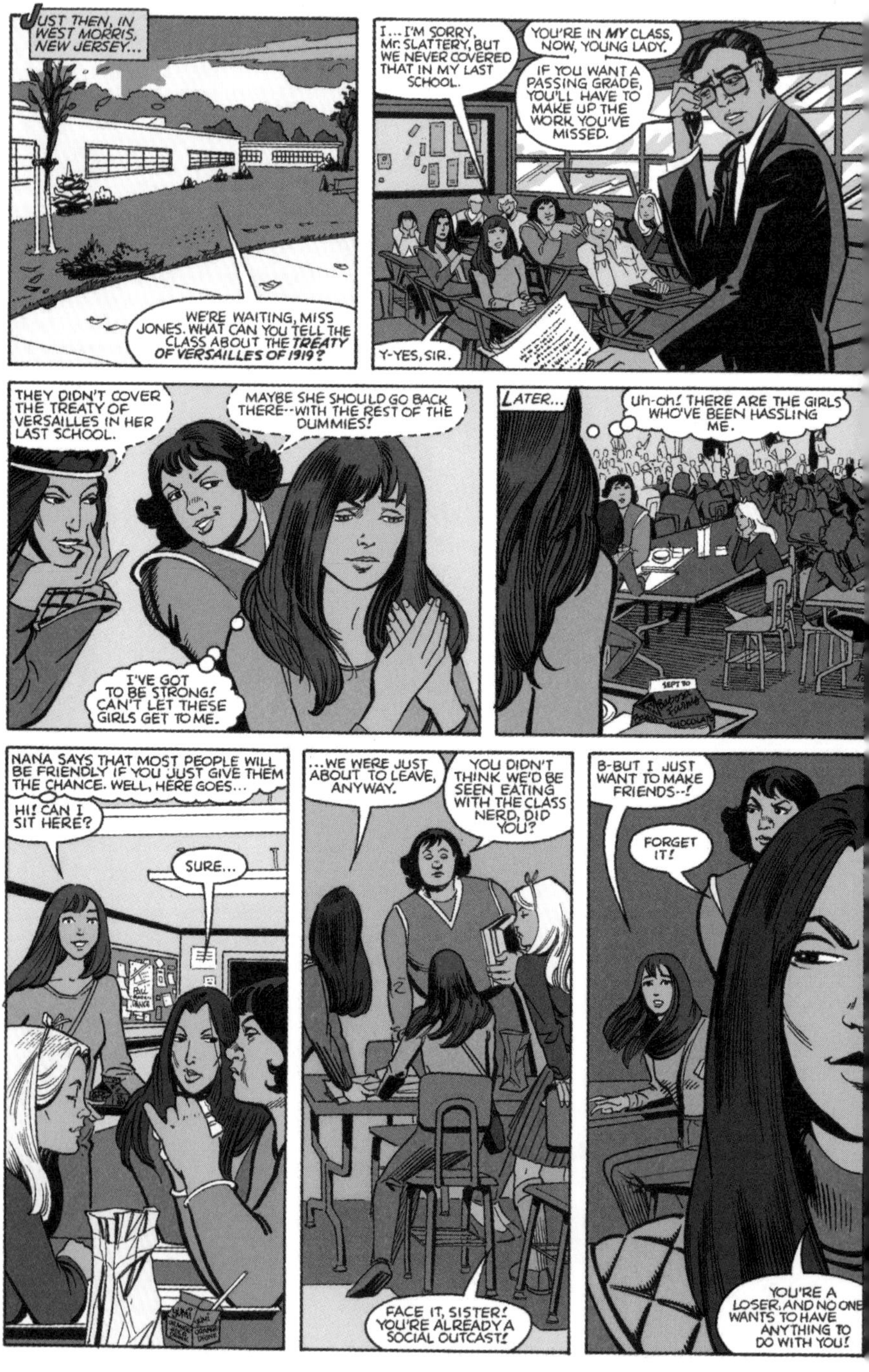
JUST THEN, IN WEST MORRIS, NEW JERSEY...
WE'RE WAITING, MISS JONES. WHAT CAN YOU TELL THE CLASS ABOUT THE TREATY OF VERSAILLES OF 1919?
I... I'M SORRY, Mr. SLATTERY, BUT WE NEVER COVERED THAT IN MY LAST SCHOOL.
YOU'RE IN MY CLASS, NOW, YOUNG LADY.
IF YOU WANT A PASSING GRADE, YOU'LL HAVE TO MAKE UP THE WORK YOU'VE MISSED.
Y-YES, SIR.
THEY DIDN'T COVER THE TREATY OF VERSAILLES IN HER LAST SCHOOL.
MAYBE SHE SHOULD GO BACK THERE--WITH THE REST OF THE DUMMIES!
I'VE GOT TO BE STRONG! CAN'T LET THESE GIRLS GET TO ME.
LATER...
Uh-oh! THERE ARE THE GIRLS WHO'VE BEEN HASSLING ME.
NANA SAYS THAT MOST PEOPLE WILL BE FRIENDLY IF YOU JUST GIVE THEM THE CHANCE. WELL, HERE GOES...
HI! CAN I SIT HERE?
SURE...
...WE WERE JUST ABOUT TO LEAVE, ANYWAY.
YOU DIDN'T THINK WE'D BE SEEN EATING WITH THE CLASS NERD, DID YOU?
FACE IT, SISTER! YOU'RE ALREADY A SOCIAL OUTCAST!
B-BUT I JUST WANT TO MAKE FRIENDS--!
FORGET IT!
YOU'RE A LOSER, AND NO ONE WANTS TO HAVE ANYTHING TO DO WITH YOU!

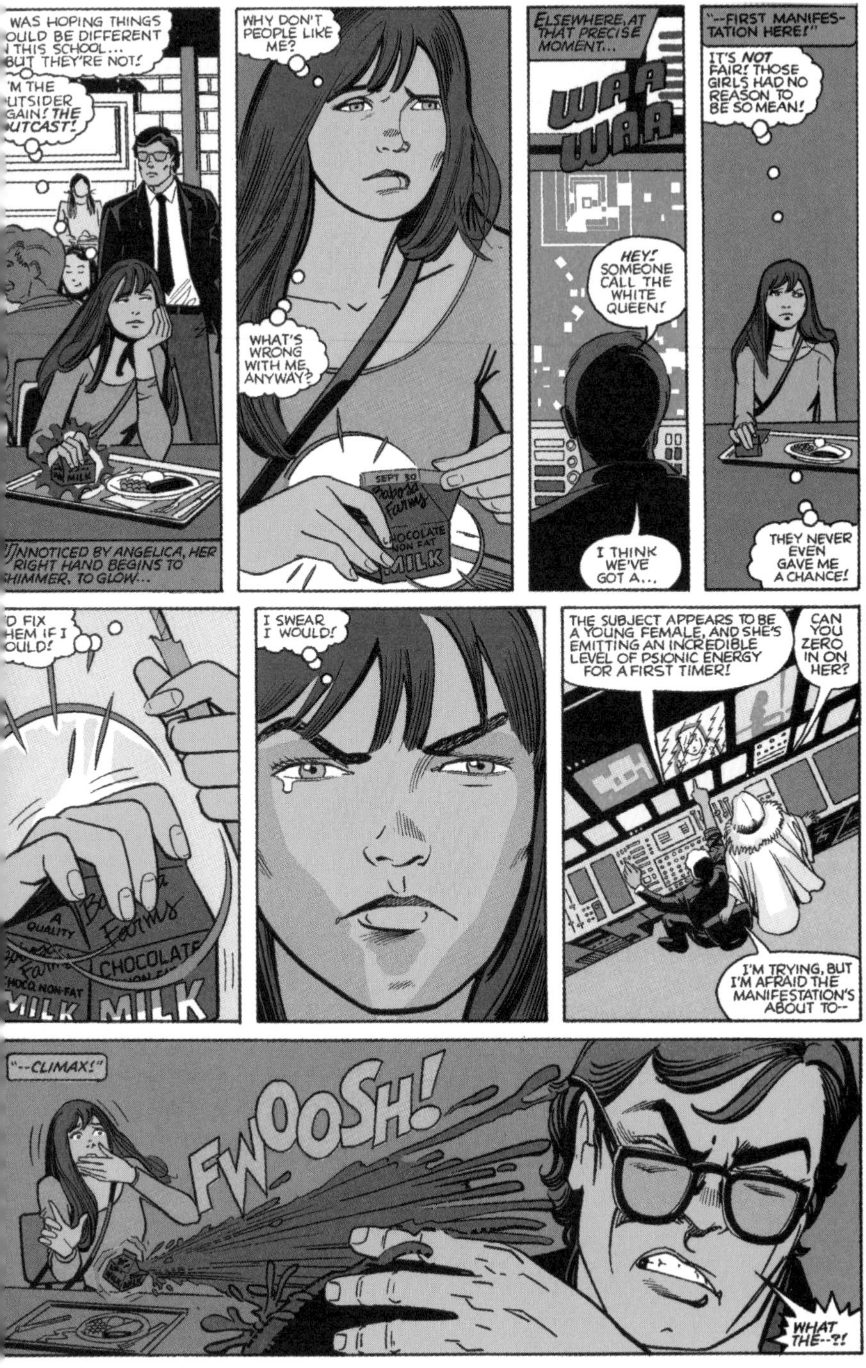
WAS HOPING THINGS OULD BE DIFFERENT N THIS SCHOOL... BUT THEY'RE NOT!
'M THE UTSIDER GAIN! THE UTCAST!
UNNOTICED BY ANGELICA, HER RIGHT HAND BEGINS TO SHIMMER, TO GLOW...
WHY DON'T PEOPLE LIKE ME?
WHAT'S WRONG WITH ME, ANYWAY?
SEPT 30
CHOCOLATE NON FAT MILK
ELSEWHERE, AT THAT PRECISE MOMENT...
WAA WAA
HEY! SOMEONE CALL THE WHITE QUEEN!
I THINK WE'VE GOT A...
"--FIRST MANIFESTATION HERE!"
IT'S NOT FAIR! THOSE GIRLS HAD NO REASON TO BE SO MEAN!
THEY NEVER EVEN GAVE ME A CHANCE!
'D FIX HEM IF I OULD!
A QUALITY
CHOCOLATE
CHOCO. NON-FAT
MILK
MILK
I SWEAR I WOULD!
THE SUBJECT APPEARS TO BE A YOUNG FEMALE, AND SHE'S EMITTING AN INCREDIBLE LEVEL OF PSIONIC ENERGY FOR A FIRST TIMER!
CAN YOU ZERO IN ON HER?
I'M TRYING, BUT I'M AFRAID THE MANIFESTATION'S ABOUT TO--
"--CLIMAX!"
FWOOSH!
WHAT THE--?!

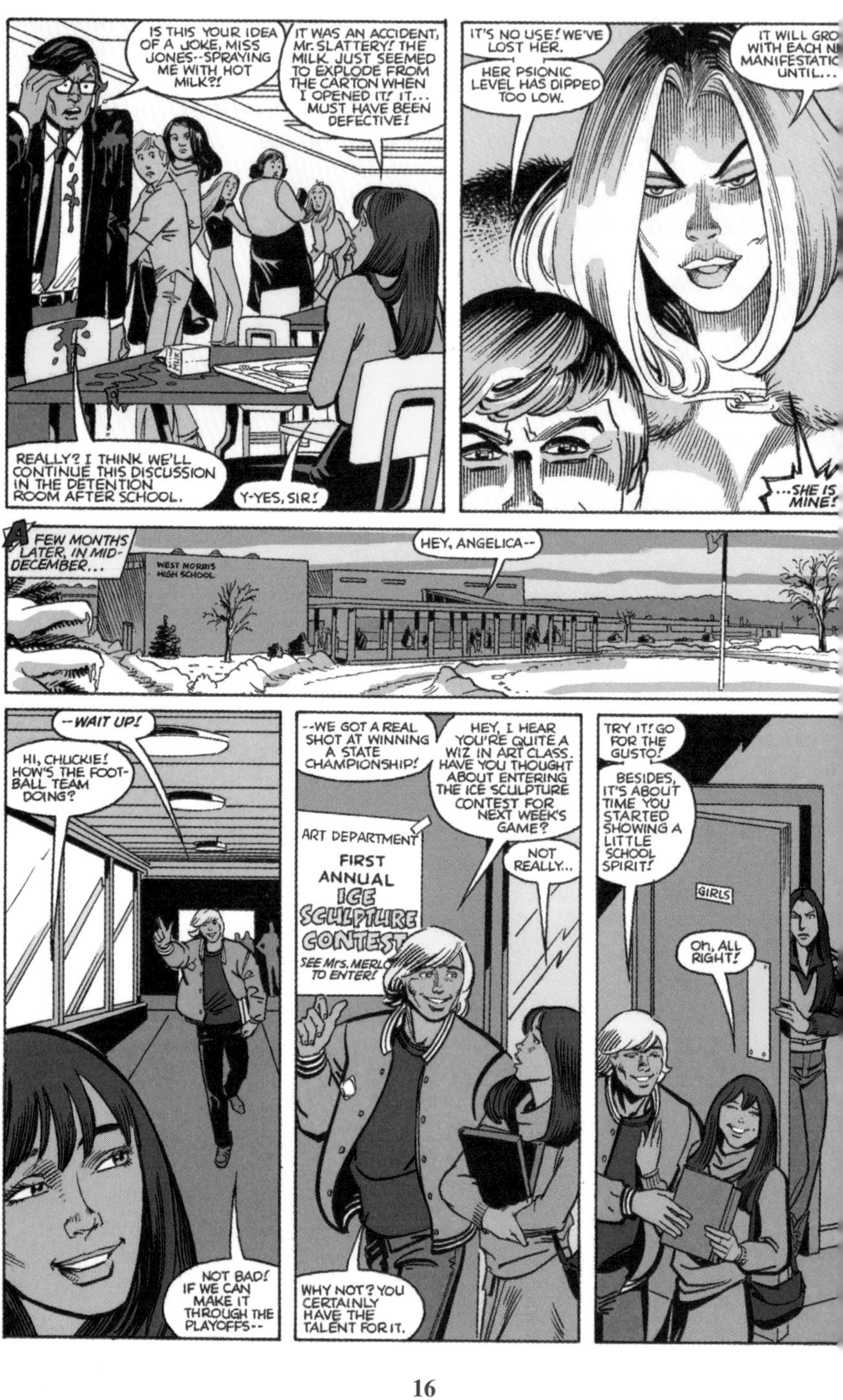
IS THIS YOUR IDEA OF A JOKE, MISS JONES--SPRAYING ME WITH HOT MILK?!
IT WAS AN ACCIDENT, Mr. SLATTERY! THE MILK JUST SEEMED TO EXPLODE FROM THE CARTON WHEN I OPENED IT! IT... MUST HAVE BEEN DEFECTIVE!
MILK
REALLY? I THINK WE'LL CONTINUE THIS DISCUSSION IN THE DETENTION ROOM AFTER SCHOOL.
Y-YES, SIR!
IT'S NO USE! WE'VE LOST HER.
HER PSIONIC LEVEL HAS DIPPED TOO LOW.
IT WILL GRO WITH EACH N MANIFESTATIC UNTIL...
...SHE IS MINE!
A FEW MONTHS LATER, IN MID-DECEMBER...
WEST MORRIS HIGH SCHOOL
HEY, ANGELICA--
--WAIT UP!
HI, CHUCKIE! HOW'S THE FOOTBALL TEAM DOING?
NOT BAD! IF WE CAN MAKE IT THROUGH THE PLAYOFFS--
--WE GOT A REAL SHOT AT WINNING A STATE CHAMPIONSHIP!
HEY, I HEAR YOU'RE QUITE A WIZ IN ART CLASS. HAVE YOU THOUGHT ABOUT ENTERING THE ICE SCULPTURE CONTEST FOR NEXT WEEK'S GAME?
ART DEPARTMENT
FIRST ANNUAL ICE SCULPTURE CONTEST
SEE Mrs. MERLO TO ENTER!
NOT REALLY...
WHY NOT? YOU CERTAINLY HAVE THE TALENT FOR IT.
TRY IT! GO FOR THE GUSTO!
BESIDES, IT'S ABOUT TIME YOU STARTED SHOWING A LITTLE SCHOOL SPIRIT!
GIRLS
Oh, ALL RIGHT!

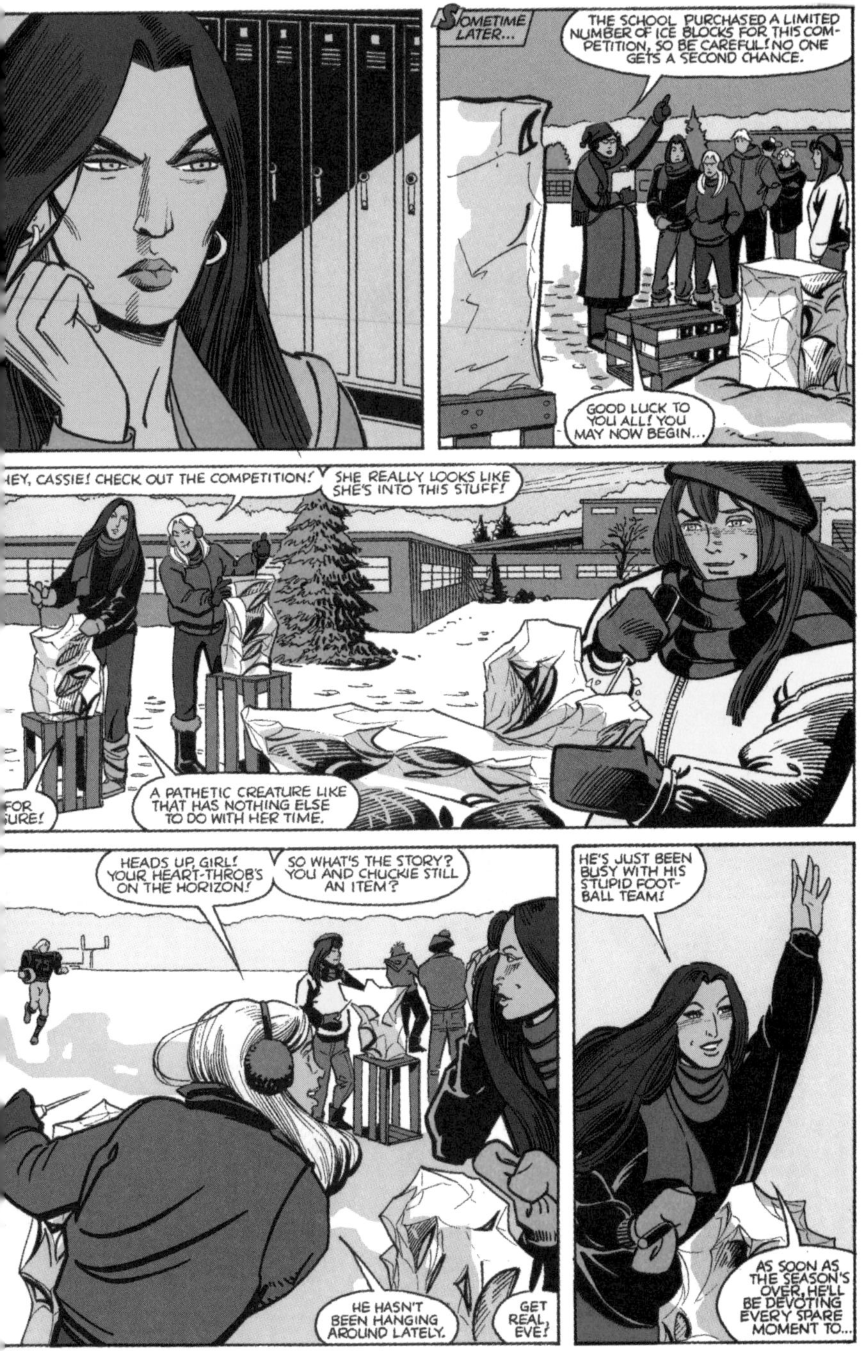
SOMETIME LATER...
THE SCHOOL PURCHASED A LIMITED NUMBER OF ICE BLOCKS FOR THIS COMPETITION, SO BE CAREFUL! NO ONE GETS A SECOND CHANCE.
GOOD LUCK TO YOU ALL! YOU MAY NOW BEGIN...
HEY, CASSIE! CHECK OUT THE COMPETITION!
SHE REALLY LOOKS LIKE SHE'S INTO THIS STUFF!
FOR SURE!
A PATHETIC CREATURE LIKE THAT HAS NOTHING ELSE TO DO WITH HER TIME.
HEADS UP, GIRL! YOUR HEART-THROB'S ON THE HORIZON!
SO WHAT'S THE STORY? YOU AND CHUCKIE STILL AN ITEM?
HE HASN'T BEEN HANGING AROUND LATELY.
GET REAL, EVE!
HE'S JUST BEEN BUSY WITH HIS STUPID FOOTBALL TEAM!
AS SOON AS THE SEASON'S OVER, HE'LL BE DEVOTING EVERY SPARE MOMENT TO...

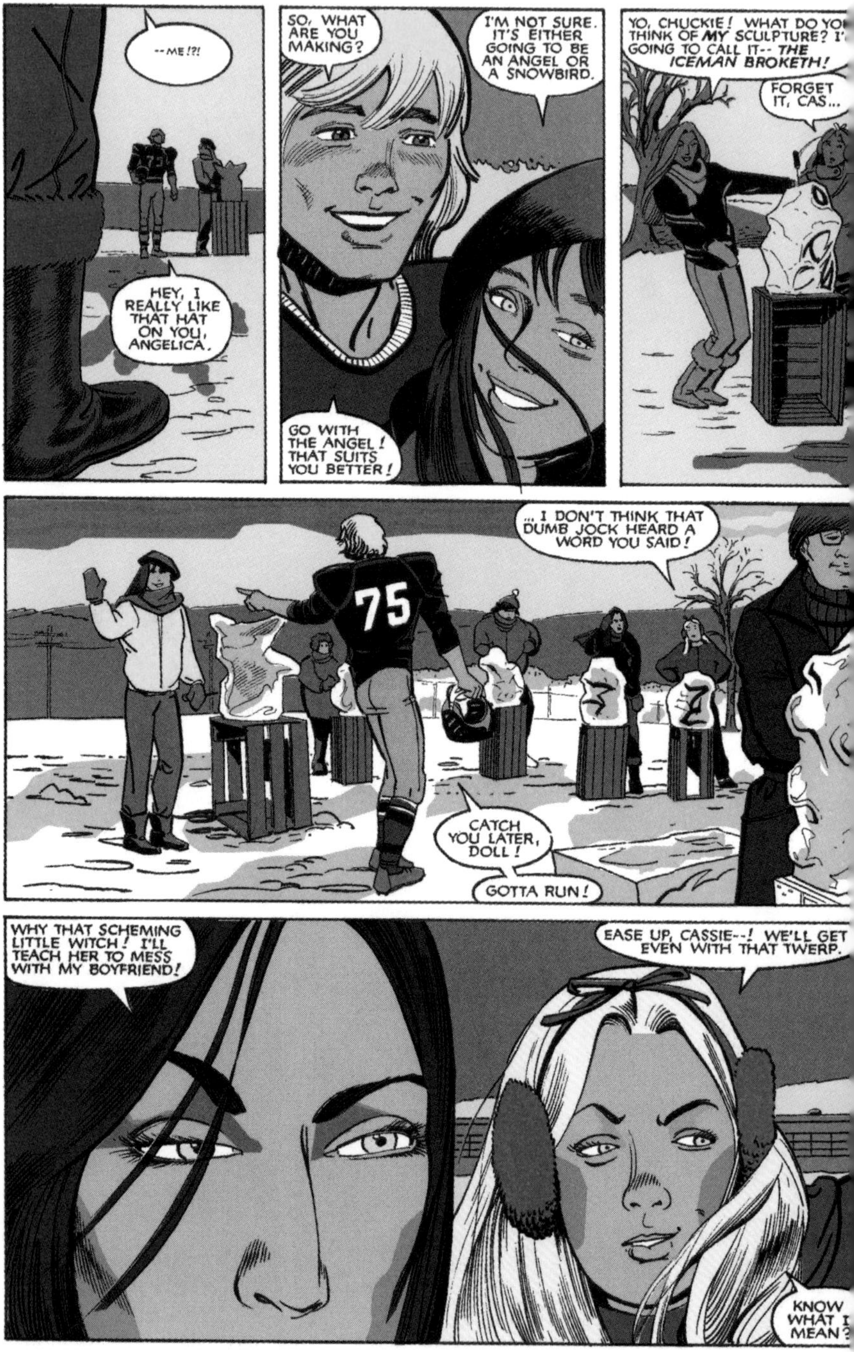
--ME!?!
HEY, I REALLY LIKE THAT HAT ON YOU, ANGELICA.
SO, WHAT ARE YOU MAKING?
I'M NOT SURE. IT'S EITHER GOING TO BE AN ANGEL OR A SNOWBIRD.
GO WITH THE ANGEL! THAT SUITS YOU BETTER!
YO, CHUCKIE! WHAT DO YO THINK OF MY SCULPTURE? I' GOING TO CALL IT-- THE ICEMAN BROKETH!
FORGET IT, CAS...
... I DON'T THINK THAT DUMB JOCK HEARD A WORD YOU SAID!
CATCH YOU LATER, DOLL!
GOTTA RUN!
WHY THAT SCHEMING LITTLE WITCH! I'LL TEACH HER TO MESS WITH MY BOYFRIEND!
EASE UP, CASSIE--! WE'LL GET EVEN WITH THAT TWERP.
KNOW WHAT I MEAN?

EARLY THE NEXT DAY...

MY, MY, YOU'RE CERTAINLY BRIGHT AND CHIPPER THIS MORNING!

THEY'RE JUDGING THE ICE SCULPTURE CONTEST TODAY, NANA-- AND I REALLY THINK I HAVE A CHANCE TO WIN IT!

ISN'T THAT RIGHT, PUM'KIN?

I WISH YOU DEVOTED AS MUCH TIME TO YOUR STUDIES AS YOU DID TO THAT SILLY CONTEST!

AH, BART, LET THE GIRL ENJOY HERSELF!

GOOD LUCK, SWEETHEART!

THANKS, NANA!

'BYE, DADDY!

Y'KNOW SOMETHING, PUM'KIN? I CAN'T REMEMBER THE LAST TIME I SAW OUR LITTLE ANGELICA SO HAPPY.

I DO BELIEVE THAT THINGS ARE FINALLY FALLING INTO PLACE FOR HER.

IT'S ABOUT TIME, TOO!

NOW, IF WE COULD ONLY DO SOMETHING ABOUT HER FATHER...

BARTHOLOMEW HAS ALWAYS BEEN A GOOD BOY, BUT MUCH TOO SERIOUS FOR HIS OWN...

UNNN

NO, NOT NOW...

19

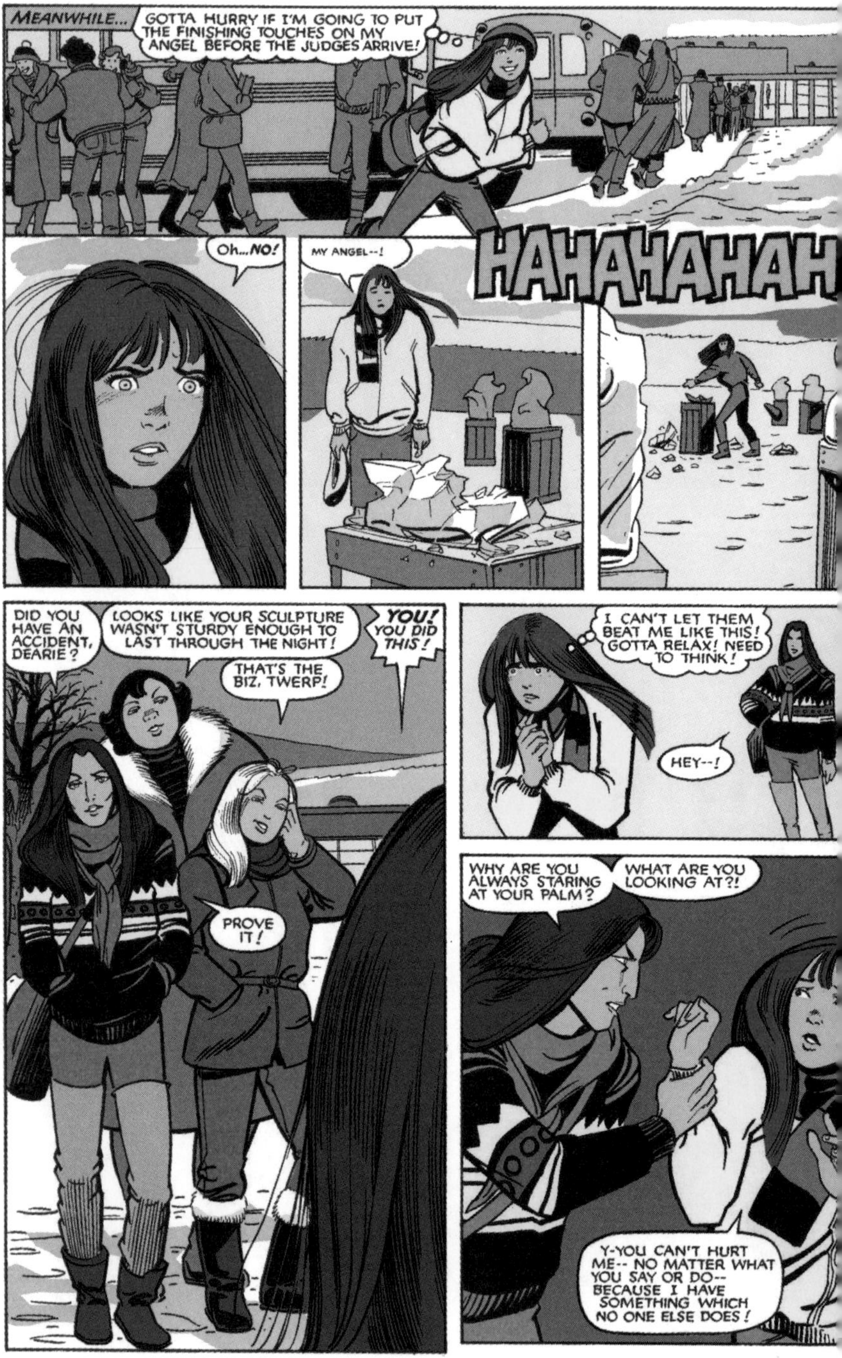
MEANWHILE...
GOTTA HURRY IF I'M GOING TO PUT THE FINISHING TOUCHES ON MY ANGEL BEFORE THE JUDGES ARRIVE!
Oh...NO!
MY ANGEL--!
HAHAHAHAH
DID YOU HAVE AN ACCIDENT, DEARIE?
LOOKS LIKE YOUR SCULPTURE WASN'T STURDY ENOUGH TO LAST THROUGH THE NIGHT!
THAT'S THE BIZ, TWERP!
YOU! YOU DID THIS!
PROVE IT!
I CAN'T LET THEM BEAT ME LIKE THIS! GOTTA RELAX! NEED TO THINK!
HEY--!
WHY ARE YOU ALWAYS STARING AT YOUR PALM?
WHAT ARE YOU LOOKING AT?!
Y-YOU CAN'T HURT ME-- NO MATTER WHAT YOU SAY OR DO-- BECAUSE I HAVE SOMETHING WHICH NO ONE ELSE DOES!

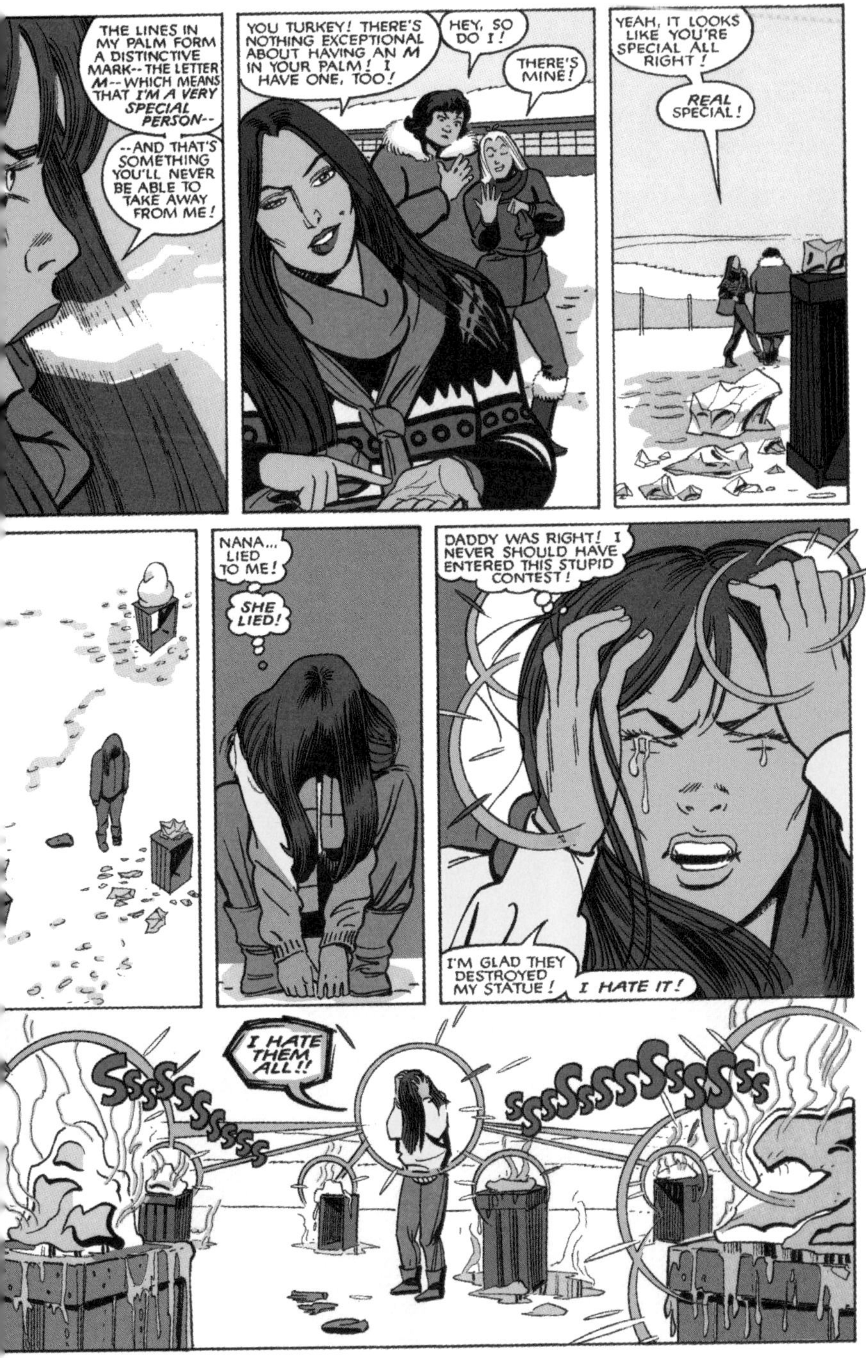
THE LINES IN MY PALM FORM A DISTINCTIVE MARK-- THE LETTER M-- WHICH MEANS THAT I'M A VERY SPECIAL PERSON--
--AND THAT'S SOMETHING YOU'LL NEVER BE ABLE TO TAKE AWAY FROM ME!
YOU TURKEY! THERE'S NOTHING EXCEPTIONAL ABOUT HAVING AN M IN YOUR PALM! I HAVE ONE, TOO!
HEY, SO DO I!
THERE'S MINE!
YEAH, IT LOOKS LIKE YOU'RE SPECIAL ALL RIGHT!
REAL SPECIAL!
NANA... LIED TO ME!
SHE LIED!
DADDY WAS RIGHT! I NEVER SHOULD HAVE ENTERED THIS STUPID CONTEST!
I'M GLAD THEY DESTROYED MY STATUE!
I HATE IT!
I HATE THEM ALL!!
SSSSSSSSSS
SSSSSSSSSSSSS

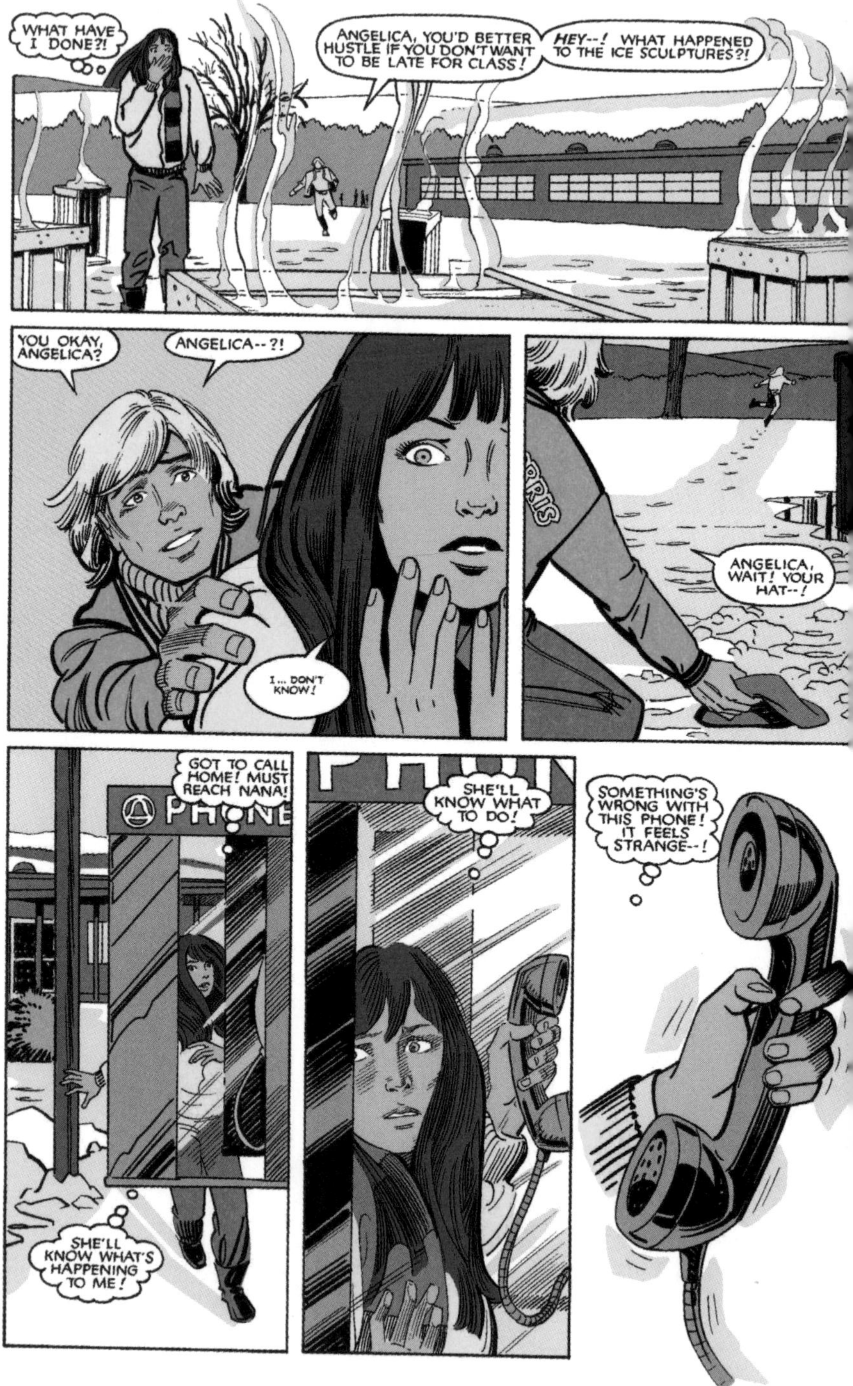
WHAT HAVE I DONE?!
ANGELICA, YOU'D BETTER HUSTLE IF YOU DON'T WANT TO BE LATE FOR CLASS!
HEY--! WHAT HAPPENED TO THE ICE SCULPTURES?!
YOU OKAY, ANGELICA?
ANGELICA--?!
I... DON'T KNOW!
ANGELICA, WAIT! YOUR HAT--!
GOT TO CALL HOME! MUST REACH NANA!
PHONE
SHE'LL KNOW WHAT'S HAPPENING TO ME!
SHE'LL KNOW WHAT TO DO!
SOMETHING'S WRONG WITH THIS PHONE! IT FEELS STRANGE--!

NO!!

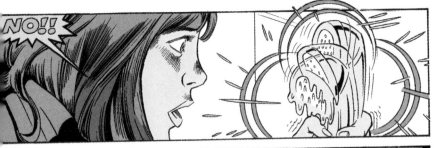

...T THAT VERY MOMENT...

CEREBRO HAS DETECTED THE PRESENCE OF A YOUNG MUTANT!

BE SILENT! CLEAR YOUR MINDS OF ALL THOUGHTS!

THERE MUST BE NO INTERFERENCE AS I USE MY OWN TELEPATHIC POWERS TO INCREASE CEREBRO'S ABILITY TO PINPOINT THE LOCATION!

GOT HER! THE COMPUTER HAS LOCKED ONTO HER COORDINATES!

SHE'S IN NEW JERSEY!

EXCELLENT! HAVE MY PRIVATE JET PREPARED FOR AN IMMEDIATE TAKE-OFF, AND ARRANGE FOR A LIMOSINE TO MEET ME WHEN I LAND.

I SHALL PERSONALLY COLLECT THIS ONE. THE POOR THING...

"...SHE MUST BE TERRIFIED!"

"WELL, SHE'LL GET USED TO IT..."

"...IF I HAVE MY WAY, *TERROR* WILL SOON BECOME A WAY OF LIFE TO HER!"

NEVER THOUGHT I'D MAKE IT ALL THE WAY HOME!

HEY! WHY IS THAT AMBULANCE-- AND THOSE COP CARS--IN FRONT OF MY HOUSE?!

23

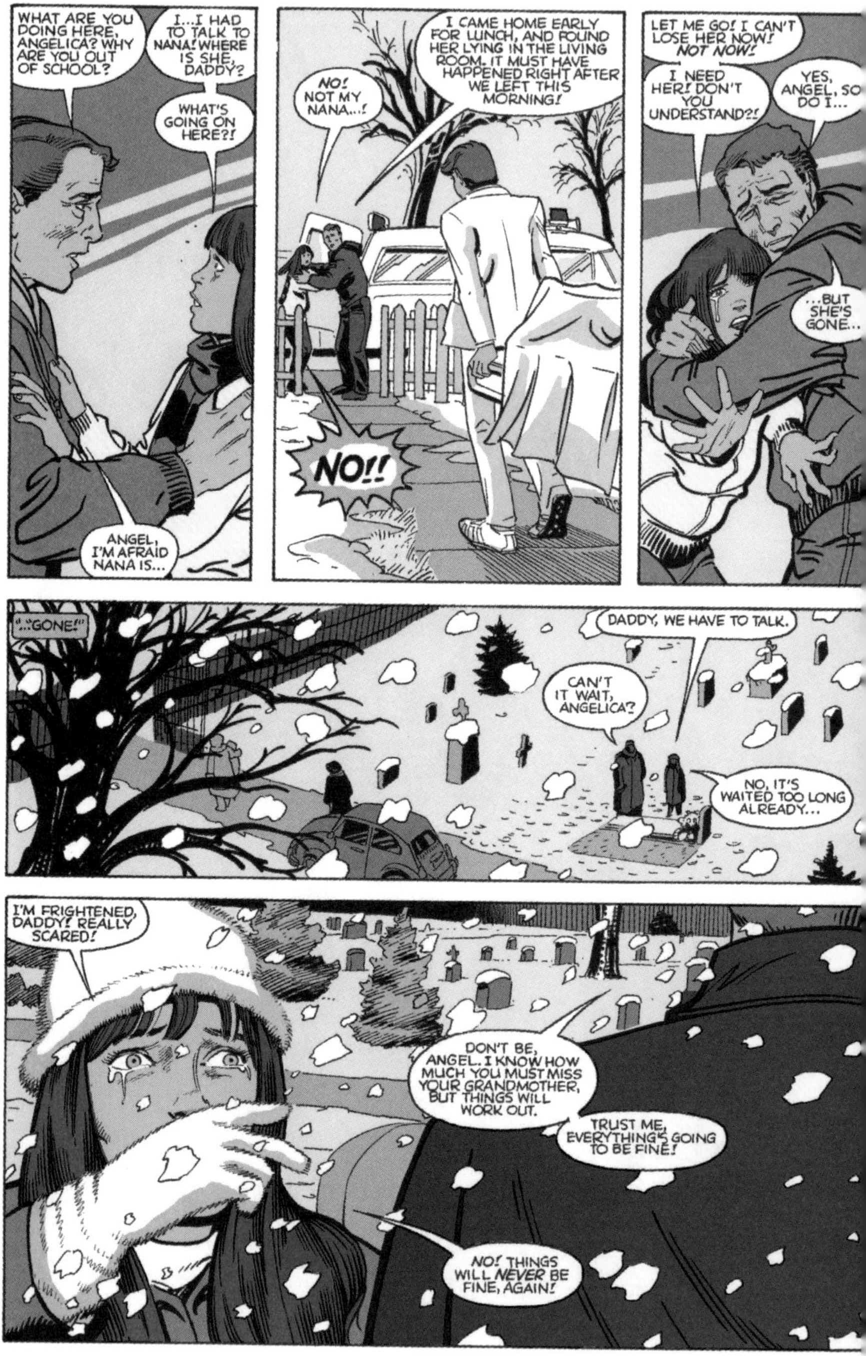
WHAT ARE YOU DOING HERE, ANGELICA? WHY ARE YOU OUT OF SCHOOL?
I...I HAD TO TALK TO NANA! WHERE IS SHE, DADDY?
WHAT'S GOING ON HERE?!
ANGEL, I'M AFRAID NANA IS...
NO! NOT MY NANA...!
I CAME HOME EARLY FOR LUNCH, AND FOUND HER LYING IN THE LIVING ROOM. IT MUST HAVE HAPPENED RIGHT AFTER WE LEFT THIS MORNING!
NO!!
LET ME GO! I CAN'T LOSE HER NOW! NOT NOW!
I NEED HER! DON'T YOU UNDERSTAND?!
YES, ANGEL, SO DO I...
...BUT SHE'S GONE...
"...GONE!"
DADDY, WE HAVE TO TALK.
CAN'T IT WAIT, ANGELICA?
NO, IT'S WAITED TOO LONG ALREADY...
I'M FRIGHTENED, DADDY! REALLY SCARED!
DON'T BE, ANGEL. I KNOW HOW MUCH YOU MUST MISS YOUR GRANDMOTHER, BUT THINGS WILL WORK OUT.
TRUST ME, EVERYTHING'S GOING TO BE FINE!
NO! THINGS WILL NEVER BE FINE, AGAIN!

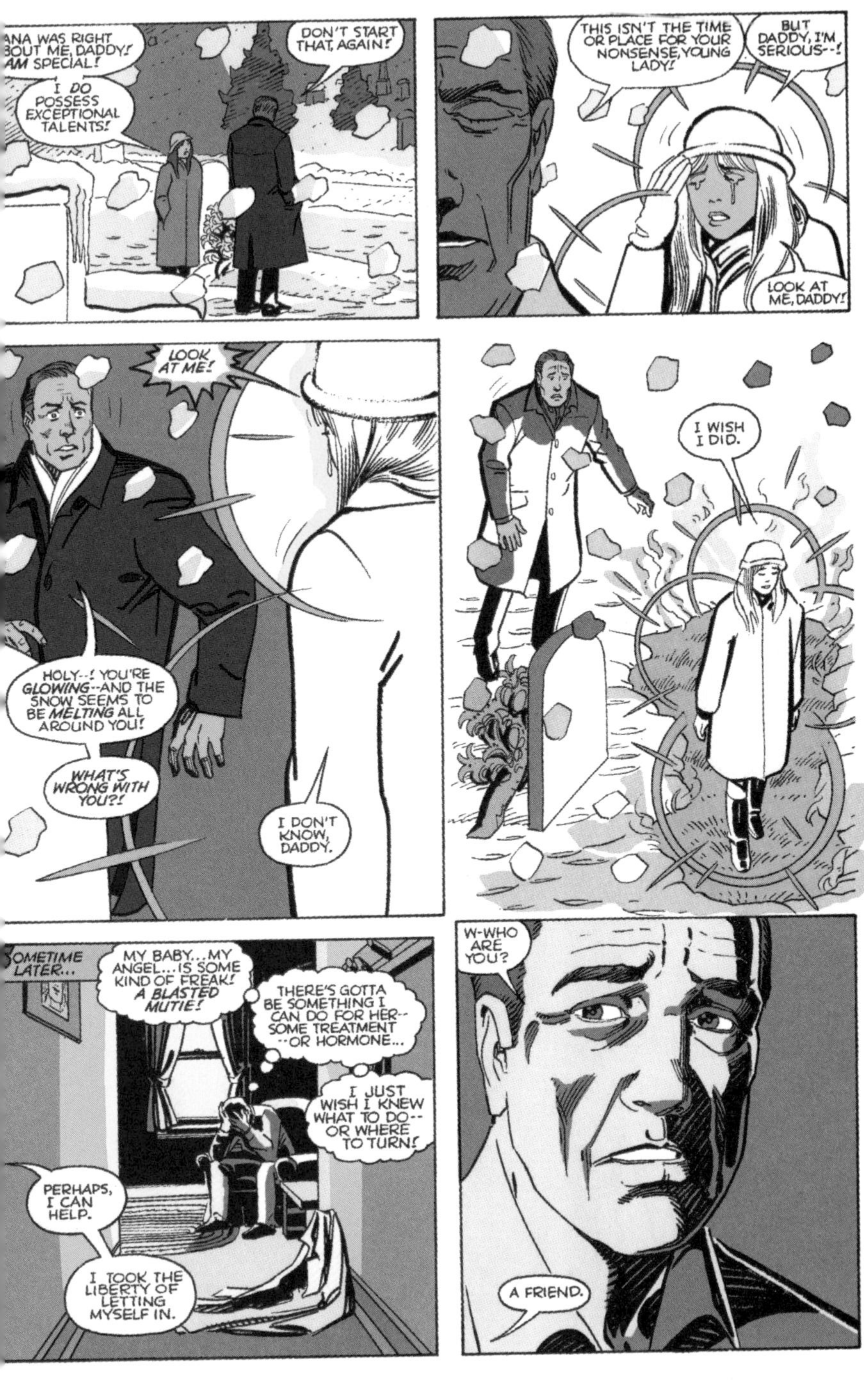

ANA WAS RIGHT BOUT ME, DADDY! AM SPECIAL!
I DO POSSESS EXCEPTIONAL TALENTS!
DON'T START THAT, AGAIN!
THIS ISN'T THE TIME OR PLACE FOR YOUR NONSENSE, YOUNG LADY!
BUT DADDY, I'M SERIOUS--!
LOOK AT ME, DADDY!
LOOK AT ME!
HOLY--! YOU'RE GLOWING--AND THE SNOW SEEMS TO BE MELTING ALL AROUND YOU!
WHAT'S WRONG WITH YOU?!
I DON'T KNOW, DADDY.
I WISH I DID.
SOMETIME LATER...
MY BABY...MY ANGEL...IS SOME KIND OF FREAK! A BLASTED MUTIE!
THERE'S GOTTA BE SOMETHING I CAN DO FOR HER--SOME TREATMENT --OR HORMONE...
I JUST WISH I KNEW WHAT TO DO--OR WHERE TO TURN!
PERHAPS, I CAN HELP.
I TOOK THE LIBERTY OF LETTING MYSELF IN.
W-WHO ARE YOU?
A FRIEND.

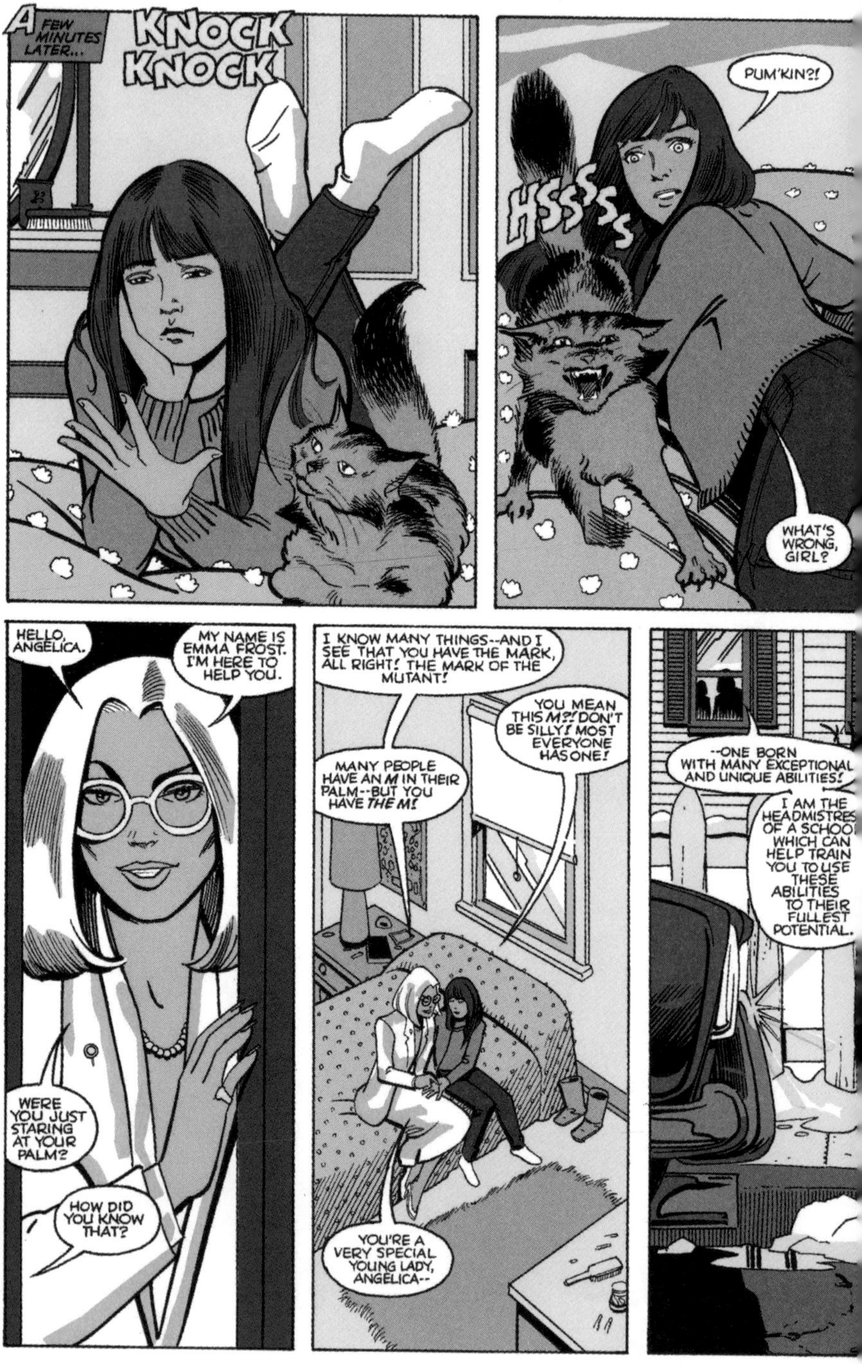
A FEW MINUTES LATER...
KNOCK KNOCK
PUM'KIN?!
HSSSSS
WHAT'S WRONG, GIRL?
HELLO, ANGELICA.
MY NAME IS EMMA FROST. I'M HERE TO HELP YOU.
WERE YOU JUST STARING AT YOUR PALM?
HOW DID YOU KNOW THAT?
I KNOW MANY THINGS--AND I SEE THAT YOU HAVE THE MARK, ALL RIGHT! THE MARK OF THE MUTANT!
YOU MEAN THIS M?! DON'T BE SILLY! MOST EVERYONE HAS ONE!
MANY PEOPLE HAVE AN M IN THEIR PALM--BUT YOU HAVE THE M!
YOU'RE A VERY SPECIAL YOUNG LADY, ANGELICA--
--ONE BORN WITH MANY EXCEPTIONAL AND UNIQUE ABILITIES!
I AM THE HEADMISTRES OF A SCHOO WHICH CAN HELP TRAIN YOU TO USE THESE ABILITIES TO THEIR FULLEST POTENTIAL.

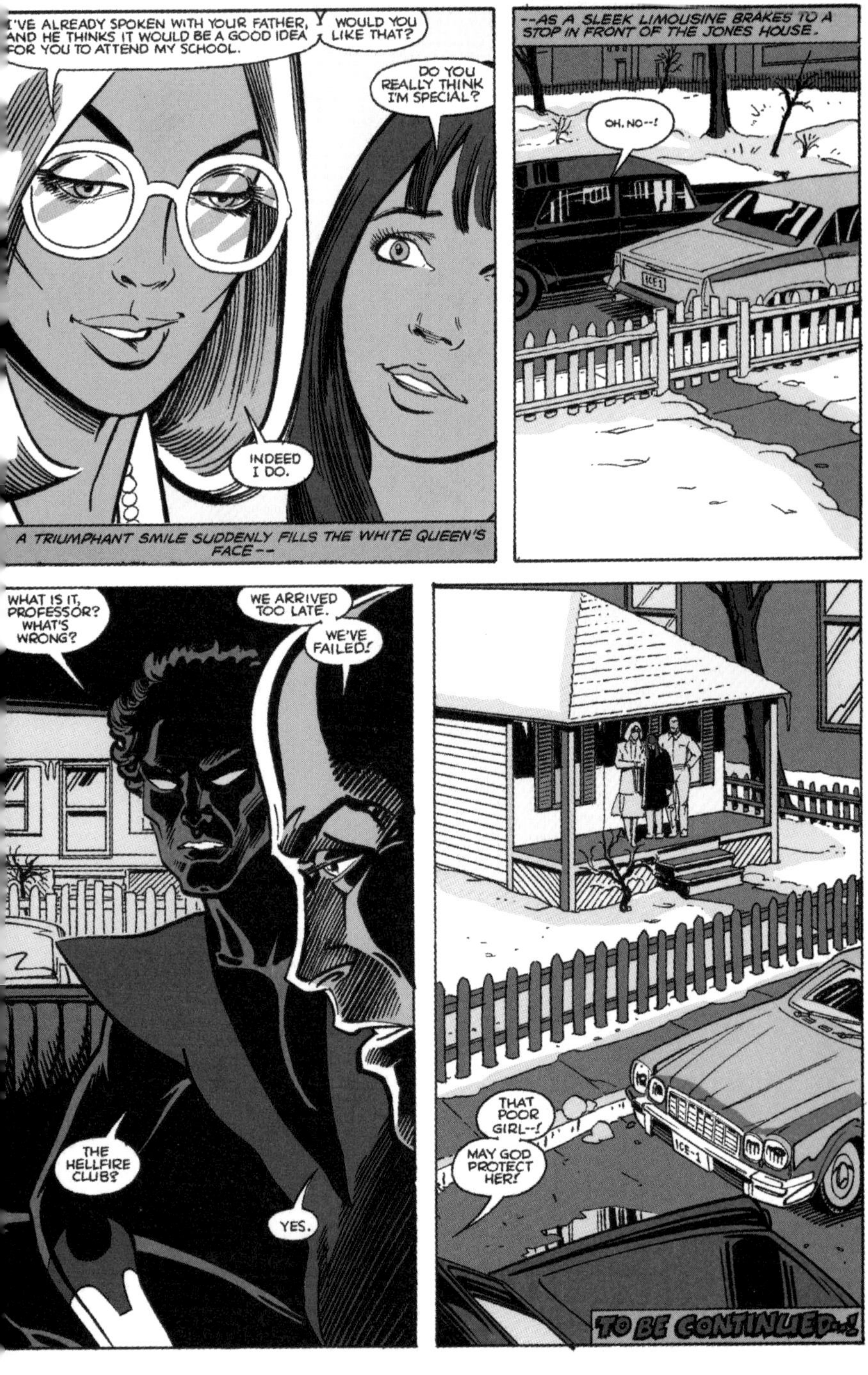
I'VE ALREADY SPOKEN WITH YOUR FATHER, AND HE THINKS IT WOULD BE A GOOD IDEA FOR YOU TO ATTEND MY SCHOOL.
WOULD YOU LIKE THAT?
DO YOU REALLY THINK I'M SPECIAL?
INDEED I DO.
A TRIUMPHANT SMILE SUDDENLY FILLS THE WHITE QUEEN'S FACE--
--AS A SLEEK LIMOUSINE BRAKES TO A STOP IN FRONT OF THE JONES HOUSE.
OH, NO--!
ICE 1
WHAT IS IT, PROFESSOR? WHAT'S WRONG?
WE ARRIVED TOO LATE.
WE'VE FAILED!
THE HELLFIRE CLUB?
YES.
THAT POOR GIRL--!
MAY GOD PROTECT HER!
ICE-1
TO BE CONTINUED--!

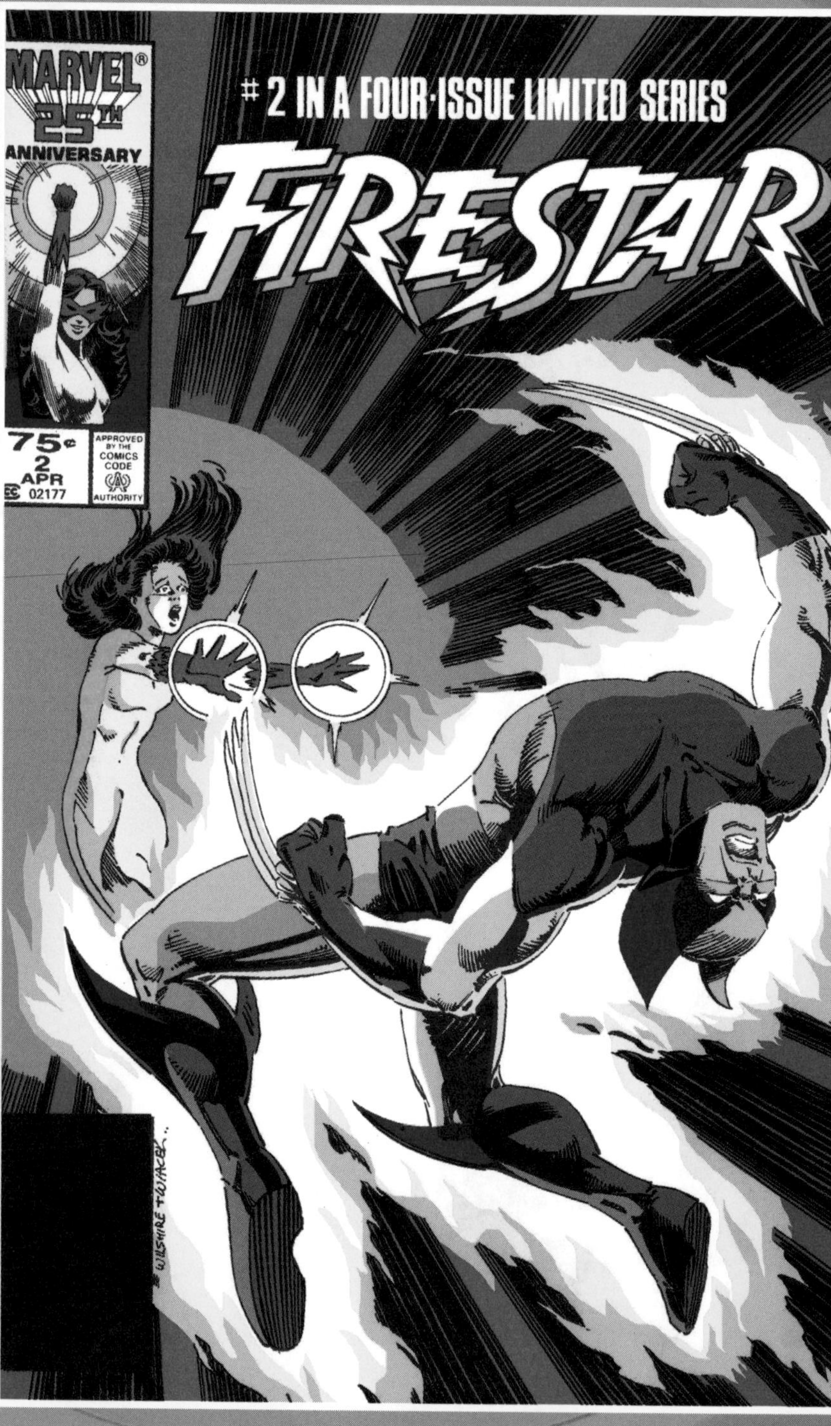

MARVEL®
25TH
ANNIVERSARY
75¢
2
APR
02177
APPROVED BY THE COMICS CODE AUTHORITY
2 IN A FOUR-ISSUE LIMITED SERIES
FIRESTAR

STAN LEE PRESENTS: FIRESTAR

Unable to cope with the fact that his only daughter is a mutant possessing strange and uncanny powers, *Bartholemew Jones* quickly entrusts her education and training to *Ms. Emma Frost*, headmistress of the prestigious *Massachusetts Academy*. Unknown to Jones, Frost is secretly a member of the *Inner Council of the Hellfire Club*, an organization determined to dominate the world!

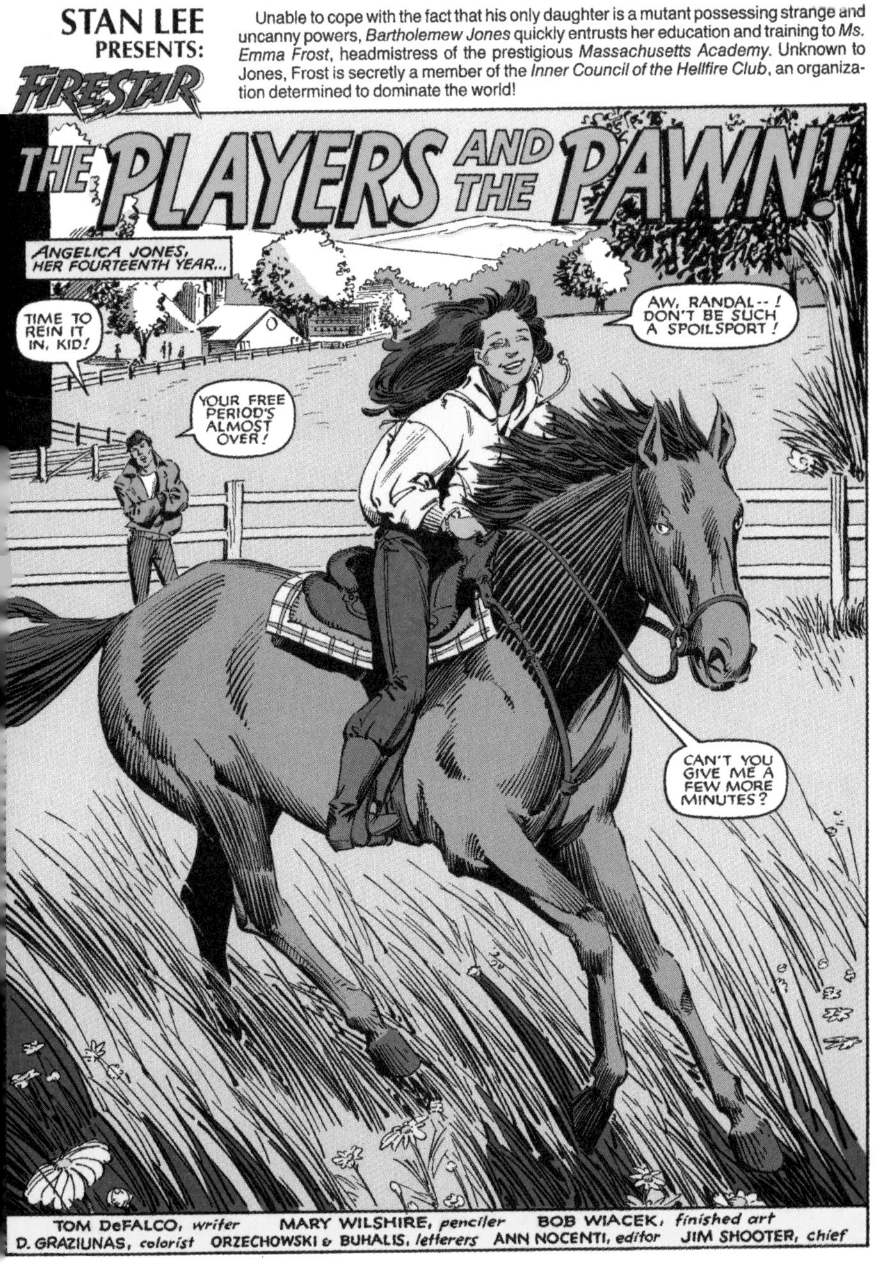
THE PLAYERS AND THE PAWN!
ANGELICA JONES, HER FOURTEENTH YEAR...
TIME TO REIN IT IN, KID!
YOUR FREE PERIOD'S ALMOST OVER!
AW, RANDAL-- ! DON'T BE SUCH A SPOILSPORT !
CAN'T YOU GIVE ME A FEW MORE MINUTES?

TOM DeFALCO, *writer* MARY WILSHIRE, *penciler* BOB WIACEK, *finished art*
D. GRAZIUNAS, *colorist* ORZECHOWSKI & BUHALIS, *letterers* ANN NOCENTI, *editor* JIM SHOOTER, *chief*

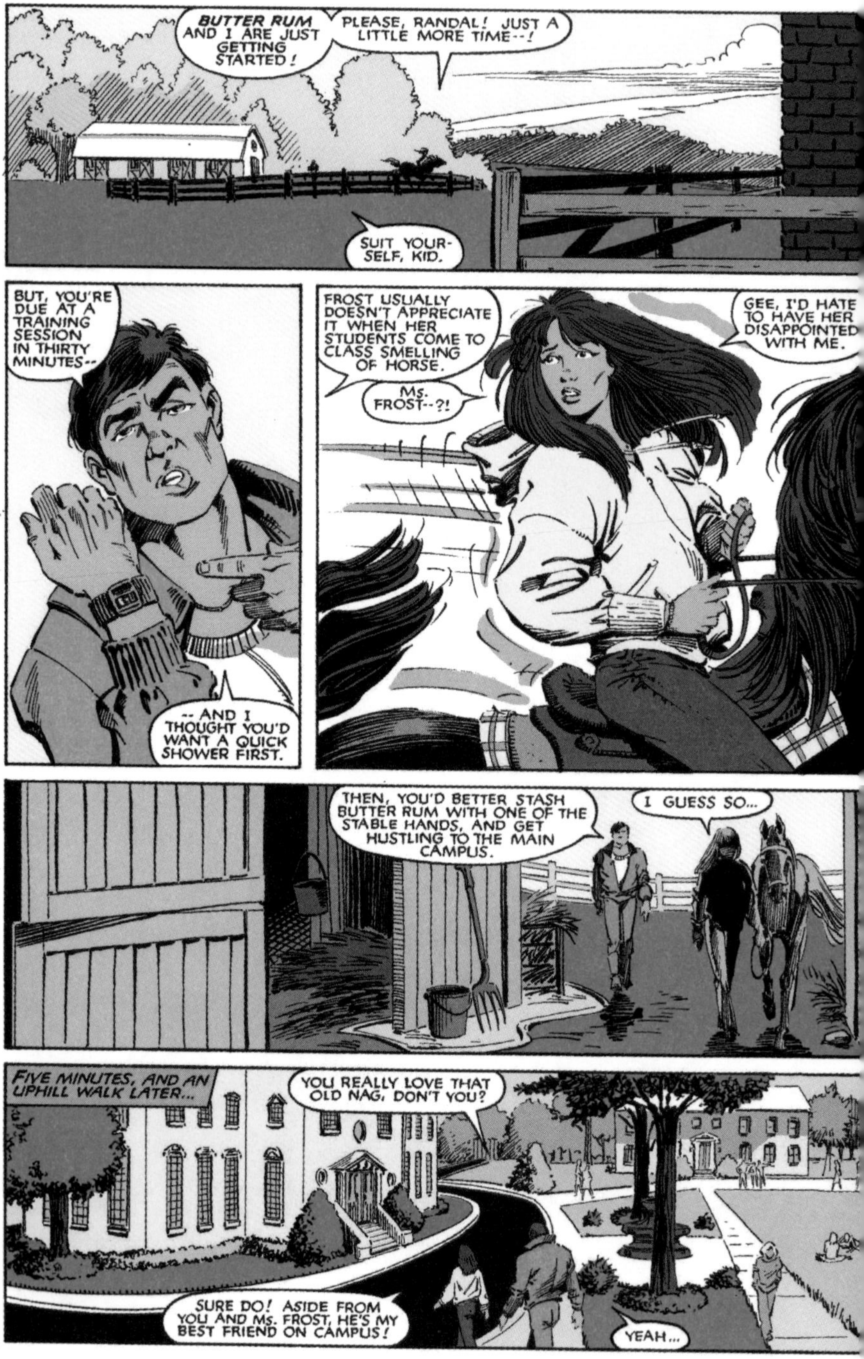
BUTTER RUM AND I ARE JUST GETTING STARTED!
PLEASE, RANDAL! JUST A LITTLE MORE TIME--!
SUIT YOURSELF, KID.
BUT, YOU'RE DUE AT A TRAINING SESSION IN THIRTY MINUTES--
--AND I THOUGHT YOU'D WANT A QUICK SHOWER FIRST.
FROST USUALLY DOESN'T APPRECIATE IT WHEN HER STUDENTS COME TO CLASS SMELLING OF HORSE.
Ms. FROST--?!
GEE, I'D HATE TO HAVE HER DISAPPOINTED WITH ME.
THEN, YOU'D BETTER STASH BUTTER RUM WITH ONE OF THE STABLE HANDS, AND GET HUSTLING TO THE MAIN CAMPUS.
I GUESS SO...
FIVE MINUTES, AND AN UPHILL WALK LATER...
YOU REALLY LOVE THAT OLD NAG, DON'T YOU?
SURE DO! ASIDE FROM YOU AND Ms. FROST, HE'S MY BEST FRIEND ON CAMPUS!
YEAH...

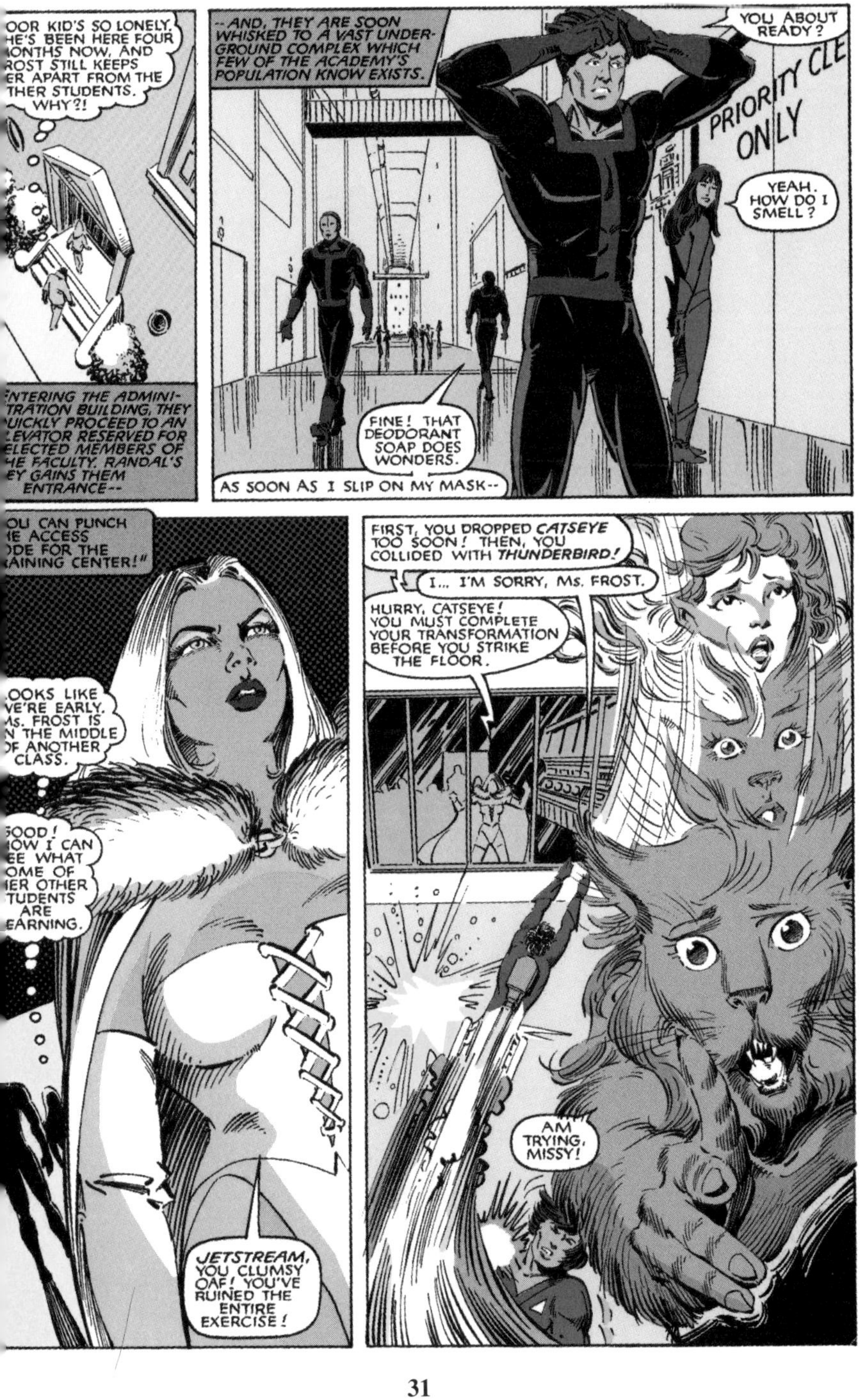
OOR KID'S SO LONELY. HE'S BEEN HERE FOUR ONTHS NOW, AND ROST STILL KEEPS ER APART FROM THE THER STUDENTS. WHY?!
NTERING THE ADMINI-TRATION BUILDING, THEY UICKLY PROCEED TO AN LEVATOR RESERVED FOR ELECTED MEMBERS OF HE FACULTY. RANDAL'S EY GAINS THEM ENTRANCE--
--AND, THEY ARE SOON WHISKED TO A VAST UNDER-GROUND COMPLEX WHICH FEW OF THE ACADEMY'S POPULATION KNOW EXISTS.
YOU ABOUT READY?
PRIORITY CLE ONLY
YEAH. HOW DO I SMELL?
FINE! THAT DEODORANT SOAP DOES WONDERS.
AS SOON AS I SLIP ON MY MASK--
OU CAN PUNCH E ACCESS ODE FOR THE AINING CENTER!"
OOKS LIKE E'RE EARLY. S. FROST IS N THE MIDDLE F ANOTHER CLASS.
OOD! OW I CAN EE WHAT OME OF ER OTHER TUDENTS ARE EARNING.
FIRST, YOU DROPPED CATSEYE TOO SOON! THEN, YOU COLLIDED WITH THUNDERBIRD!
I... I'M SORRY, Ms. FROST.
HURRY, CATSEYE! YOU MUST COMPLETE YOUR TRANSFORMATION BEFORE YOU STRIKE THE FLOOR.
AM TRYING, MISSY!
JETSTREAM, YOU CLUMSY OAF! YOU'VE RUINED THE ENTIRE EXERCISE!

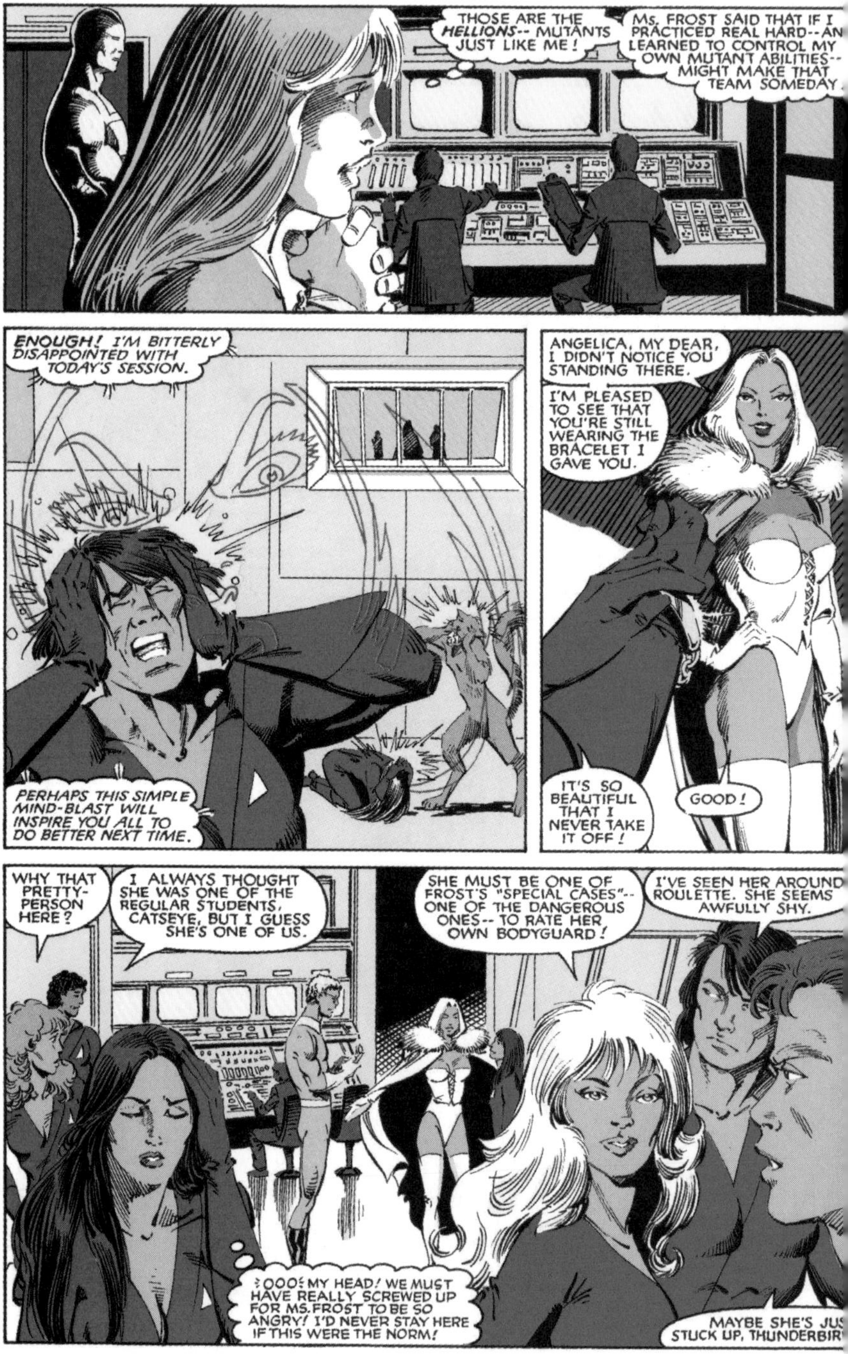
THOSE ARE THE HELLIONS-- MUTANTS JUST LIKE ME!
Ms. FROST SAID THAT IF I PRACTICED REAL HARD--AN LEARNED TO CONTROL MY OWN MUTANT ABILITIES-- MIGHT MAKE THAT TEAM SOMEDAY.
ENOUGH! I'M BITTERLY DISAPPOINTED WITH TODAY'S SESSION.
PERHAPS THIS SIMPLE MIND-BLAST WILL INSPIRE YOU ALL TO DO BETTER NEXT TIME.
ANGELICA, MY DEAR, I DIDN'T NOTICE YOU STANDING THERE.
I'M PLEASED TO SEE THAT YOU'RE STILL WEARING THE BRACELET I GAVE YOU.
IT'S SO BEAUTIFUL THAT I NEVER TAKE IT OFF!
GOOD!
WHY THAT PRETTY-PERSON HERE?
I ALWAYS THOUGHT SHE WAS ONE OF THE REGULAR STUDENTS, CATSEYE, BUT I GUESS SHE'S ONE OF US.
SHE MUST BE ONE OF FROST'S "SPECIAL CASES"-- ONE OF THE DANGEROUS ONES-- TO RATE HER OWN BODYGUARD!
I'VE SEEN HER AROUND ROULETTE. SHE SEEMS AWFULLY SHY.
OOO! MY HEAD! WE MUST HAVE REALLY SCREWED UP FOR MS. FROST TO BE SO ANGRY! I'D NEVER STAY HERE IF THIS WERE THE NORM!
MAYBE SHE'S JUS STUCK UP, THUNDERBIR

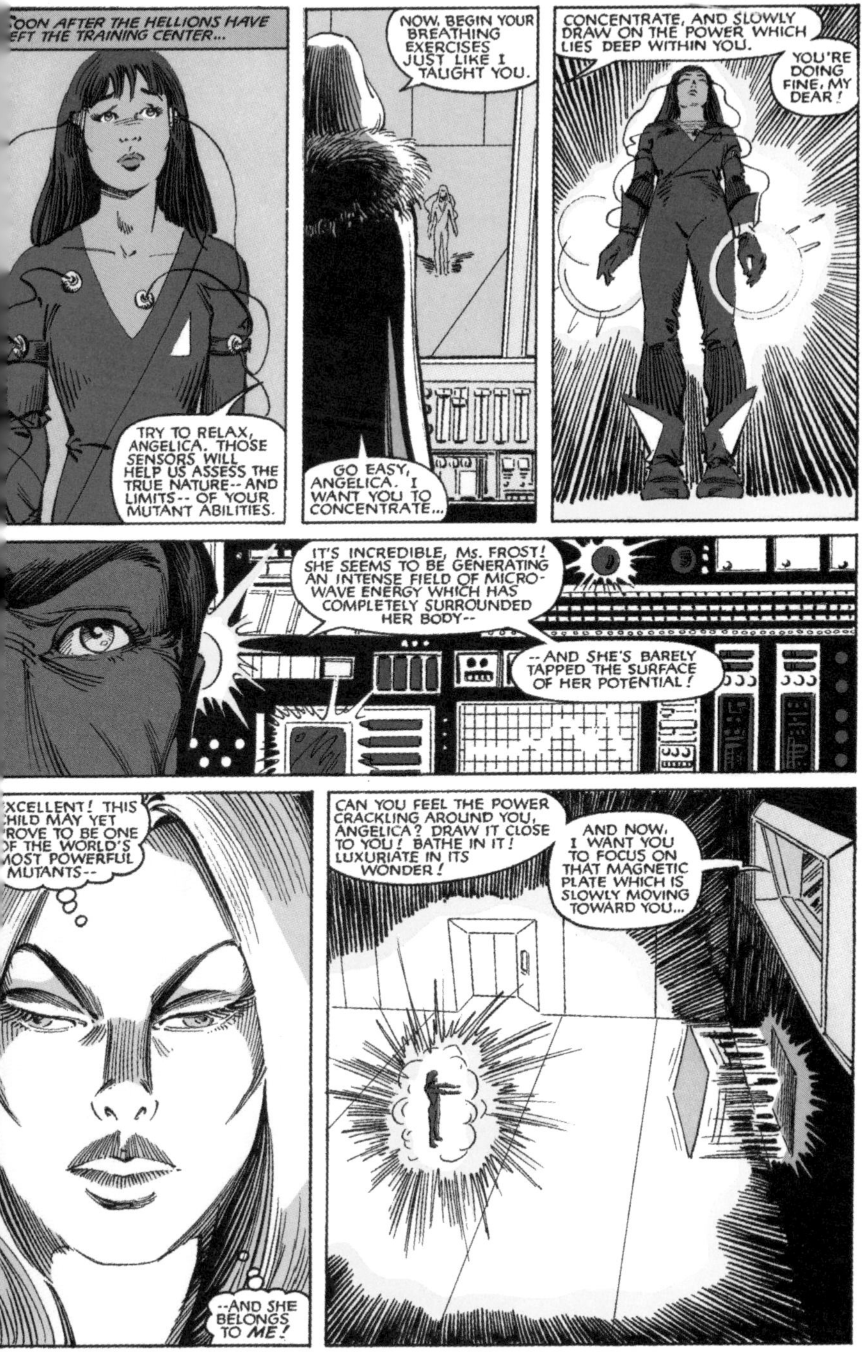

SOON AFTER THE HELLIONS HAVE LEFT THE TRAINING CENTER...
TRY TO RELAX, ANGELICA. THOSE SENSORS WILL HELP US ASSESS THE TRUE NATURE-- AND LIMITS-- OF YOUR MUTANT ABILITIES.
NOW, BEGIN YOUR BREATHING EXERCISES JUST LIKE I TAUGHT YOU.
GO EASY, ANGELICA. I WANT YOU TO CONCENTRATE...
CONCENTRATE, AND SLOWLY DRAW ON THE POWER WHICH LIES DEEP WITHIN YOU.
YOU'RE DOING FINE, MY DEAR!
IT'S INCREDIBLE, Ms. FROST! SHE SEEMS TO BE GENERATING AN INTENSE FIELD OF MICRO-WAVE ENERGY WHICH HAS COMPLETELY SURROUNDED HER BODY--
--AND SHE'S BARELY TAPPED THE SURFACE OF HER POTENTIAL!
EXCELLENT! THIS CHILD MAY YET PROVE TO BE ONE OF THE WORLD'S MOST POWERFUL MUTANTS--
--AND SHE BELONGS TO ME!
CAN YOU FEEL THE POWER CRACKLING AROUND YOU, ANGELICA? DRAW IT CLOSE TO YOU! BATHE IN IT! LUXURIATE IN ITS WONDER!
AND NOW, I WANT YOU TO FOCUS ON THAT MAGNETIC PLATE WHICH IS SLOWLY MOVING TOWARD YOU...

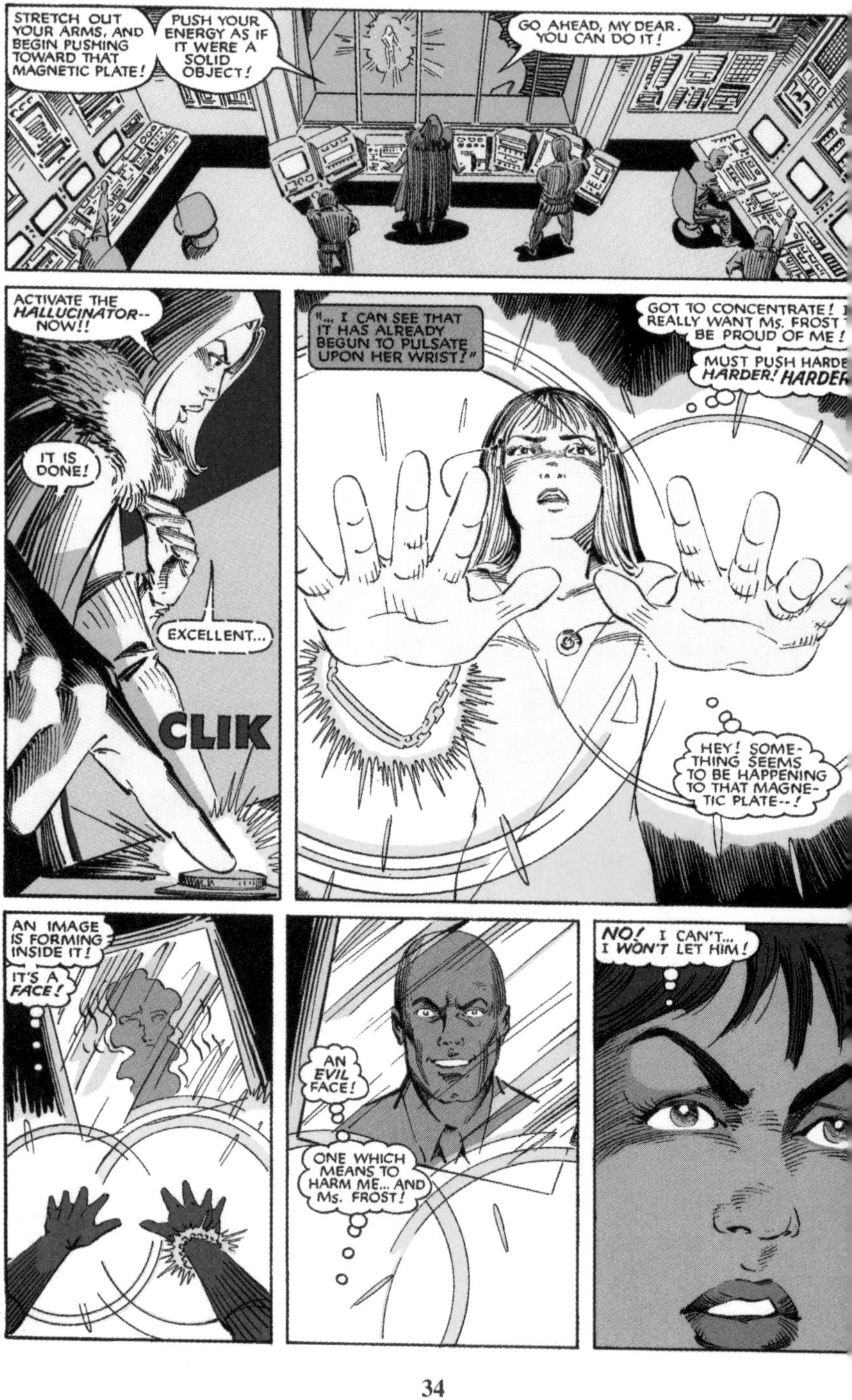
STRETCH OUT YOUR ARMS, AND BEGIN PUSHING TOWARD THAT MAGNETIC PLATE!
PUSH YOUR ENERGY AS IF IT WERE A SOLID OBJECT!
GO AHEAD, MY DEAR. YOU CAN DO IT!
ACTIVATE THE HALLUCINATOR-- NOW!!
IT IS DONE!
EXCELLENT...
CLIK
"... I CAN SEE THAT IT HAS ALREADY BEGUN TO PULSATE UPON HER WRIST!"
GOT TO CONCENTRATE! I REALLY WANT Ms. FROST TO BE PROUD OF ME!
MUST PUSH HARDER! HARDER! HARDER!
HEY! SOMETHING SEEMS TO BE HAPPENING TO THAT MAGNETIC PLATE--!
AN IMAGE IS FORMING INSIDE IT!
IT'S A FACE!
AN EVIL FACE!
ONE WHICH MEANS TO HARM ME... AND Ms. FROST!
NO! I CAN'T... I WON'T LET HIM!

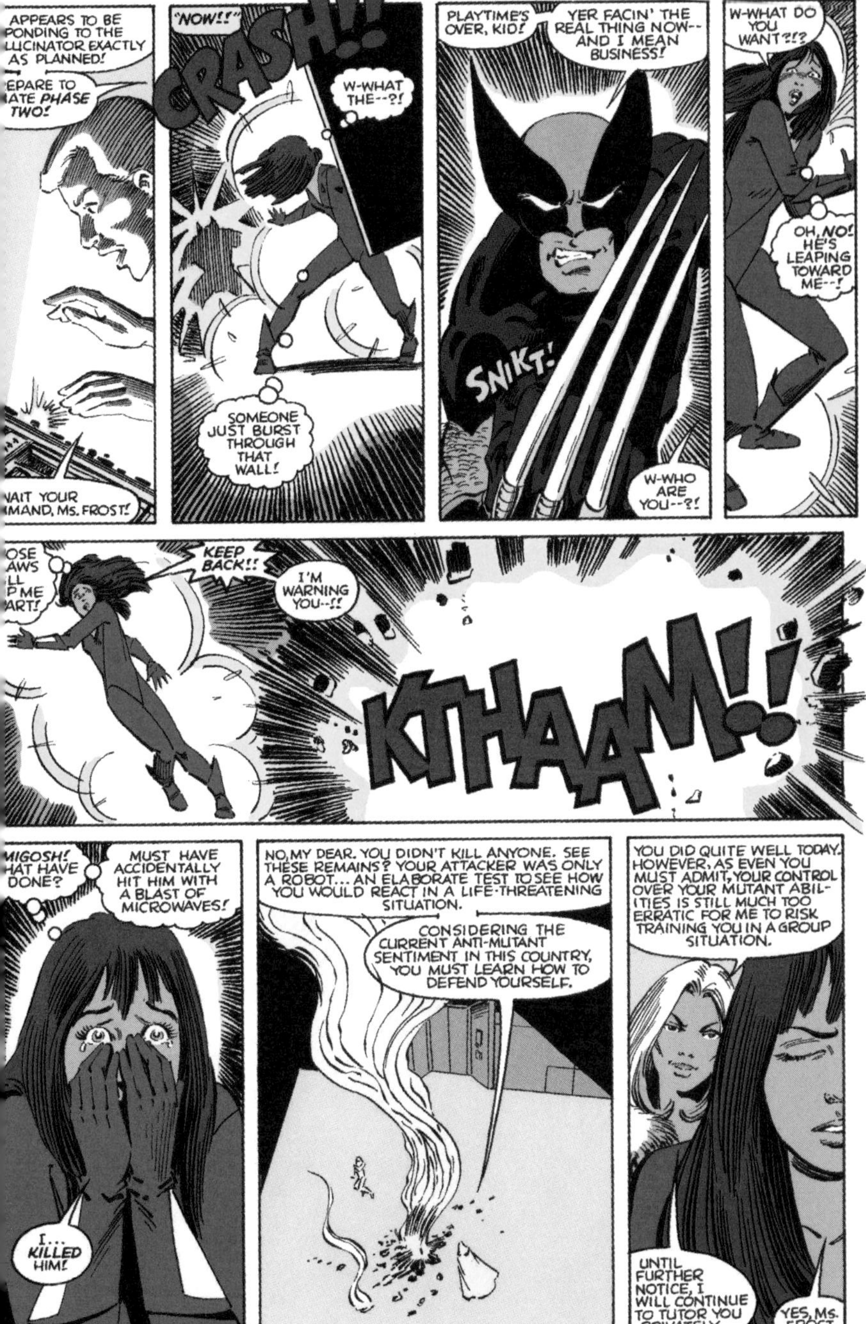

APPEARS TO BE
PONDING TO THE
LLUCINATOR EXACTLY
AS PLANNED!
EPARE TO
IATE PHASE
TWO!
AIT YOUR
MMAND, MS. FROST!
"NOW!!"
CRASH!!
W-WHAT
THE--?!
SOMEONE
JUST BURST
THROUGH
THAT
WALL!
PLAYTIME'S
OVER, KID!
YER FACIN' THE
REAL THING NOW--
AND I MEAN
BUSINESS!
SNIKT!
W-WHO
ARE
YOU--?!
W-WHAT DO
YOU
WANT?!?
OH, NO!
HE'S
LEAPING
TOWARD
ME--!
OSE
AWS
LL
P ME
ART!
KEEP
BACK!!
I'M
WARNING
YOU--!!
KTHAAM!!
MIGOSH!
HAT HAVE
DONE?
MUST HAVE
ACCIDENTALLY
HIT HIM WITH
A BLAST OF
MICROWAVES!
I...
KILLED
HIM!
NO, MY DEAR. YOU DIDN'T KILL ANYONE. SEE THESE REMAINS? YOUR ATTACKER WAS ONLY A ROBOT... AN ELABORATE TEST TO SEE HOW YOU WOULD REACT IN A LIFE-THREATENING SITUATION.
CONSIDERING THE CURRENT ANTI-MUTANT SENTIMENT IN THIS COUNTRY, YOU MUST LEARN HOW TO DEFEND YOURSELF.
YOU DID QUITE WELL TODAY. HOWEVER, AS EVEN YOU MUST ADMIT, YOUR CONTROL OVER YOUR MUTANT ABILITIES IS STILL MUCH TOO ERRATIC FOR ME TO RISK TRAINING YOU IN A GROUP SITUATION.
UNTIL FURTHER NOTICE, I WILL CONTINUE TO TUTOR YOU PRIVATELY.
YES, MS. FROST.

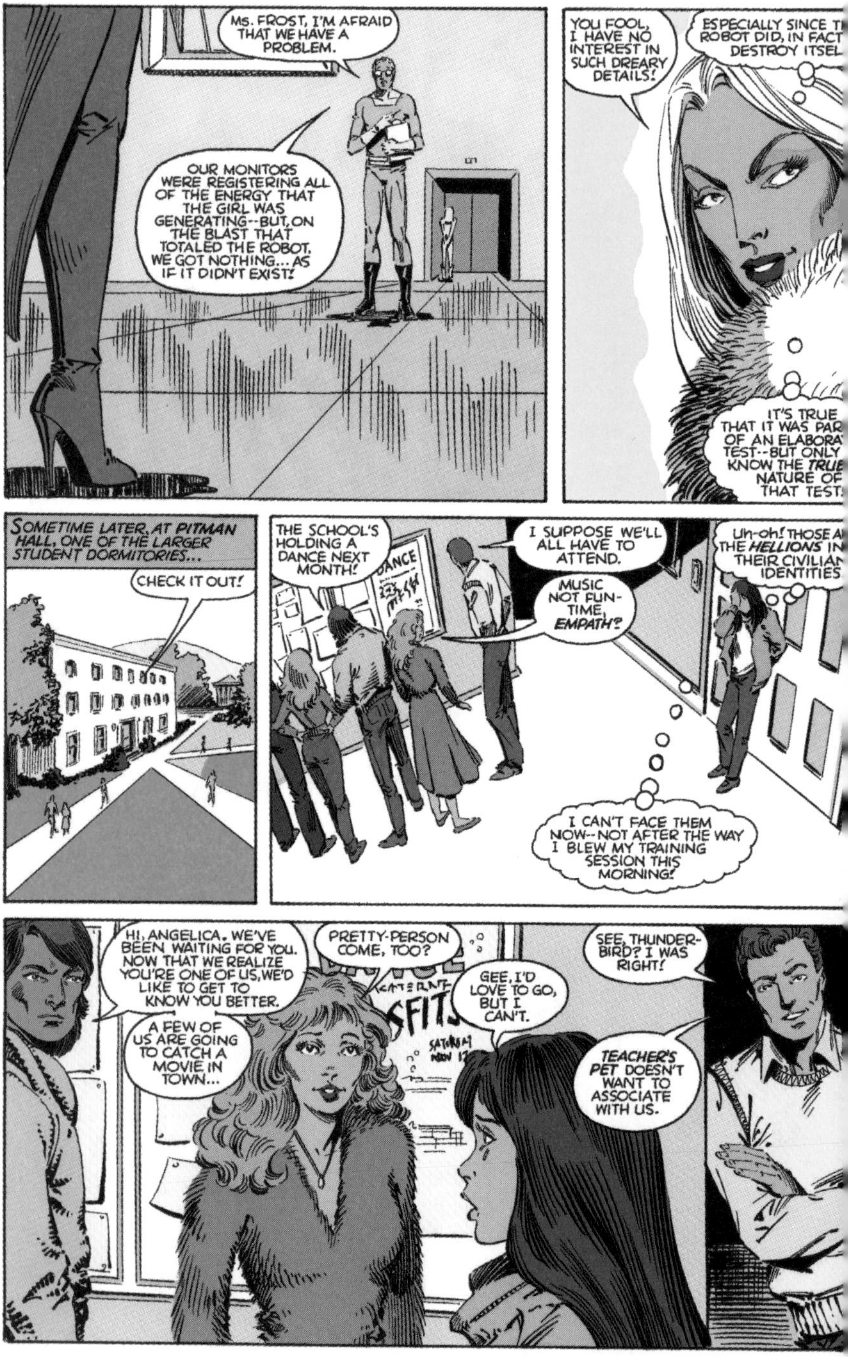
MS. FROST, I'M AFRAID THAT WE HAVE A PROBLEM.
OUR MONITORS WERE REGISTERING ALL OF THE ENERGY THAT THE GIRL WAS GENERATING--BUT, ON THE BLAST THAT TOTALED THE ROBOT, WE GOT NOTHING... AS IF IT DIDN'T EXIST!
YOU FOOL, I HAVE NO INTEREST IN SUCH DREARY DETAILS!
ESPECIALLY SINCE T ROBOT DID, IN FACT DESTROY ITSEL
IT'S TRUE THAT IT WAS PAR OF AN ELABORA TEST--BUT ONLY KNOW THE TRUE NATURE OF THAT TEST.
SOMETIME LATER, AT PITMAN HALL, ONE OF THE LARGER STUDENT DORMITORIES...
CHECK IT OUT!
THE SCHOOL'S HOLDING A DANCE NEXT MONTH!
I SUPPOSE WE'LL ALL HAVE TO ATTEND.
MUSIC NOT FUN-TIME, EMPATH?
Uh-oh! THOSE A THE HELLIONS IN THEIR CIVILIAN IDENTITIES
I CAN'T FACE THEM NOW--NOT AFTER THE WAY I BLEW MY TRAINING SESSION THIS MORNING!
HI, ANGELICA. WE'VE BEEN WAITING FOR YOU. NOW THAT WE REALIZE YOU'RE ONE OF US, WE'D LIKE TO GET TO KNOW YOU BETTER.
A FEW OF US ARE GOING TO CATCH A MOVIE IN TOWN...
PRETTY-PERSON COME, TOO?
GEE, I'D LOVE TO GO, BUT I CAN'T.
SEE, THUNDER-BIRD? I WAS RIGHT!
TEACHER'S PET DOESN'T WANT TO ASSOCIATE WITH US.

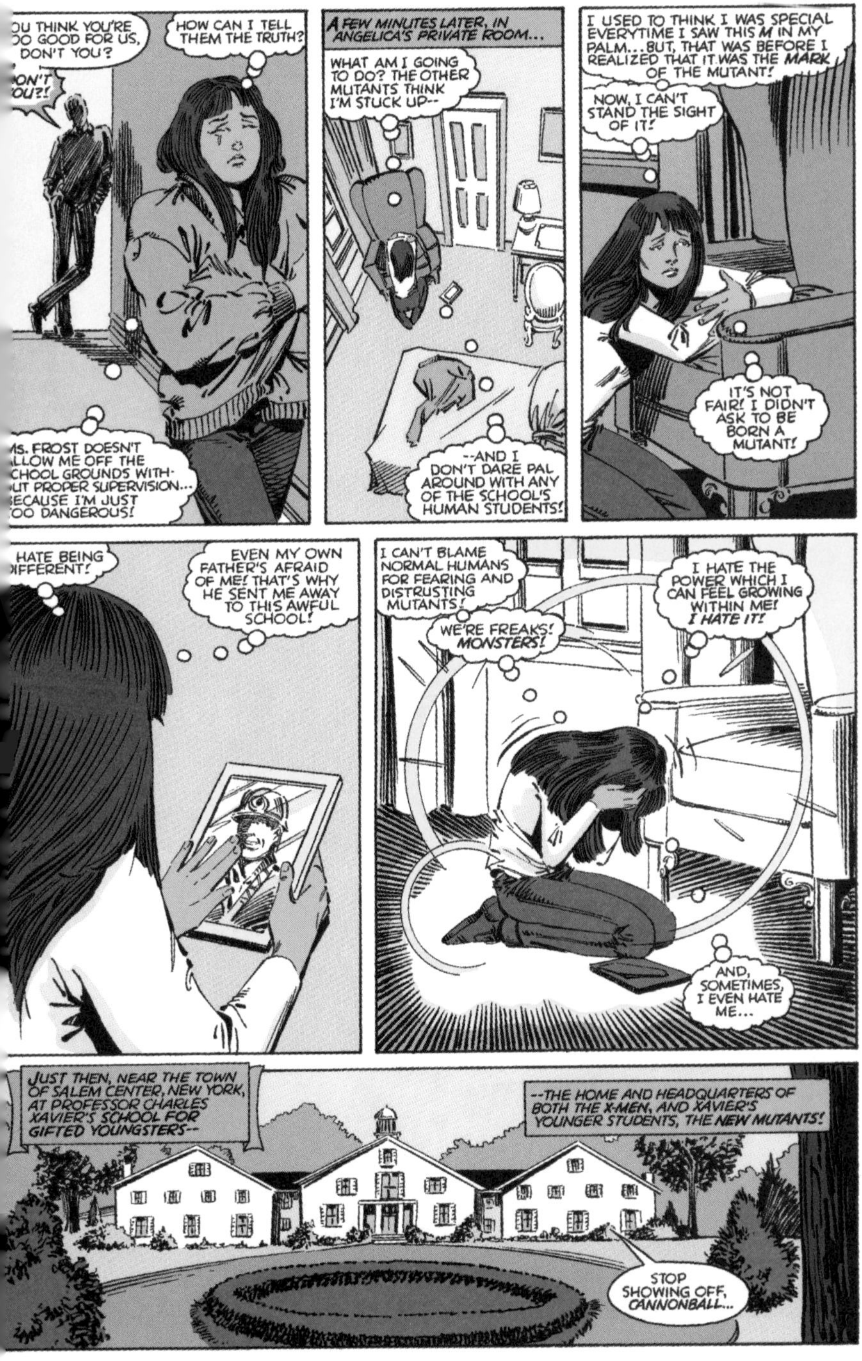
OU THINK YOU'RE
OO GOOD FOR US,
DON'T YOU?
ON'T
OU?!
HOW CAN I TELL THEM THE TRUTH?
MS. FROST DOESN'T ALLOW ME OFF THE SCHOOL GROUNDS WITH-OUT PROPER SUPERVISION... BECAUSE I'M JUST TOO DANGEROUS!
A FEW MINUTES LATER, IN ANGELICA'S PRIVATE ROOM...
WHAT AM I GOING TO DO? THE OTHER MUTANTS THINK I'M STUCK UP--
--AND I DON'T DARE PAL AROUND WITH ANY OF THE SCHOOL'S HUMAN STUDENTS!
I USED TO THINK I WAS SPECIAL EVERYTIME I SAW THIS M IN MY PALM...BUT, THAT WAS BEFORE I REALIZED THAT IT WAS THE MARK OF THE MUTANT!
NOW, I CAN'T STAND THE SIGHT OF IT!
IT'S NOT FAIR! I DIDN'T ASK TO BE BORN A MUTANT!
HATE BEING DIFFERENT!
EVEN MY OWN FATHER'S AFRAID OF ME! THAT'S WHY HE SENT ME AWAY TO THIS AWFUL SCHOOL!
I CAN'T BLAME NORMAL HUMANS FOR FEARING AND DISTRUSTING MUTANTS!
WE'RE FREAKS! MONSTERS!
I HATE THE POWER WHICH I CAN FEEL GROWING WITHIN ME! I HATE IT!
AND, SOMETIMES, I EVEN HATE ME...
JUST THEN, NEAR THE TOWN OF SALEM CENTER, NEW YORK, AT PROFESSOR CHARLES XAVIER'S SCHOOL FOR GIFTED YOUNGSTERS--
--THE HOME AND HEADQUARTERS OF BOTH THE X-MEN, AND XAVIER'S YOUNGER STUDENTS, THE NEW MUTANTS!
STOP SHOWING OFF, CANNONBALL...

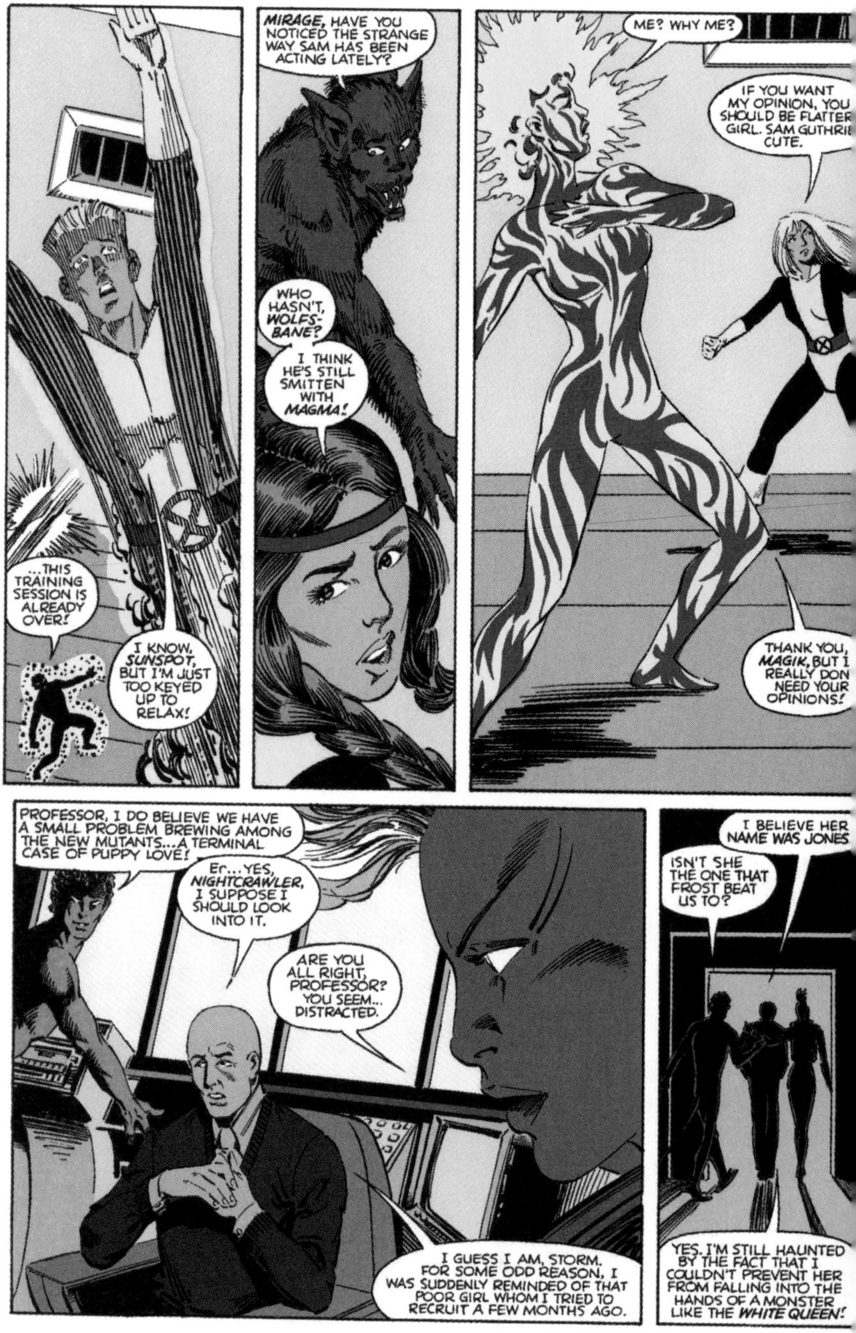
...THIS TRAINING SESSION IS ALREADY OVER!
I KNOW, SUNSPOT, BUT I'M JUST TOO KEYED UP TO RELAX!
MIRAGE, HAVE YOU NOTICED THE STRANGE WAY SAM HAS BEEN ACTING LATELY?
WHO HASN'T, WOLFSBANE?
I THINK HE'S STILL SMITTEN WITH MAGMA!
ME? WHY ME?
IF YOU WANT MY OPINION, YOU SHOULD BE FLATTER GIRL. SAM GUTHRI CUTE.
THANK YOU, MAGIK, BUT I REALLY DON NEED YOUR OPINIONS!
PROFESSOR, I DO BELIEVE WE HAVE A SMALL PROBLEM BREWING AMONG THE NEW MUTANTS...A TERMINAL CASE OF PUPPY LOVE!
Er...YES, NIGHTCRAWLER, I SUPPOSE I SHOULD LOOK INTO IT.
ARE YOU ALL RIGHT, PROFESSOR? YOU SEEM... DISTRACTED.
I GUESS I AM, STORM. FOR SOME ODD REASON, I WAS SUDDENLY REMINDED OF THAT POOR GIRL WHOM I TRIED TO RECRUIT A FEW MONTHS AGO.
I BELIEVE HER NAME WAS JONES
ISN'T SHE THE ONE THAT FROST BEAT US TO?
YES. I'M STILL HAUNTED BY THE FACT THAT I COULDN'T PREVENT HER FROM FALLING INTO THE HANDS OF A MONSTER LIKE THE WHITE QUEEN!

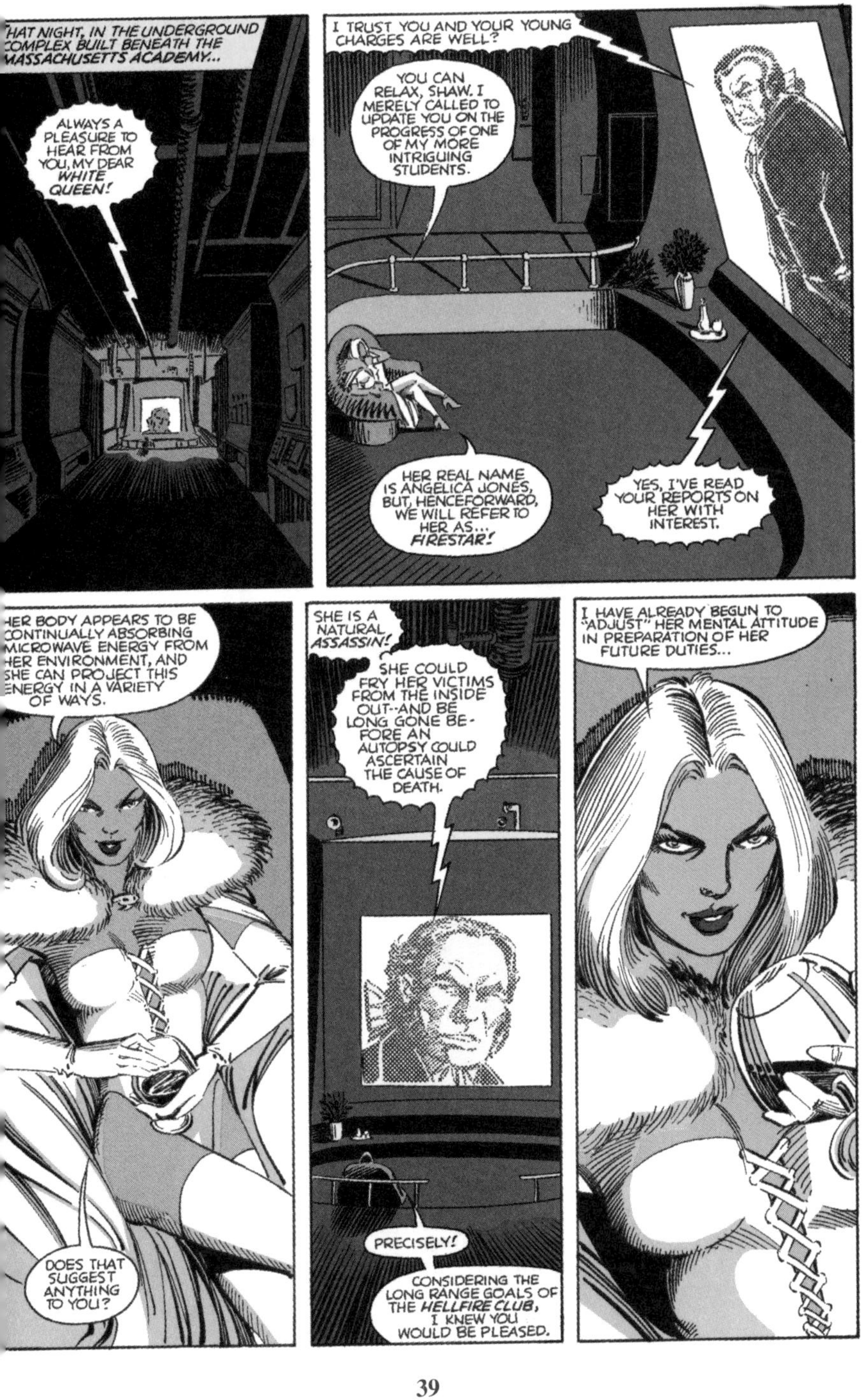
THAT NIGHT, IN THE UNDERGROUND COMPLEX BUILT BENEATH THE MASSACHUSETTS ACADEMY...
ALWAYS A PLEASURE TO HEAR FROM YOU, MY DEAR WHITE QUEEN!
I TRUST YOU AND YOUR YOUNG CHARGES ARE WELL?
YOU CAN RELAX, SHAW. I MERELY CALLED TO UPDATE YOU ON THE PROGRESS OF ONE OF MY MORE INTRIGUING STUDENTS.
HER REAL NAME IS ANGELICA JONES, BUT, HENCEFORWARD, WE WILL REFER TO HER AS... FIRESTAR!
YES, I'VE READ YOUR REPORTS ON HER WITH INTEREST.
HER BODY APPEARS TO BE CONTINUALLY ABSORBING MICROWAVE ENERGY FROM HER ENVIRONMENT, AND SHE CAN PROJECT THIS ENERGY IN A VARIETY OF WAYS.
DOES THAT SUGGEST ANYTHING TO YOU?
SHE IS A NATURAL ASSASSIN!
SHE COULD FRY HER VICTIMS FROM THE INSIDE OUT--AND BE LONG GONE BE-FORE AN AUTOPSY COULD ASCERTAIN THE CAUSE OF DEATH.
PRECISELY!
CONSIDERING THE LONG RANGE GOALS OF THE HELLFIRE CLUB, I KNEW YOU WOULD BE PLEASED.
I HAVE ALREADY BEGUN TO "ADJUST" HER MENTAL ATTITUDE IN PREPARATION OF HER FUTURE DUTIES...

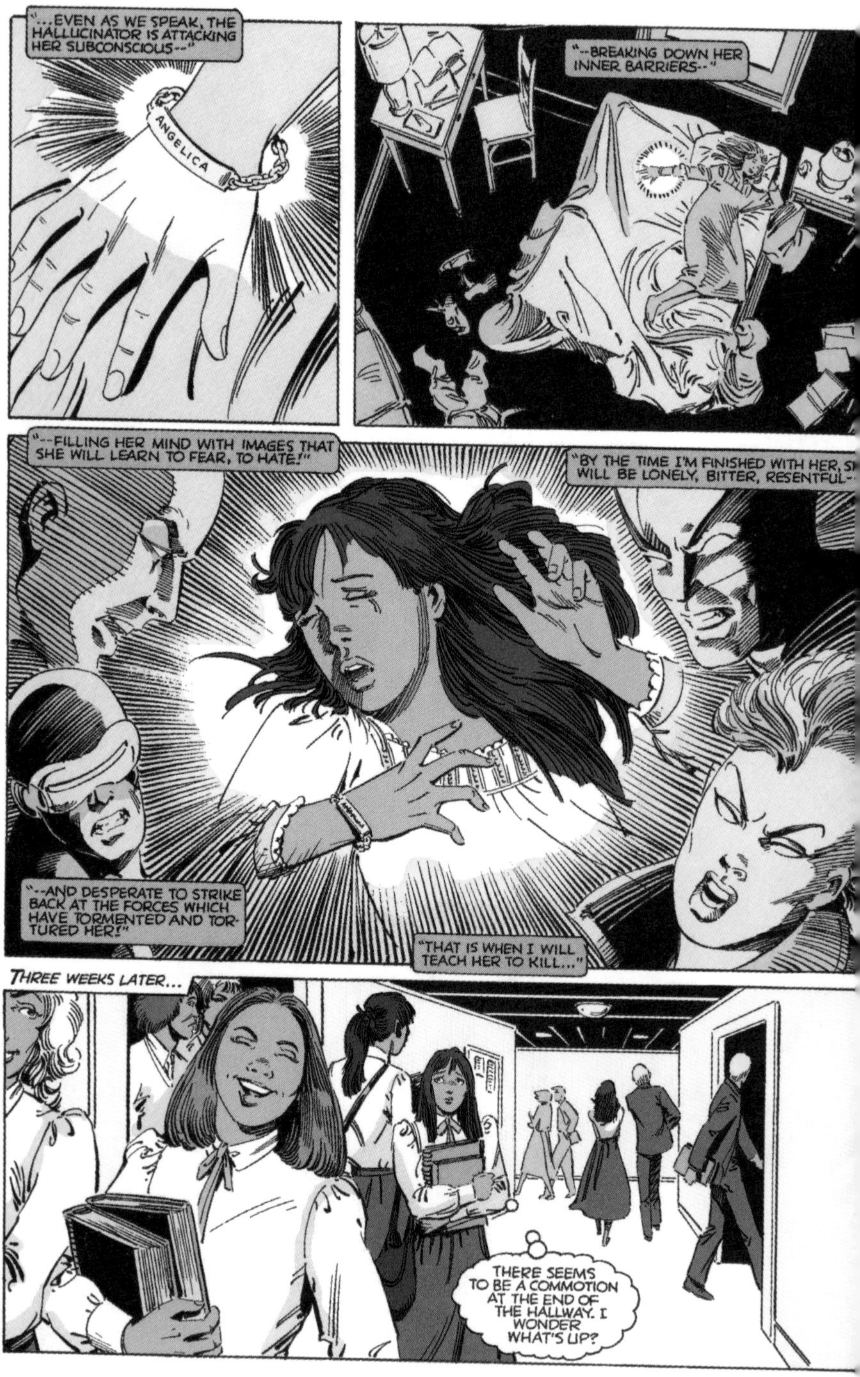
"...EVEN AS WE SPEAK, THE HALLUCINATOR IS ATTACKING HER SUBCONSCIOUS--"
ANGELICA
"--BREAKING DOWN HER INNER BARRIERS--"
"--FILLING HER MIND WITH IMAGES THAT SHE WILL LEARN TO FEAR, TO HATE!"
"BY THE TIME I'M FINISHED WITH HER, SH
WILL BE LONELY, BITTER, RESENTFUL--
"--AND DESPERATE TO STRIKE BACK AT THE FORCES WHICH HAVE TORMENTED AND TORTURED HER!"
"THAT IS WHEN I WILL TEACH HER TO KILL..."
THREE WEEKS LATER...
THERE SEEMS TO BE A COMMOTION AT THE END OF THE HALLWAY. I WONDER WHAT'S UP?

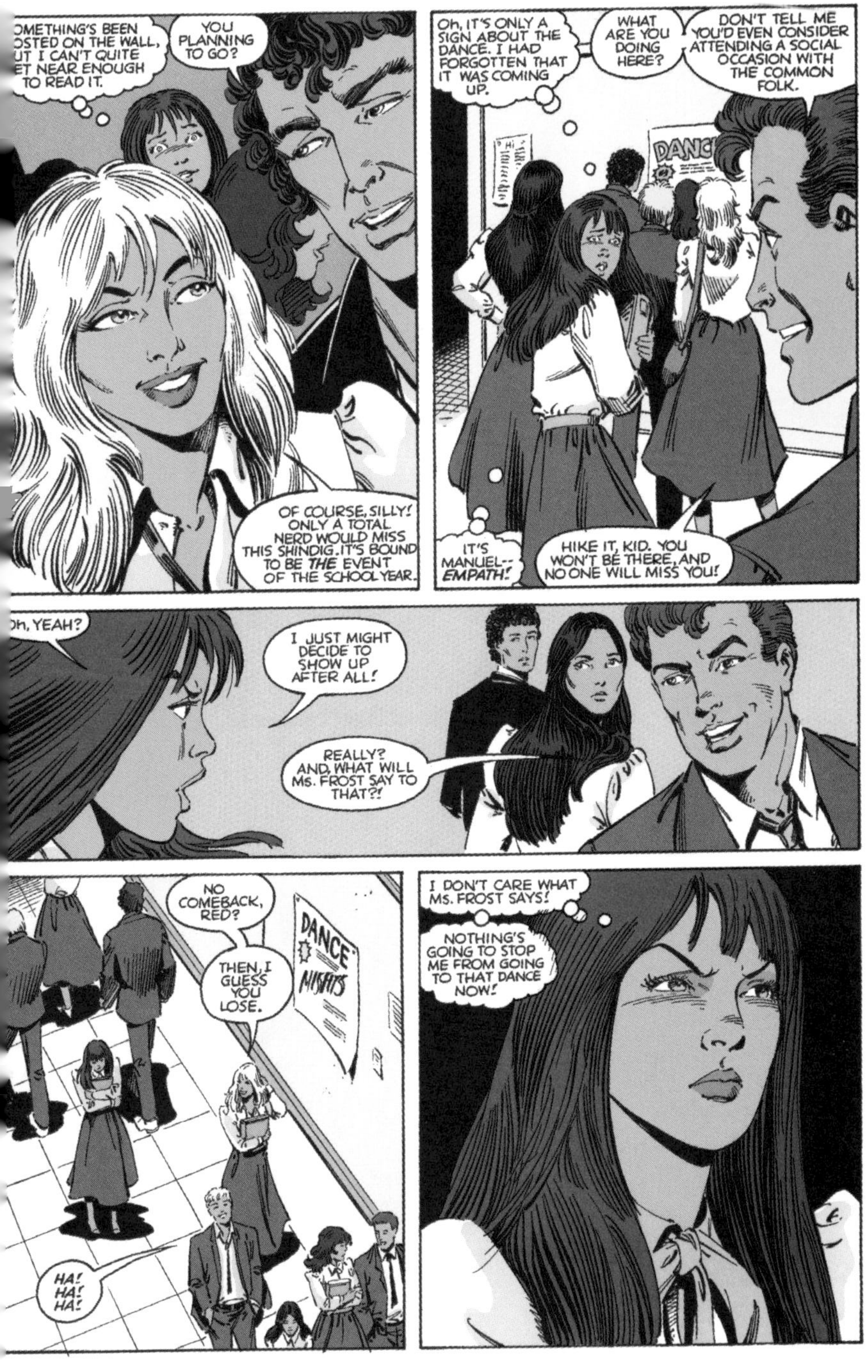
OMETHING'S BEEN OSTED ON THE WALL, UT I CAN'T QUITE ET NEAR ENOUGH TO READ IT.
YOU PLANNING TO GO?
OF COURSE, SILLY! ONLY A TOTAL NERD WOULD MISS THIS SHINDIG. IT'S BOUND TO BE *THE* EVENT OF THE SCHOOL YEAR.
Oh, IT'S ONLY A SIGN ABOUT THE DANCE. I HAD FORGOTTEN THAT IT WAS COMING UP.
WHAT ARE YOU DOING HERE?
DON'T TELL ME YOU'D EVEN CONSIDER ATTENDING A SOCIAL OCCASION WITH THE COMMON FOLK.
IT'S MANUEL-- *EMPATH!*
HIKE IT, KID. YOU WON'T BE THERE, AND NO ONE WILL MISS YOU!
DANCE
Oh, YEAH?
I JUST MIGHT DECIDE TO SHOW UP AFTER ALL!
REALLY? AND, WHAT WILL Ms. FROST SAY TO THAT?!
NO COMEBACK, RED?
THEN, I GUESS YOU LOSE.
DANCE
MISFITS
HA! HA! HA!
I DON'T CARE WHAT Ms. FROST SAYS!
NOTHING'S GOING TO STOP ME FROM GOING TO THAT DANCE NOW!

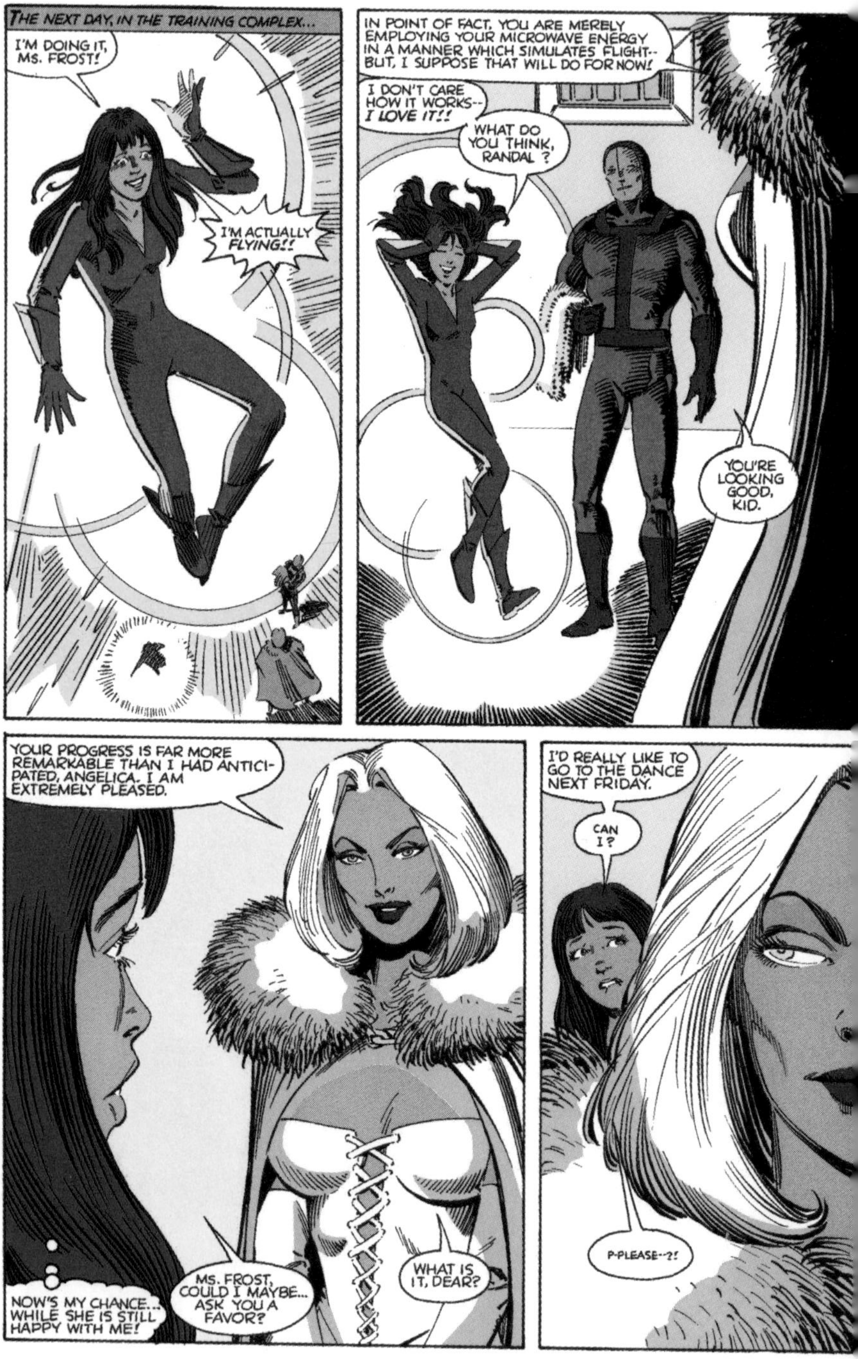
THE NEXT DAY, IN THE TRAINING COMPLEX...
I'M DOING IT, MS. FROST!
I'M ACTUALLY FLYING!!
IN POINT OF FACT, YOU ARE MERELY EMPLOYING YOUR MICROWAVE ENERGY IN A MANNER WHICH SIMULATES FLIGHT-- BUT, I SUPPOSE THAT WILL DO FOR NOW!
I DON'T CARE HOW IT WORKS-- I LOVE IT!!
WHAT DO YOU THINK, RANDAL ?
YOU'RE LOOKING GOOD, KID.
YOUR PROGRESS IS FAR MORE REMARKABLE THAN I HAD ANTICIPATED, ANGELICA. I AM EXTREMELY PLEASED.
NOW'S MY CHANCE... WHILE SHE IS STILL HAPPY WITH ME!
MS. FROST, COULD I MAYBE... ASK YOU A FAVOR?
WHAT IS IT, DEAR?
I'D REALLY LIKE TO GO TO THE DANCE NEXT FRIDAY.
CAN I?
P-PLEASE--?!

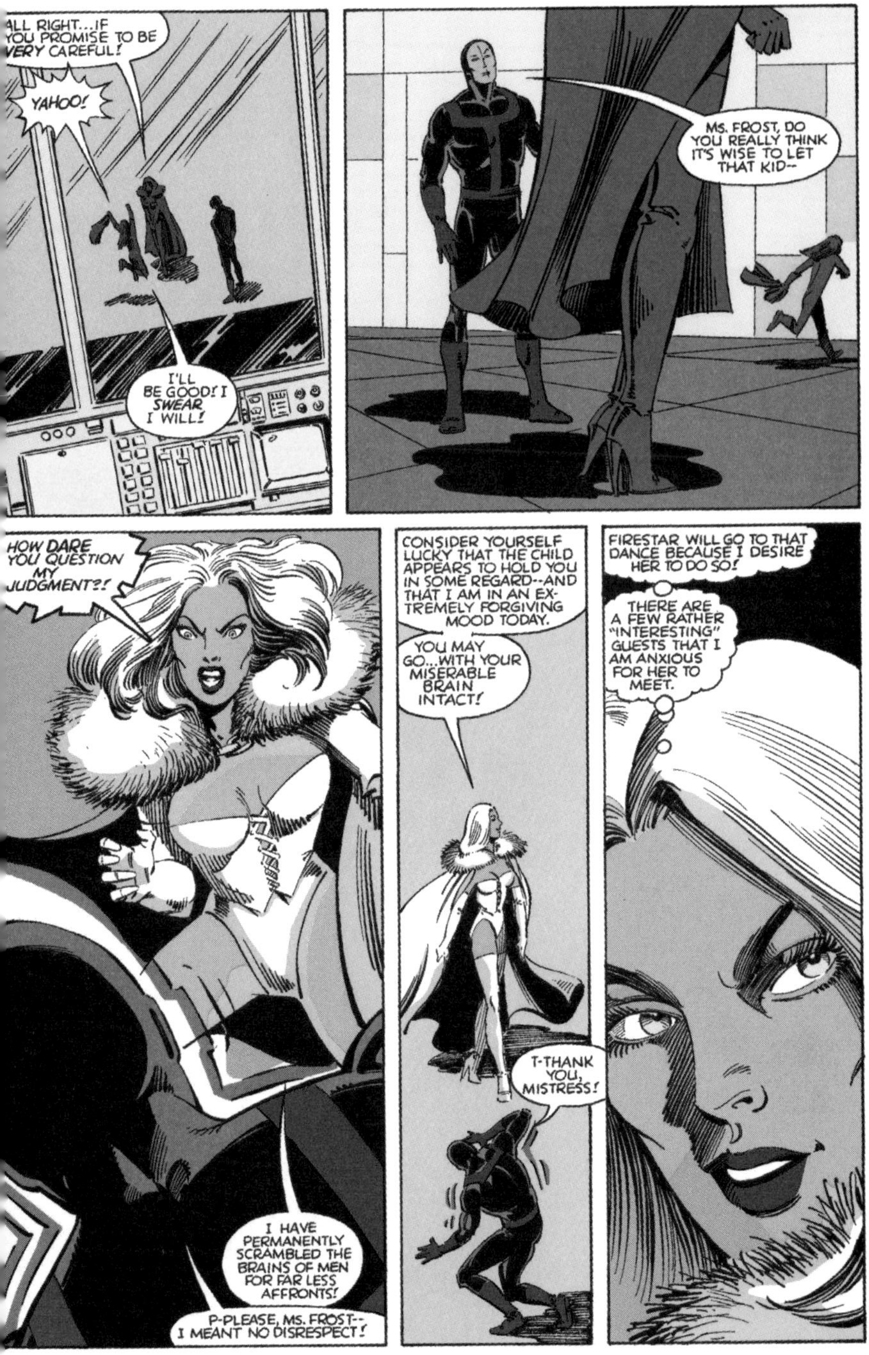

ALL RIGHT...IF YOU PROMISE TO BE VERY CAREFUL!
YAHOO!
I'LL BE GOOD! I SWEAR I WILL!
MS. FROST, DO YOU REALLY THINK IT'S WISE TO LET THAT KID--
HOW DARE YOU QUESTION MY JUDGMENT?!
I HAVE PERMANENTLY SCRAMBLED THE BRAINS OF MEN FOR FAR LESS AFFRONTS!
P-PLEASE, MS. FROST-- I MEANT NO DISRESPECT!
CONSIDER YOURSELF LUCKY THAT THE CHILD APPEARS TO HOLD YOU IN SOME REGARD--AND THAT I AM IN AN EXTREMELY FORGIVING MOOD TODAY.
YOU MAY GO...WITH YOUR MISERABLE BRAIN INTACT!
T-THANK YOU, MISTRESS!
FIRESTAR WILL GO TO THAT DANCE BECAUSE I DESIRE HER TO DO SO!
THERE ARE A FEW RATHER "INTERESTING" GUESTS THAT I AM ANXIOUS FOR HER TO MEET.

ELSEWHERE, AT THAT VERY MOMENT...

GO AHEAD, SAM. I'LL LET YOU EXPLAIN THE SITUATION.

WELL, PROFESSOR, IT'S LIKE THIS... WE ALL GOT INVITATIONS TO THIS HERE DANCE AT THE MASSACHUSETTS ACADEMY... AND, WELL, WE'D LIKE TO GO.

MS. FROST'S SCHOOL? HAVE YOU FORGOTTEN YOUR PAST EXPERIENCES WITH THE WHITE QUEEN'S HELLIONS--AND THE HELLFIRE CLUB ITSELF?*

NO, SIR, BUT WE DON'T THINK FROS WILL TRY ANYTHIN FUNNY AT A DANCE HER OWN STUDENT WILL BE ATTENDIN

*SEE NEW MUTANTS GRAPH NOVEL AND NEW MUTANT #15-17. --Ann.

I DON'T LIKE IT. IT'S JUST PLAIN STUPID TO PUT YOURSELF IN YOUR ENEMY'S HANDS WHEN YOU HAVE NOTHING TO GAIN.

AH, BUT I AM HOPING TO END UP IN THE HANDS OF SOME VERY PRETTY COEDS!

BE QUIET, ROBERTO!

I AM FOR IT, PROFESSOR.

THESE YOUNG ONES SHOULD BE EXPOSED TO MORE SOCIAL SITUATIONS. YOU CAN'T KEEP THEM IN THIS NEST FOREVER.

The Pleas of your c Mas

I'M WITH STORM, AND I'LL EVEN VOLUNTEER TO ACT AS A CHAPERONE.

WAY TO GO, COLOSSUS!

WELL, I SUPPOSE IT WILL BE ALL RIGHT... JUST THIS ONCE!

YAY!

I MUST BE MELLOWING IN MY OLD AGE. I'M CERTAIN THAT I NEVER WOULD HAVE PERMITTED THE ORIGINAL X-MEN TO GO.

CHANGE IS ALWAYS GOOD WHEN IT IS TEMPERED BY WISDOM AND EXPERIENCE.

JUST MAKE SURE YOU SEE HOW THE JONES GIRL IS DOING.

44

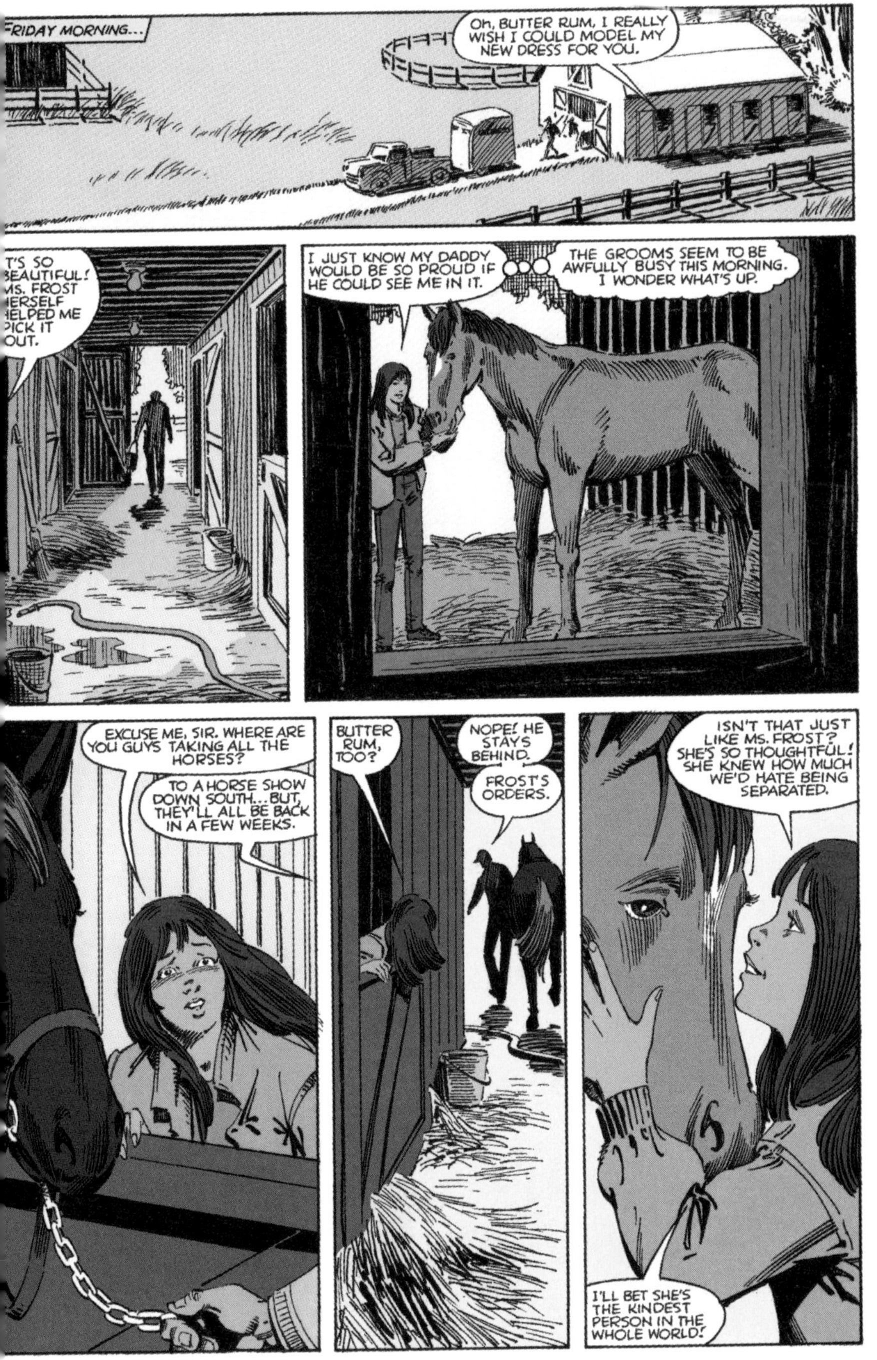
FRIDAY MORNING...
Oh, BUTTER RUM, I REALLY WISH I COULD MODEL MY NEW DRESS FOR YOU.
T'S SO BEAUTIFUL! MS. FROST HERSELF HELPED ME PICK IT OUT.
I JUST KNOW MY DADDY WOULD BE SO PROUD IF HE COULD SEE ME IN IT.
THE GROOMS SEEM TO BE AWFULLY BUSY THIS MORNING. I WONDER WHAT'S UP.
EXCUSE ME, SIR. WHERE ARE YOU GUYS TAKING ALL THE HORSES?
TO A HORSE SHOW DOWN SOUTH... BUT, THEY'LL ALL BE BACK IN A FEW WEEKS.
BUTTER RUM, TOO?
NOPE! HE STAYS BEHIND.
FROST'S ORDERS.
ISN'T THAT JUST LIKE MS. FROST? SHE'S SO THOUGHTFUL! SHE KNEW HOW MUCH WE'D HATE BEING SEPARATED.
I'LL BET SHE'S THE KINDEST PERSON IN THE WHOLE WORLD!

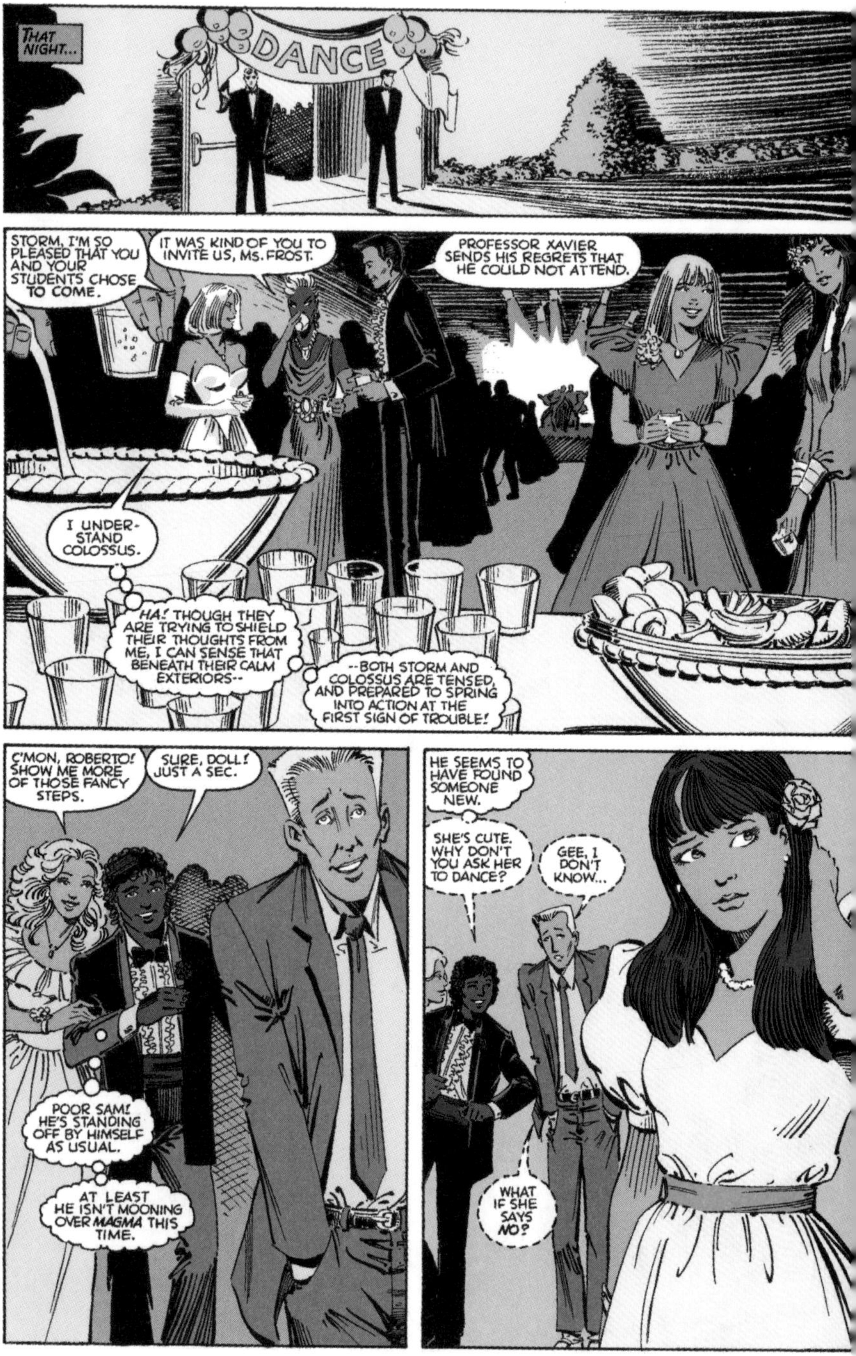
THAT NIGHT...
DANCE
STORM, I'M SO PLEASED THAT YOU AND YOUR STUDENTS CHOSE TO COME.
IT WAS KIND OF YOU TO INVITE US, MS. FROST.
PROFESSOR XAVIER SENDS HIS REGRETS THAT HE COULD NOT ATTEND.
I UNDER-STAND COLOSSUS.
HA! THOUGH THEY ARE TRYING TO SHIELD THEIR THOUGHTS FROM ME, I CAN SENSE THAT BENEATH THEIR CALM EXTERIORS--
--BOTH STORM AND COLOSSUS ARE TENSED, AND PREPARED TO SPRING INTO ACTION AT THE FIRST SIGN OF TROUBLE!
C'MON, ROBERTO! SHOW ME MORE OF THOSE FANCY STEPS.
SURE, DOLL! JUST A SEC.
POOR SAM! HE'S STANDING OFF BY HIMSELF AS USUAL.
AT LEAST HE ISN'T MOONING OVER MAGMA THIS TIME.
HE SEEMS TO HAVE FOUND SOMEONE NEW.
SHE'S CUTE. WHY DON'T YOU ASK HER TO DANCE?
GEE, I DON'T KNOW...
WHAT IF SHE SAYS NO?

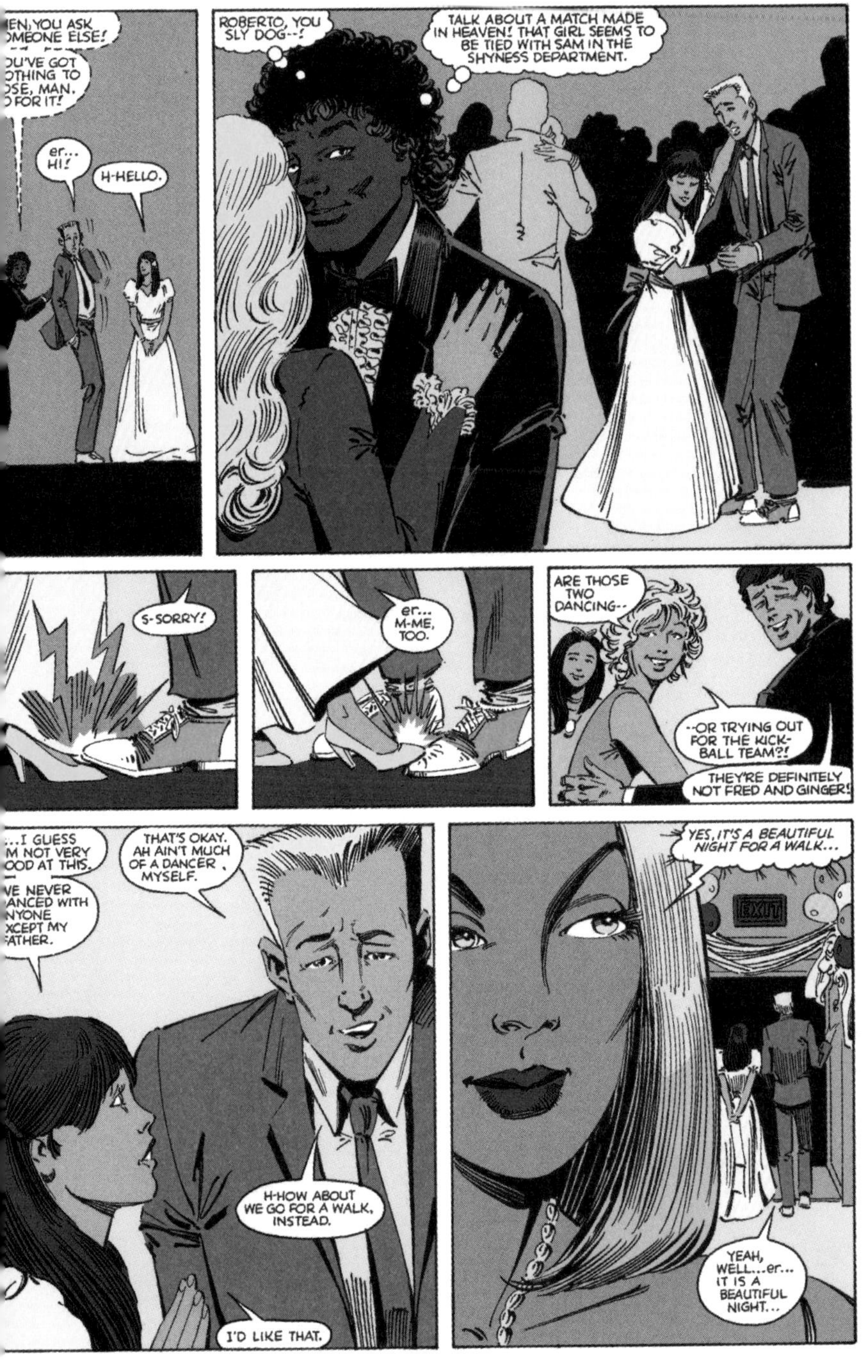

...EN, YOU ASK
...MEONE ELSE!
...OU'VE GOT
...OTHING TO
...OSE, MAN.
...O FOR IT!
er... HI!
H-HELLO.
ROBERTO, YOU SLY DOG--!
TALK ABOUT A MATCH MADE IN HEAVEN! THAT GIRL SEEMS TO BE TIED WITH SAM IN THE SHYNESS DEPARTMENT.
S-SORRY!
er... M-ME, TOO.
ARE THOSE TWO DANCING--
--OR TRYING OUT FOR THE KICK-BALL TEAM?!
THEY'RE DEFINITELY NOT FRED AND GINGER!
...I GUESS
...M NOT VERY
...OOD AT THIS.
...VE NEVER
...ANCED WITH
...NYONE
...XCEPT MY
...ATHER.
THAT'S OKAY. AH AIN'T MUCH OF A DANCER MYSELF.
H-HOW ABOUT WE GO FOR A WALK, INSTEAD.
I'D LIKE THAT.
YES, IT'S A BEAUTIFUL NIGHT FOR A WALK...
EXIT
YEAH, WELL...er... IT IS A BEAUTIFUL NIGHT...

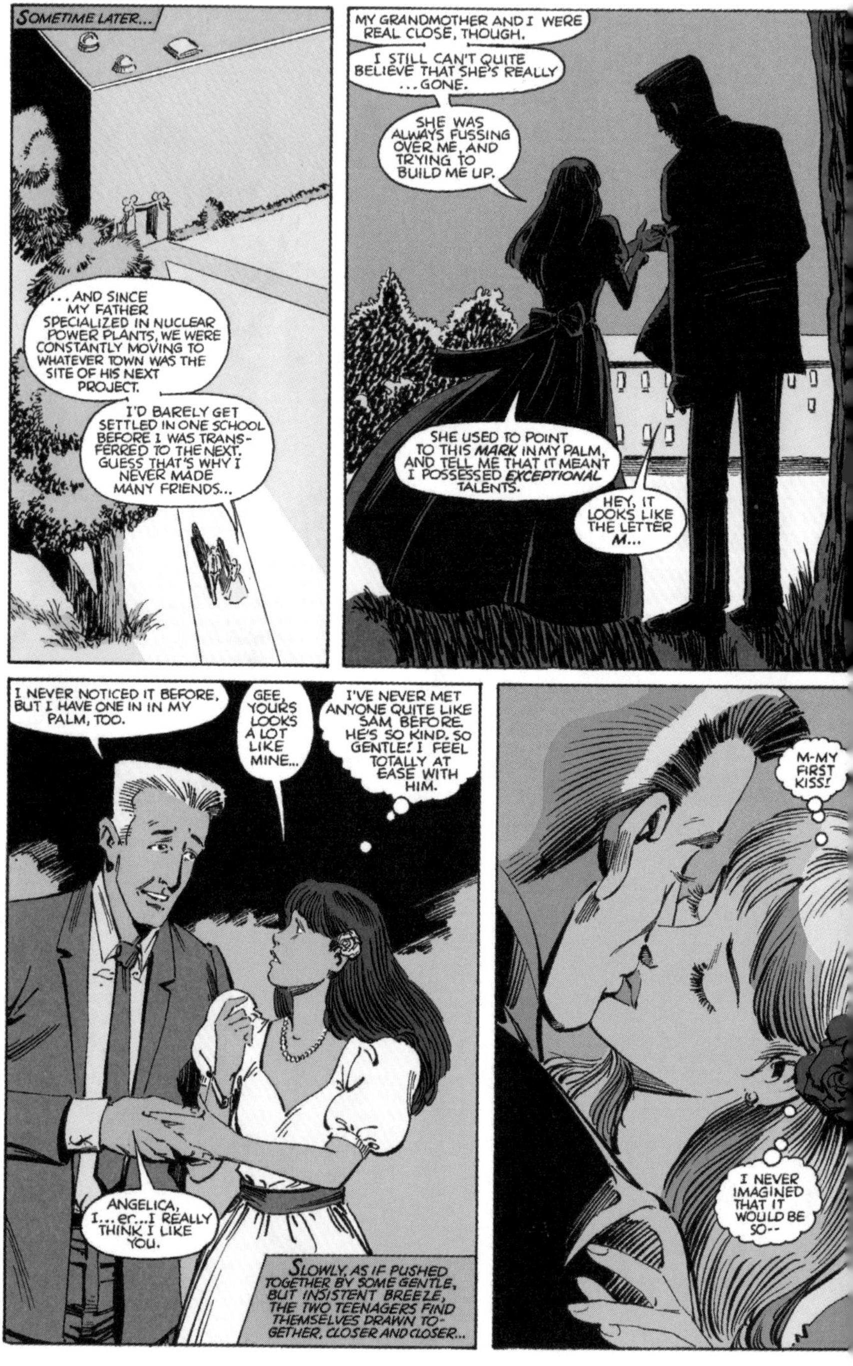
SOMETIME LATER...
...AND SINCE MY FATHER SPECIALIZED IN NUCLEAR POWER PLANTS, WE WERE CONSTANTLY MOVING TO WHATEVER TOWN WAS THE SITE OF HIS NEXT PROJECT.
I'D BARELY GET SETTLED IN ONE SCHOOL BEFORE I WAS TRANSFERRED TO THE NEXT. GUESS THAT'S WHY I NEVER MADE MANY FRIENDS...
MY GRANDMOTHER AND I WERE REAL CLOSE, THOUGH.
I STILL CAN'T QUITE BELIEVE THAT SHE'S REALLY ...GONE.
SHE WAS ALWAYS FUSSING OVER ME, AND TRYING TO BUILD ME UP.
SHE USED TO POINT TO THIS MARK IN MY PALM, AND TELL ME THAT IT MEANT I POSSESSED EXCEPTIONAL TALENTS.
HEY, IT LOOKS LIKE THE LETTER M...
I NEVER NOTICED IT BEFORE, BUT I HAVE ONE IN IN MY PALM, TOO.
GEE, YOURS LOOKS A LOT LIKE MINE...
I'VE NEVER MET ANYONE QUITE LIKE SAM BEFORE. HE'S SO KIND. SO GENTLE! I FEEL TOTALLY AT EASE WITH HIM.
ANGELICA, I...er...I REALLY THINK I LIKE YOU.
SLOWLY, AS IF PUSHED TOGETHER BY SOME GENTLE, BUT INSISTENT BREEZE, THE TWO TEENAGERS FIND THEMSELVES DRAWN TOGETHER, CLOSER AND CLOSER...
M-MY FIRST KISS!
I NEVER IMAGINED THAT IT WOULD BE SO--

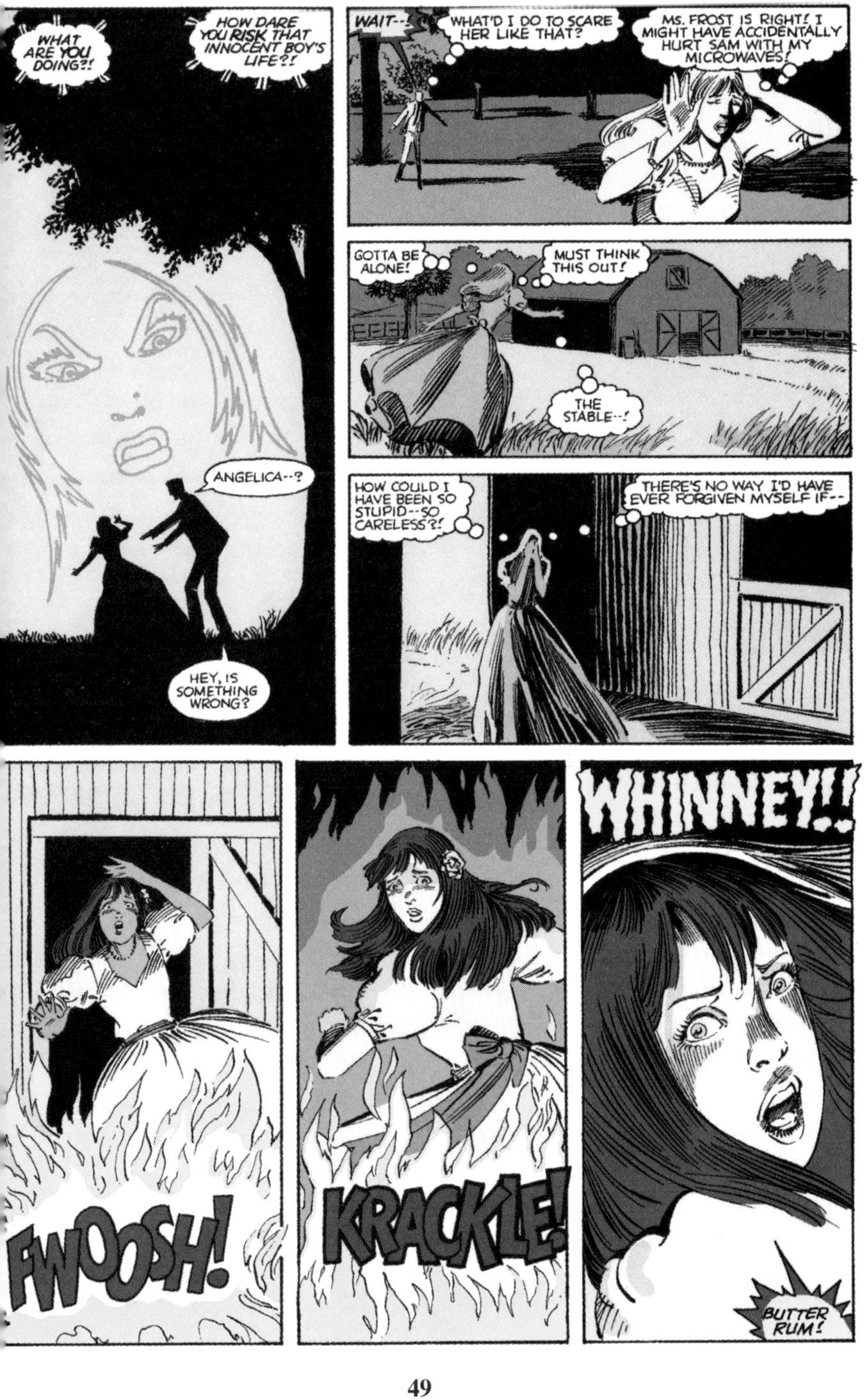
WHAT ARE YOU DOING?!
HOW DARE YOU RISK THAT INNOCENT BOY'S LIFE?!
ANGELICA--?
HEY, IS SOMETHING WRONG?
WAIT--!
WHAT'D I DO TO SCARE HER LIKE THAT?
MS. FROST IS RIGHT! I MIGHT HAVE ACCIDENTALLY HURT SAM WITH MY MICROWAVES!
GOTTA BE ALONE!
MUST THINK THIS OUT!
THE STABLE--!
HOW COULD I HAVE BEEN SO STUPID--SO CARELESS?!
THERE'S NO WAY I'D HAVE EVER FORGIVEN MYSELF IF--
FWOOSH!
KRACKLE!
WHINNEY!!
BUTTER RUM!

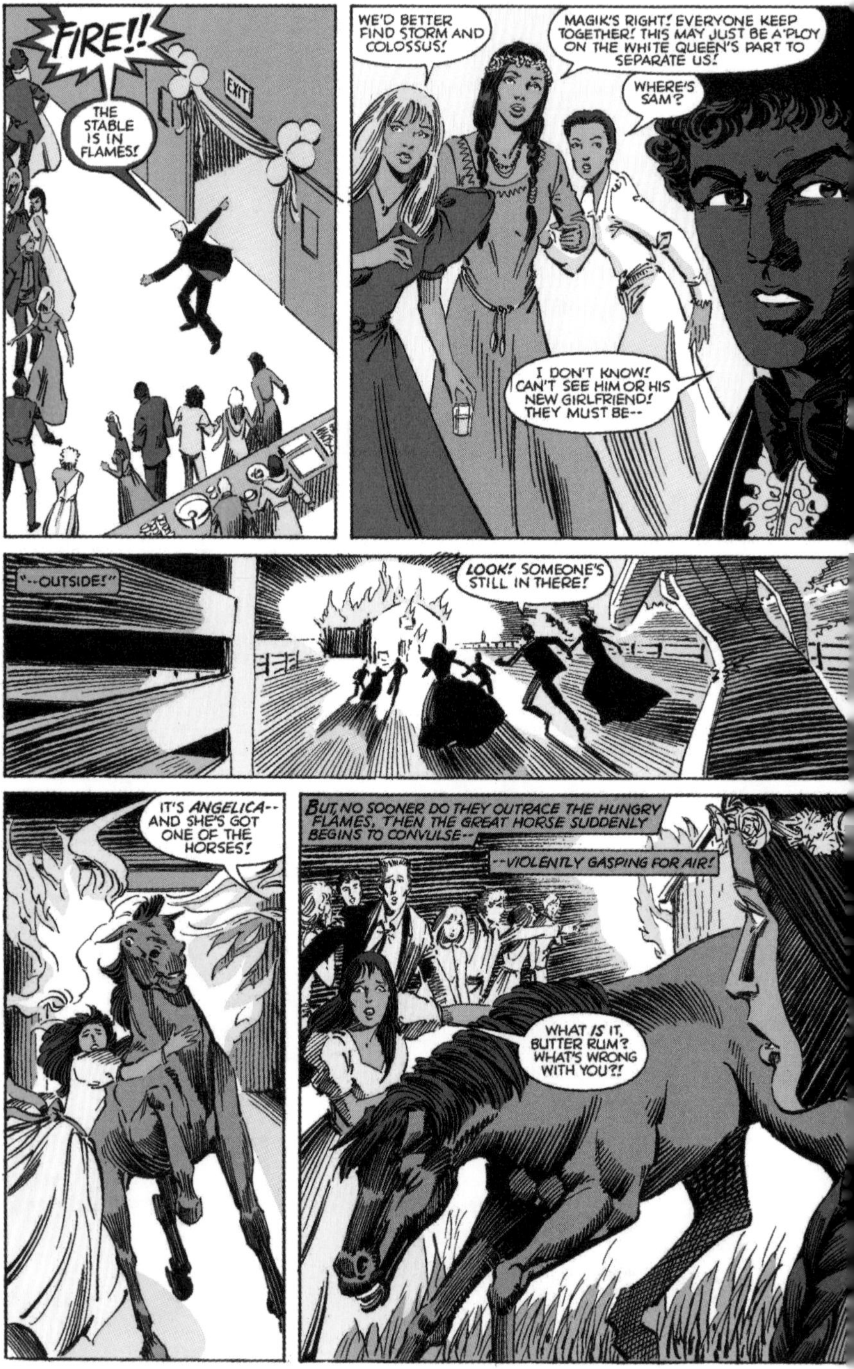
FIRE!!
THE STABLE IS IN FLAMES!
WE'D BETTER FIND STORM AND COLOSSUS!
MAGIK'S RIGHT! EVERYONE KEEP TOGETHER! THIS MAY JUST BE A PLOY ON THE WHITE QUEEN'S PART TO SEPARATE US!
WHERE'S SAM?
I DON'T KNOW! CAN'T SEE HIM OR HIS NEW GIRLFRIEND! THEY MUST BE--
"--OUTSIDE!"
LOOK! SOMEONE'S STILL IN THERE!
IT'S ANGELICA-- AND SHE'S GOT ONE OF THE HORSES!
BUT, NO SOONER DO THEY OUTRACE THE HUNGRY FLAMES, THEN THE GREAT HORSE SUDDENLY BEGINS TO CONVULSE--
--VIOLENTLY GASPING FOR AIR!
WHAT IS IT, BUTTER RUM? WHAT'S WRONG WITH YOU?!

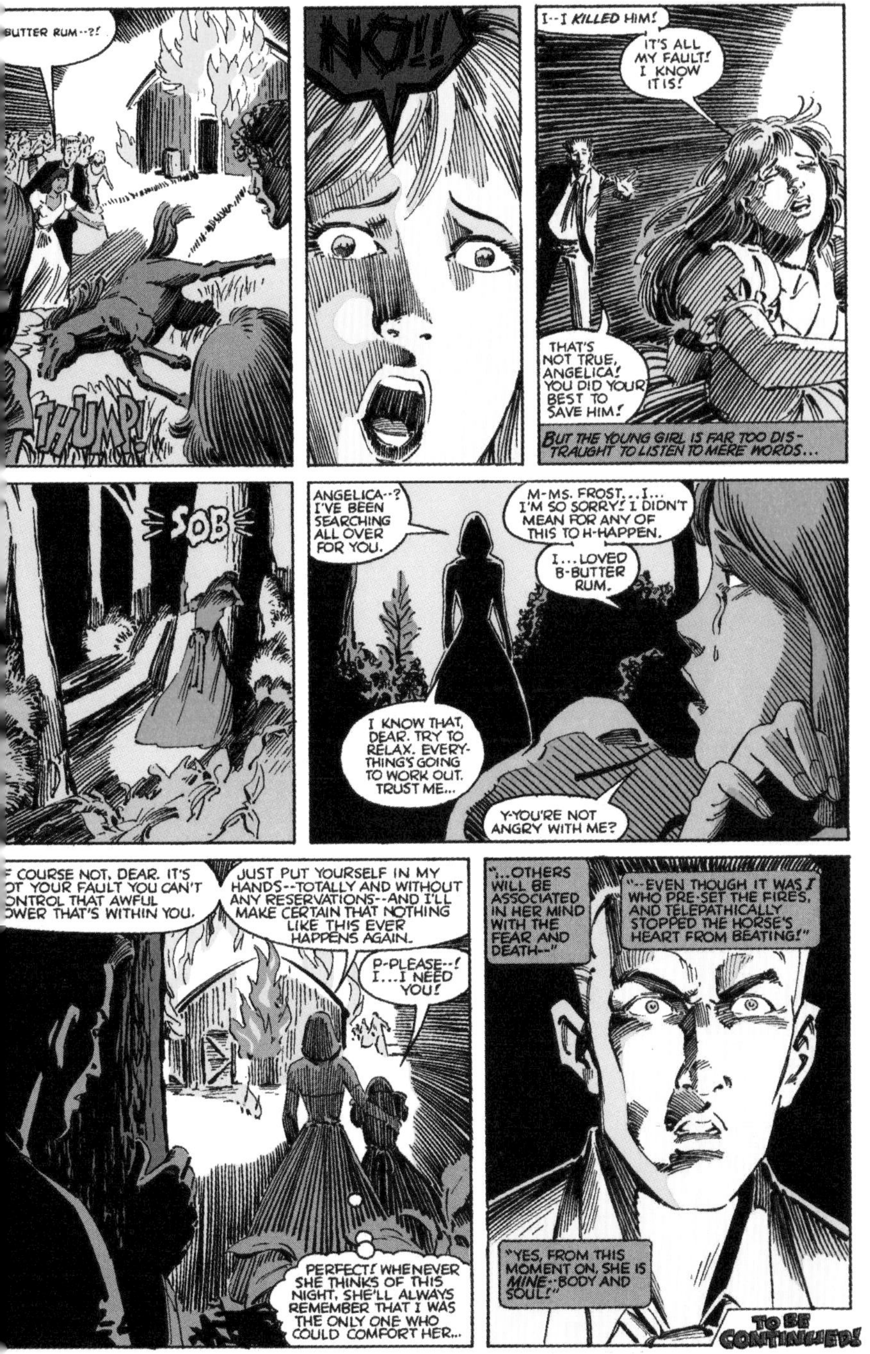
BUTTER RUM--?!
THUMP!
NO!!
I--I KILLED HIM!
IT'S ALL MY FAULT! I KNOW IT IS!
THAT'S NOT TRUE, ANGELICA! YOU DID YOUR BEST TO SAVE HIM!
BUT THE YOUNG GIRL IS FAR TOO DISTRAUGHT TO LISTEN TO MERE WORDS...
SOB
ANGELICA--? I'VE BEEN SEARCHING ALL OVER FOR YOU.
M-MS. FROST...I... I'M SO SORRY! I DIDN'T MEAN FOR ANY OF THIS TO H-HAPPEN.
I...LOVED B-BUTTER RUM.
I KNOW THAT, DEAR. TRY TO RELAX. EVERYTHING'S GOING TO WORK OUT. TRUST ME...
Y-YOU'RE NOT ANGRY WITH ME?
F COURSE NOT, DEAR. IT'S OT YOUR FAULT YOU CAN'T ONTROL THAT AWFUL OWER THAT'S WITHIN YOU.
JUST PUT YOURSELF IN MY HANDS--TOTALLY AND WITHOUT ANY RESERVATIONS--AND I'LL MAKE CERTAIN THAT NOTHING LIKE THIS EVER HAPPENS AGAIN.
P-PLEASE--! I...I NEED YOU!
PERFECT! WHENEVER SHE THINKS OF THIS NIGHT, SHE'LL ALWAYS REMEMBER THAT I WAS THE ONLY ONE WHO COULD COMFORT HER...
"...OTHERS WILL BE ASSOCIATED IN HER MIND WITH THE FEAR AND DEATH--"
"--EVEN THOUGH IT WAS I WHO PRE-SET THE FIRES, AND TELEPATHICALLY STOPPED THE HORSE'S HEART FROM BEATING!"
"YES, FROM THIS MOMENT ON, SHE IS MINE--BODY AND SOUL!"
TO BE CONTINUED!

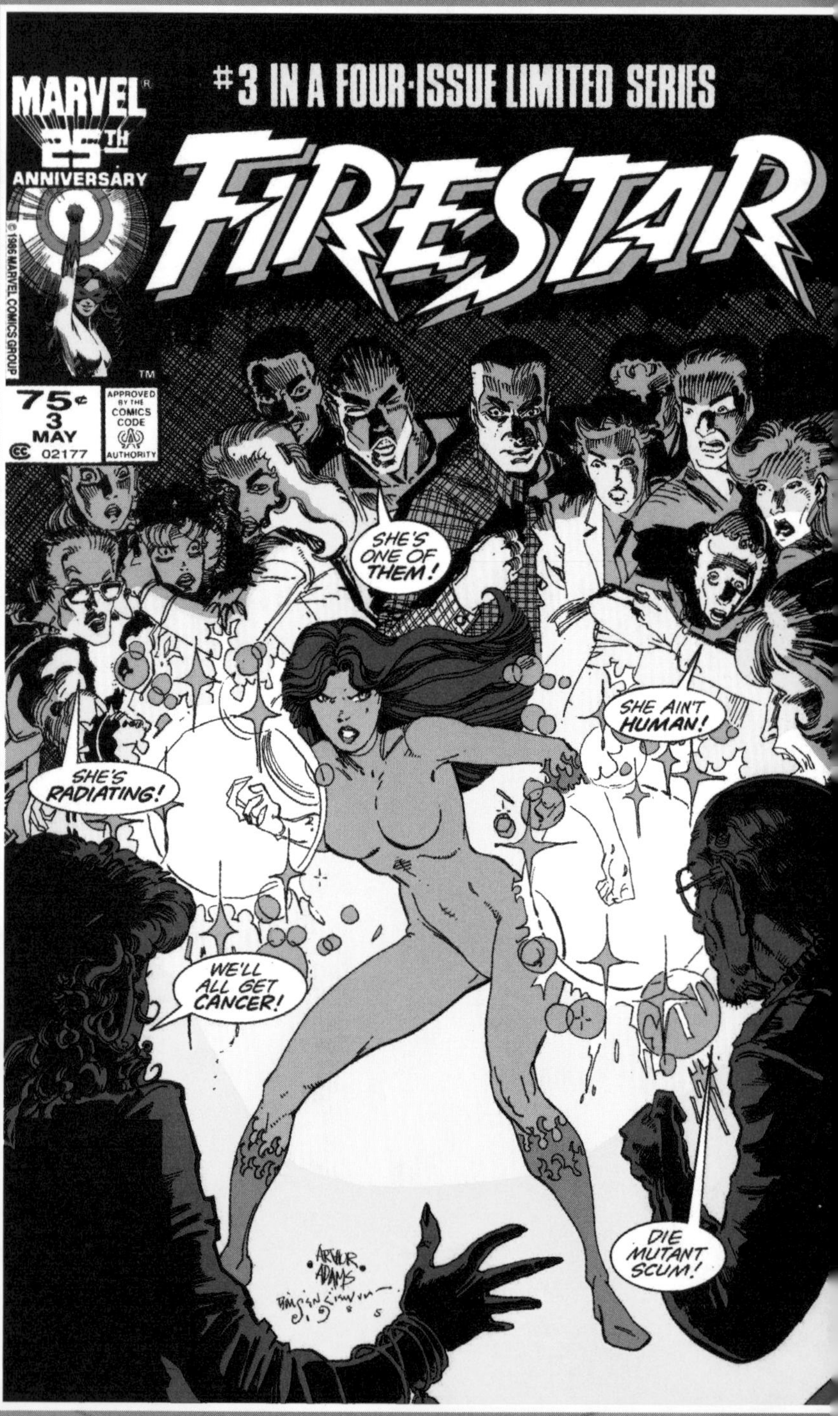
MARVEL
25TH ANNIVERSARY
© 1986 MARVEL COMICS GROUP
#3 IN A FOUR-ISSUE LIMITED SERIES
FIRESTAR
TM
75¢
3
MAY
02177
APPROVED BY THE COMICS CODE AUTHORITY
SHE'S ONE OF THEM!
SHE AIN'T HUMAN!
SHE'S RADIATING!
WE'LL ALL GET CANCER!
DIE MUTANT SCUM!

nable to cope with the fact that his only daughter is a mutant possessing strange and anny powers, *Bartholomew Jones* quickly entrusts her education and training to *Ms. ma Frost*, headmistress of the prestigious *Massachusetts Academy*. Secretly a member he *Inner Council of the Hellfire Club*, an organization determined to dominate the world, st plans to mold young *Angelica* into the ultimate weapon—a human killing machine!!

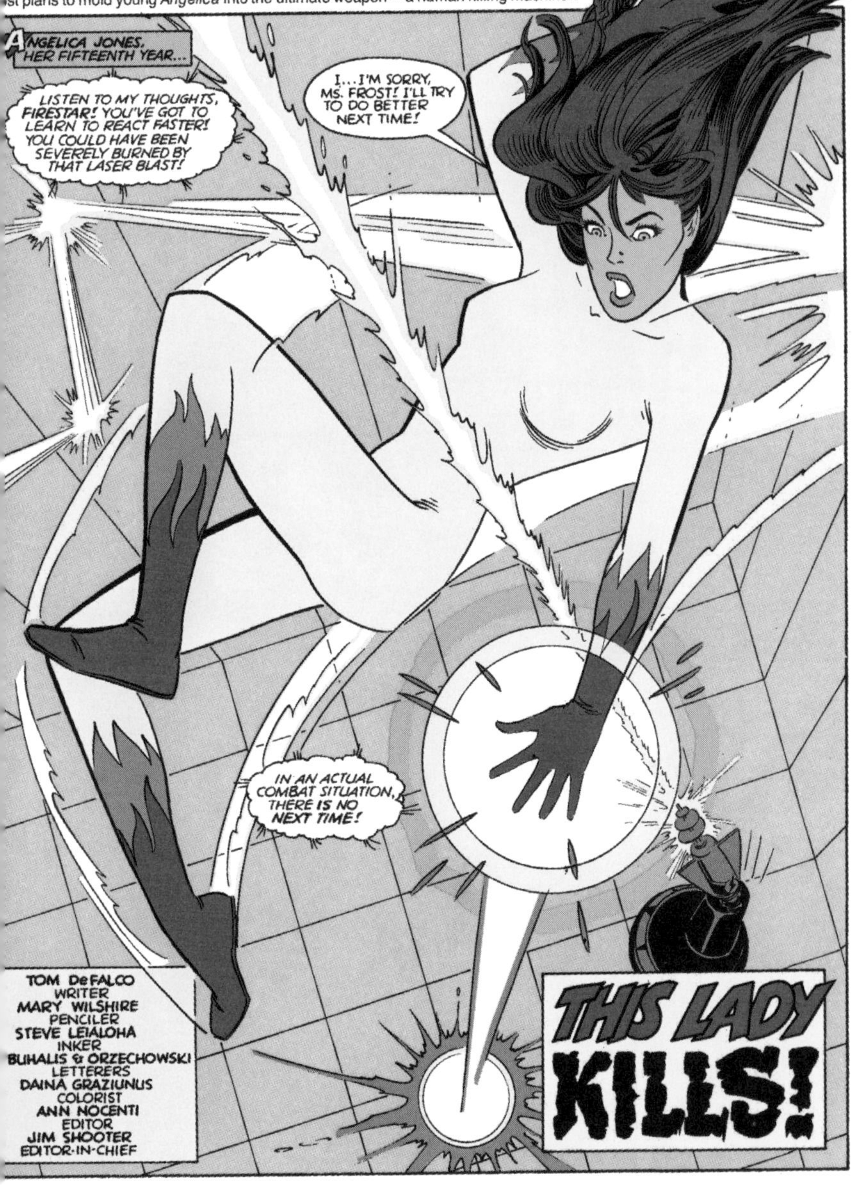
ANGELICA JONES, HER FIFTEENTH YEAR...
LISTEN TO MY THOUGHTS, FIRESTAR! YOU'VE GOT TO LEARN TO REACT FASTER! YOU COULD HAVE BEEN SEVERELY BURNED BY THAT LASER BLAST!
I... I'M SORRY, MS. FROST! I'LL TRY TO DO BETTER NEXT TIME!
IN AN ACTUAL COMBAT SITUATION, THERE IS NO NEXT TIME!
TOM DeFALCO WRITER
MARY WILSHIRE PENCILER
STEVE LEIALOHA INKER
BUHALIS & ORZECHOWSKI LETTERERS
DAINA GRAZIUNUS COLORIST
ANN NOCENTI EDITOR
JIM SHOOTER EDITOR-IN-CHIEF
THIS LADY KILLS!

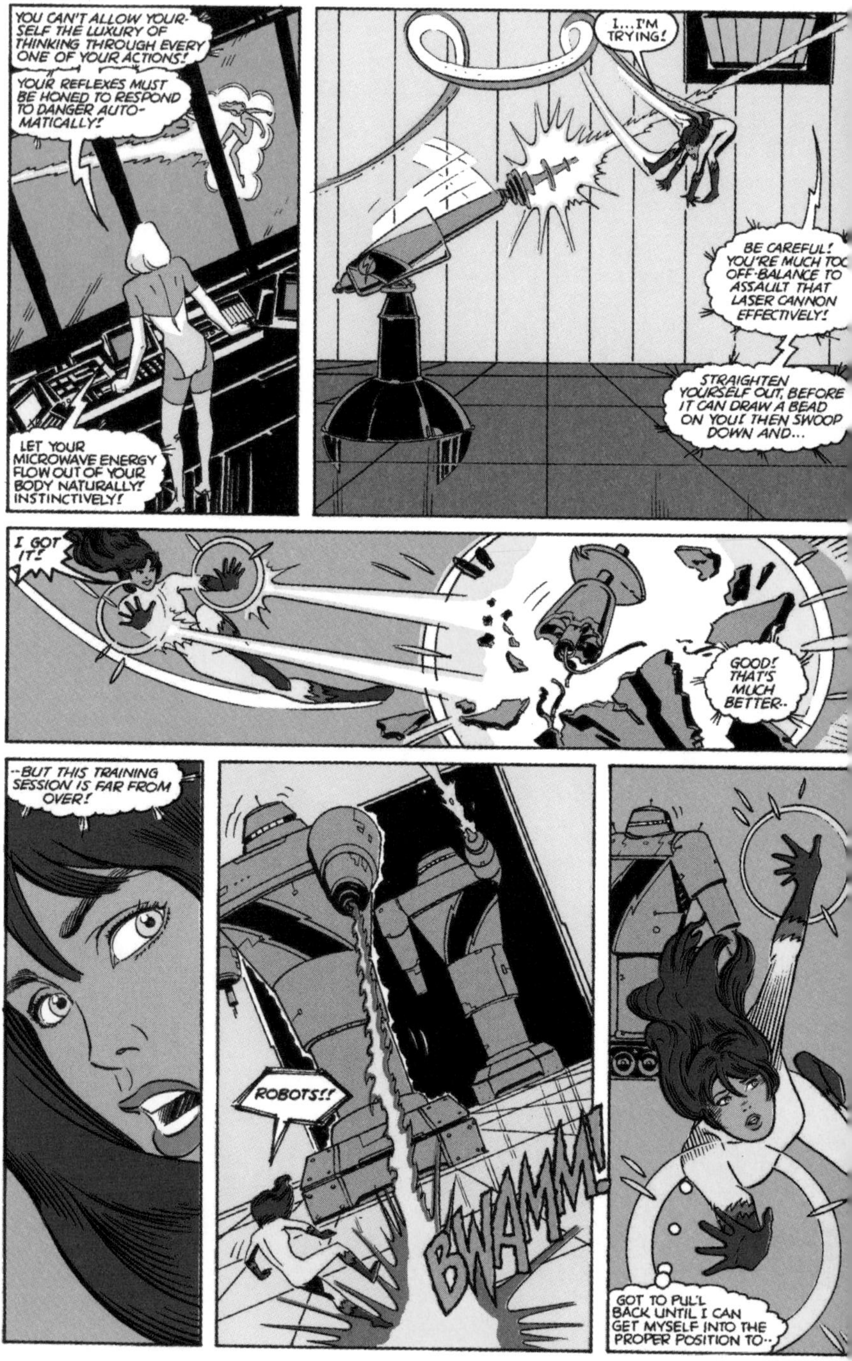
YOU CAN'T ALLOW YOURSELF THE LUXURY OF THINKING THROUGH EVERY ONE OF YOUR ACTIONS!
YOUR REFLEXES MUST BE HONED TO RESPOND TO DANGER AUTOMATICALLY!
LET YOUR MICROWAVE ENERGY FLOW OUT OF YOUR BODY NATURALLY! INSTINCTIVELY!
I...I'M TRYING!
BE CAREFUL! YOU'RE MUCH TOO OFF-BALANCE TO ASSAULT THAT LASER CANNON EFFECTIVELY!
STRAIGHTEN YOURSELF OUT, BEFORE IT CAN DRAW A BEAD ON YOU! THEN SWOOP DOWN AND...
I GOT IT!
GOOD! THAT'S MUCH BETTER..
--BUT THIS TRAINING SESSION IS FAR FROM OVER!
ROBOTS!!
BWAMM!
GOT TO PULL BACK UNTIL I CAN GET MYSELF INTO THE PROPER POSITION TO..

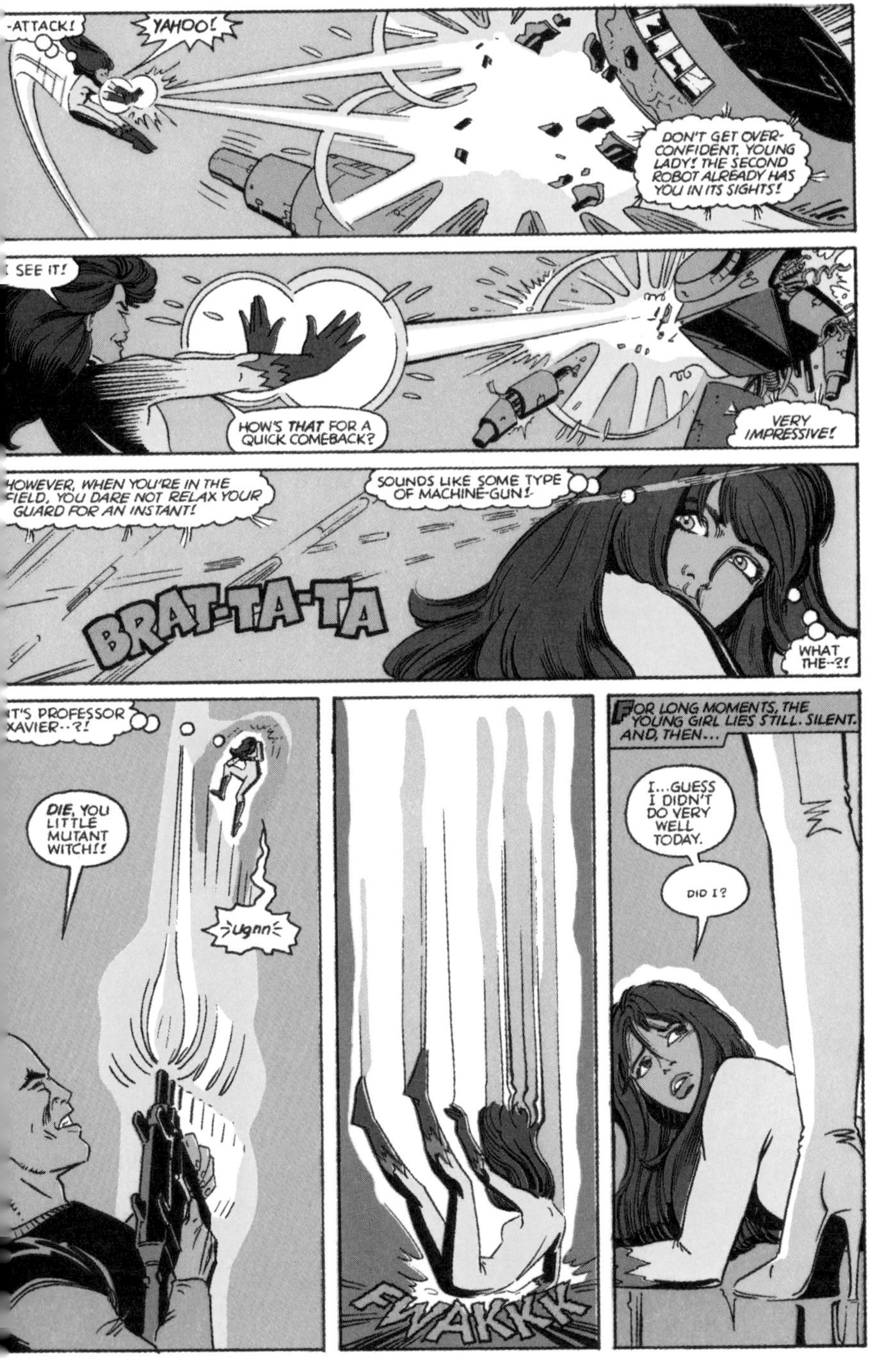

-ATTACK!
YAHOO!
DON'T GET OVER-CONFIDENT, YOUNG LADY! THE SECOND ROBOT ALREADY HAS YOU IN ITS SIGHTS!
I SEE IT!
HOW'S THAT FOR A QUICK COMEBACK?
VERY IMPRESSIVE!
HOWEVER, WHEN YOU'RE IN THE FIELD, YOU DARE NOT RELAX YOUR GUARD FOR AN INSTANT!
SOUNDS LIKE SOME TYPE OF MACHINE-GUN!
BRAT-TA-TA
WHAT THE--?!
IT'S PROFESSOR XAVIER--?!
DIE, YOU LITTLE MUTANT WITCH!!
Ugnn
FWAKKK
FOR LONG MOMENTS, THE YOUNG GIRL LIES STILL. SILENT. AND, THEN...
I...GUESS I DIDN'T DO VERY WELL TODAY.
DID I?

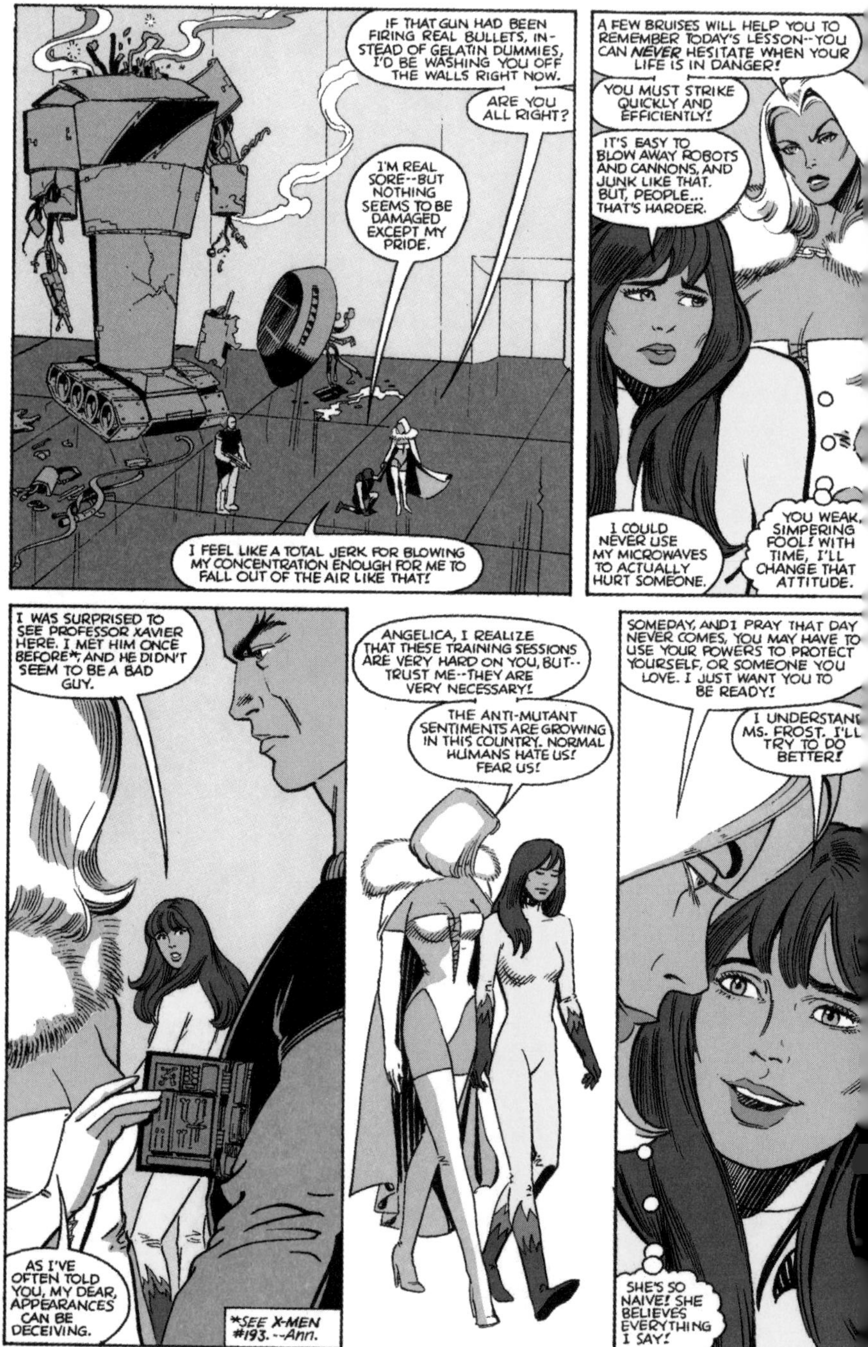
IF THAT GUN HAD BEEN FIRING REAL BULLETS, INSTEAD OF GELATIN DUMMIES, I'D BE WASHING YOU OFF THE WALLS RIGHT NOW.
ARE YOU ALL RIGHT?
I'M REAL SORE--BUT NOTHING SEEMS TO BE DAMAGED EXCEPT MY PRIDE.
I FEEL LIKE A TOTAL JERK FOR BLOWING MY CONCENTRATION ENOUGH FOR ME TO FALL OUT OF THE AIR LIKE THAT!
A FEW BRUISES WILL HELP YOU TO REMEMBER TODAY'S LESSON--YOU CAN *NEVER* HESITATE WHEN YOUR LIFE IS IN DANGER!
YOU MUST STRIKE QUICKLY AND EFFICIENTLY!
IT'S EASY TO BLOW AWAY ROBOTS AND CANNONS, AND JUNK LIKE THAT. BUT, PEOPLE... THAT'S HARDER.
I COULD NEVER USE MY MICROWAVES TO ACTUALLY HURT SOMEONE.
YOU WEAK, SIMPERING FOOL! WITH TIME, I'LL CHANGE THAT ATTITUDE.
I WAS SURPRISED TO SEE PROFESSOR XAVIER HERE. I MET HIM ONCE BEFORE*; AND HE DIDN'T SEEM TO BE A BAD GUY.
AS I'VE OFTEN TOLD YOU, MY DEAR, APPEARANCES CAN BE DECEIVING.
*SEE X-MEN #193.--Ann.
ANGELICA, I REALIZE THAT THESE TRAINING SESSIONS ARE VERY HARD ON YOU, BUT--TRUST ME--THEY ARE VERY NECESSARY!
THE ANTI-MUTANT SENTIMENTS ARE GROWING IN THIS COUNTRY. NORMAL HUMANS HATE US! FEAR US!
SOMEDAY, AND I PRAY THAT DAY NEVER COMES, YOU MAY HAVE TO USE YOUR POWERS TO PROTECT YOURSELF, OR SOMEONE YOU LOVE. I JUST WANT YOU TO BE READY!
I UNDERSTAND MS. FROST. I'LL TRY TO DO BETTER!
SHE'S SO NAIVE! SHE BELIEVES EVERYTHING I SAY!

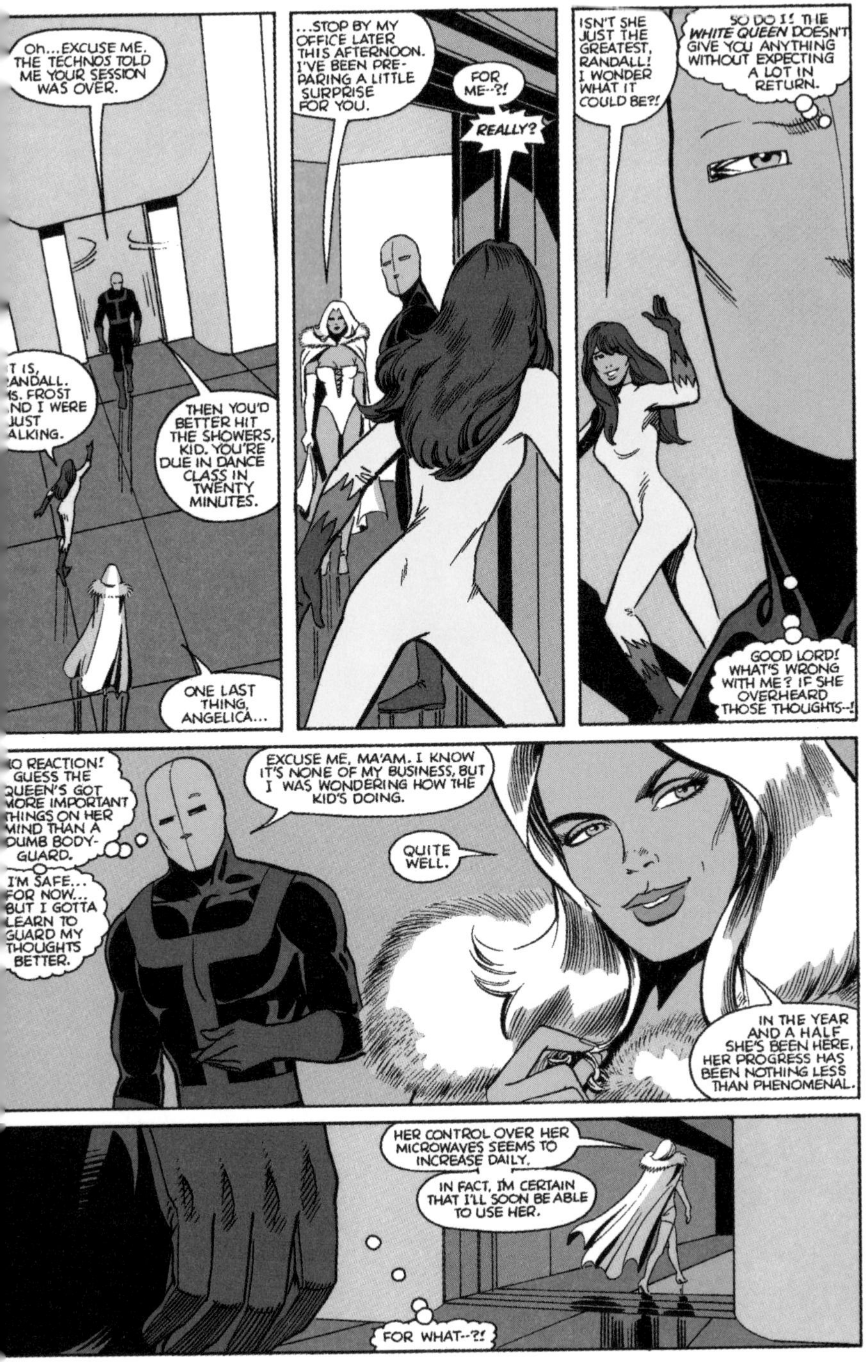
Oh...EXCUSE ME. THE TECHNOS TOLD ME YOUR SESSION WAS OVER.
...T IS, RANDALL. MS. FROST AND I WERE JUST TALKING.
THEN YOU'D BETTER HIT THE SHOWERS, KID. YOU'RE DUE IN DANCE CLASS IN TWENTY MINUTES.
ONE LAST THING, ANGELICA...
...STOP BY MY OFFICE LATER THIS AFTERNOON. I'VE BEEN PRE-PARING A LITTLE SURPRISE FOR YOU.
FOR ME--?!
REALLY?
ISN'T SHE JUST THE GREATEST, RANDALL! I WONDER WHAT IT COULD BE?!
SO DO I! THE WHITE QUEEN DOESN'T GIVE YOU ANYTHING WITHOUT EXPECTING A LOT IN RETURN.
GOOD LORD! WHAT'S WRONG WITH ME? IF SHE OVERHEARD THOSE THOUGHTS--!
NO REACTION! GUESS THE QUEEN'S GOT MORE IMPORTANT THINGS ON HER MIND THAN A DUMB BODY-GUARD.
I'M SAFE... FOR NOW... BUT I GOTTA LEARN TO GUARD MY THOUGHTS BETTER.
EXCUSE ME, MA'AM. I KNOW IT'S NONE OF MY BUSINESS, BUT I WAS WONDERING HOW THE KID'S DOING.
QUITE WELL.
IN THE YEAR AND A HALF SHE'S BEEN HERE, HER PROGRESS HAS BEEN NOTHING LESS THAN PHENOMENAL.
HER CONTROL OVER HER MICROWAVES SEEMS TO INCREASE DAILY.
IN FACT, I'M CERTAIN THAT I'LL SOON BE ABLE TO USE HER.
FOR WHAT--?!

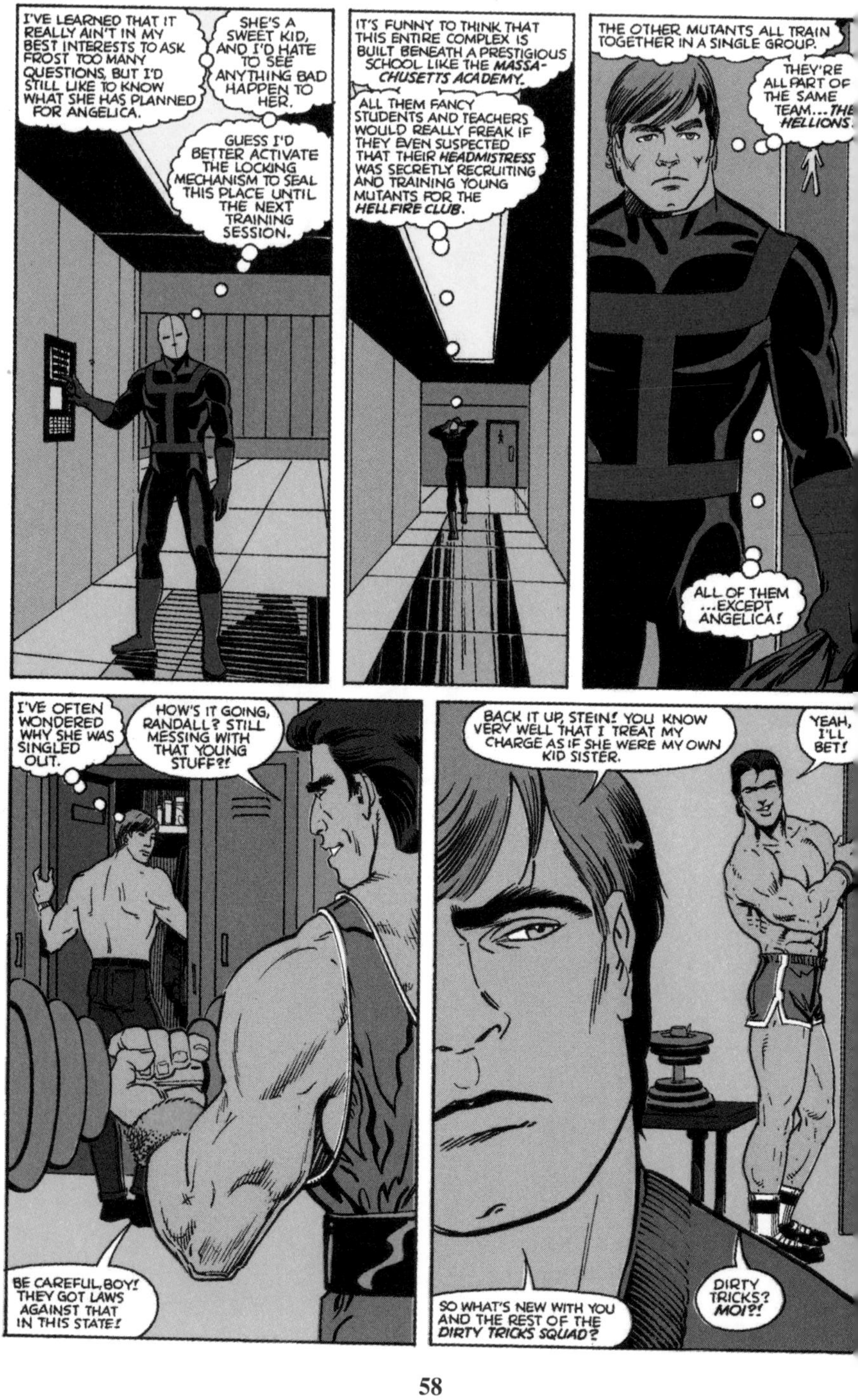
I'VE LEARNED THAT IT REALLY AIN'T IN MY BEST INTERESTS TO ASK FROST TOO MANY QUESTIONS, BUT I'D STILL LIKE TO KNOW WHAT SHE HAS PLANNED FOR ANGELICA.
SHE'S A SWEET KID, AND I'D HATE TO SEE ANYTHING BAD HAPPEN TO HER.
GUESS I'D BETTER ACTIVATE THE LOCKING MECHANISM TO SEAL THIS PLACE UNTIL THE NEXT TRAINING SESSION.
IT'S FUNNY TO THINK THAT THIS ENTIRE COMPLEX IS BUILT BENEATH A PRESTIGIOUS SCHOOL LIKE THE MASSA-CHUSETTS ACADEMY.
ALL THEM FANCY STUDENTS AND TEACHERS WOULD REALLY FREAK IF THEY EVEN SUSPECTED THAT THEIR HEADMISTRESS WAS SECRETLY RECRUITING AND TRAINING YOUNG MUTANTS FOR THE HELLFIRE CLUB.
THE OTHER MUTANTS ALL TRAIN TOGETHER IN A SINGLE GROUP.
THEY'RE ALL PART OF THE SAME TEAM... THE HELLIONS.
ALL OF THEM ...EXCEPT ANGELICA!
I'VE OFTEN WONDERED WHY SHE WAS SINGLED OUT.
HOW'S IT GOING, RANDALL? STILL MESSING WITH THAT YOUNG STUFF?!
BE CAREFUL, BOY! THEY GOT LAWS AGAINST THAT IN THIS STATE!
BACK IT UP, STEIN! YOU KNOW VERY WELL THAT I TREAT MY CHARGE AS IF SHE WERE MY OWN KID SISTER.
YEAH, I'LL BET!
SO WHAT'S NEW WITH YOU AND THE REST OF THE DIRTY TRICKS SQUAD?
DIRTY TRICKS? MOI?!

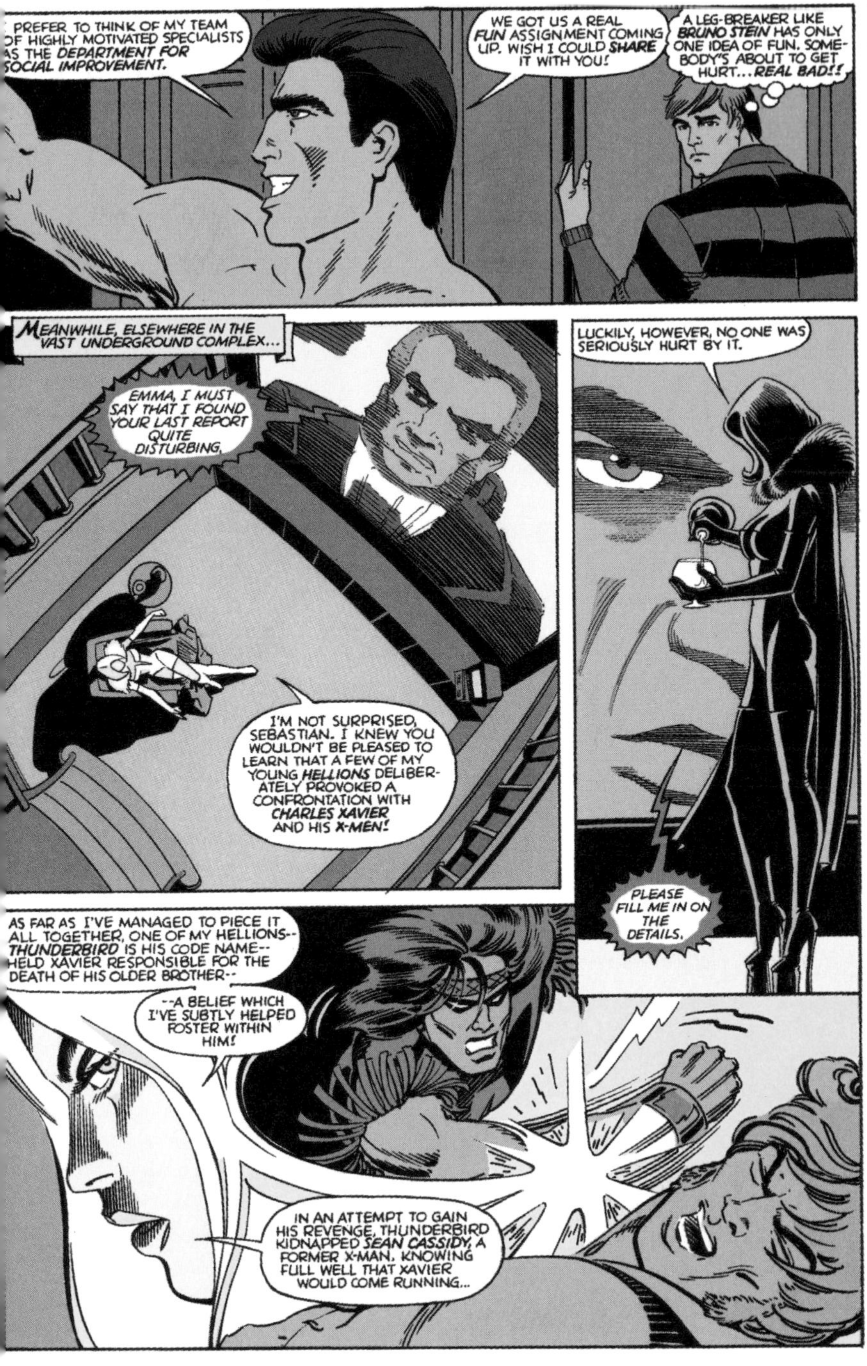
I PREFER TO THINK OF MY TEAM OF HIGHLY MOTIVATED SPECIALISTS AS THE DEPARTMENT FOR SOCIAL IMPROVEMENT.
WE GOT US A REAL FUN ASSIGNMENT COMING UP. WISH I COULD SHARE IT WITH YOU!
A LEG-BREAKER LIKE BRUNO STEIN HAS ONLY ONE IDEA OF FUN. SOMEBODY'S ABOUT TO GET HURT... REAL BAD!!
MEANWHILE, ELSEWHERE IN THE VAST UNDERGROUND COMPLEX...
EMMA, I MUST SAY THAT I FOUND YOUR LAST REPORT QUITE DISTURBING.
I'M NOT SURPRISED, SEBASTIAN. I KNEW YOU WOULDN'T BE PLEASED TO LEARN THAT A FEW OF MY YOUNG HELLIONS DELIBERATELY PROVOKED A CONFRONTATION WITH CHARLES XAVIER AND HIS X-MEN!
LUCKILY, HOWEVER, NO ONE WAS SERIOUSLY HURT BY IT.
PLEASE FILL ME IN ON THE DETAILS.
AS FAR AS I'VE MANAGED TO PIECE IT ALL TOGETHER, ONE OF MY HELLIONS-- THUNDERBIRD IS HIS CODE NAME-- HELD XAVIER RESPONSIBLE FOR THE DEATH OF HIS OLDER BROTHER--
--A BELIEF WHICH I'VE SUBTLY HELPED FOSTER WITHIN HIM!
IN AN ATTEMPT TO GAIN HIS REVENGE, THUNDERBIRD KIDNAPPED SEAN CASSIDY, A FORMER X-MAN, KNOWING FULL WELL THAT XAVIER WOULD COME RUNNING...

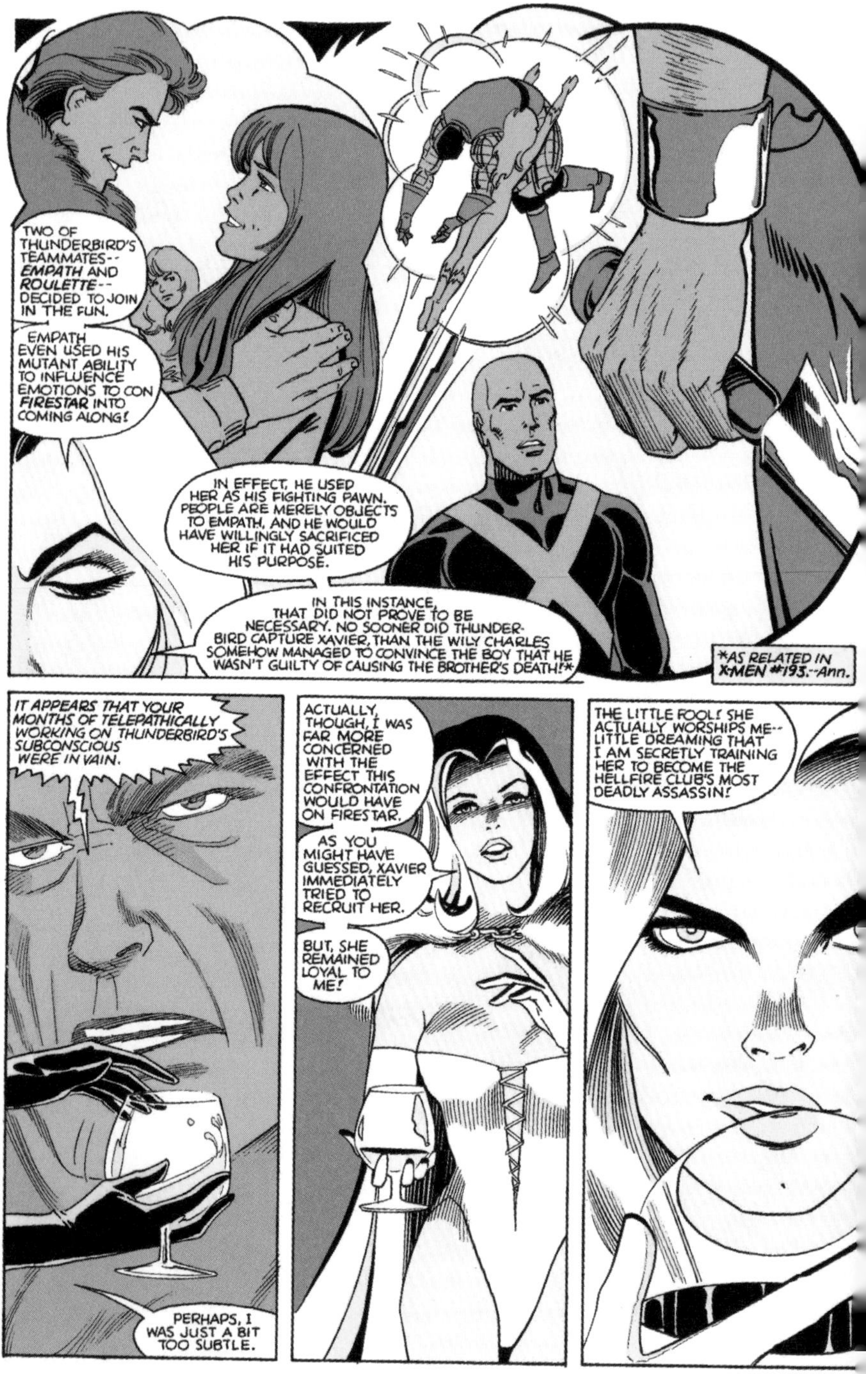
TWO OF THUNDERBIRD'S TEAMMATES-- EMPATH AND ROULETTE-- DECIDED TO JOIN IN THE FUN.
EMPATH EVEN USED HIS MUTANT ABILITY TO INFLUENCE EMOTIONS TO CON FIRESTAR INTO COMING ALONG!
IN EFFECT, HE USED HER AS HIS FIGHTING PAWN. PEOPLE ARE MERELY OBJECTS TO EMPATH, AND HE WOULD HAVE WILLINGLY SACRIFICED HER IF IT HAD SUITED HIS PURPOSE.
IN THIS INSTANCE, THAT DID NOT PROVE TO BE NECESSARY. NO SOONER DID THUNDER-BIRD CAPTURE XAVIER, THAN THE WILY CHARLES SOMEHOW MANAGED TO CONVINCE THE BOY THAT HE WASN'T GUILTY OF CAUSING THE BROTHER'S DEATH!*
*AS RELATED IN X-MEN #193.--Ann.
IT APPEARS THAT YOUR MONTHS OF TELEPATHICALLY WORKING ON THUNDERBIRD'S SUBCONSCIOUS WERE IN VAIN.
PERHAPS, I WAS JUST A BIT TOO SUBTLE.
ACTUALLY, THOUGH, I WAS FAR MORE CONCERNED WITH THE EFFECT THIS CONFRONTATION WOULD HAVE ON FIRESTAR.
AS YOU MIGHT HAVE GUESSED, XAVIER IMMEDIATELY TRIED TO RECRUIT HER.
BUT, SHE REMAINED LOYAL TO ME!
THE LITTLE FOOL! SHE ACTUALLY WORSHIPS ME-- LITTLE DREAMING THAT I AM SECRETLY TRAINING HER TO BECOME THE HELLFIRE CLUB'S MOST DEADLY ASSASSIN!

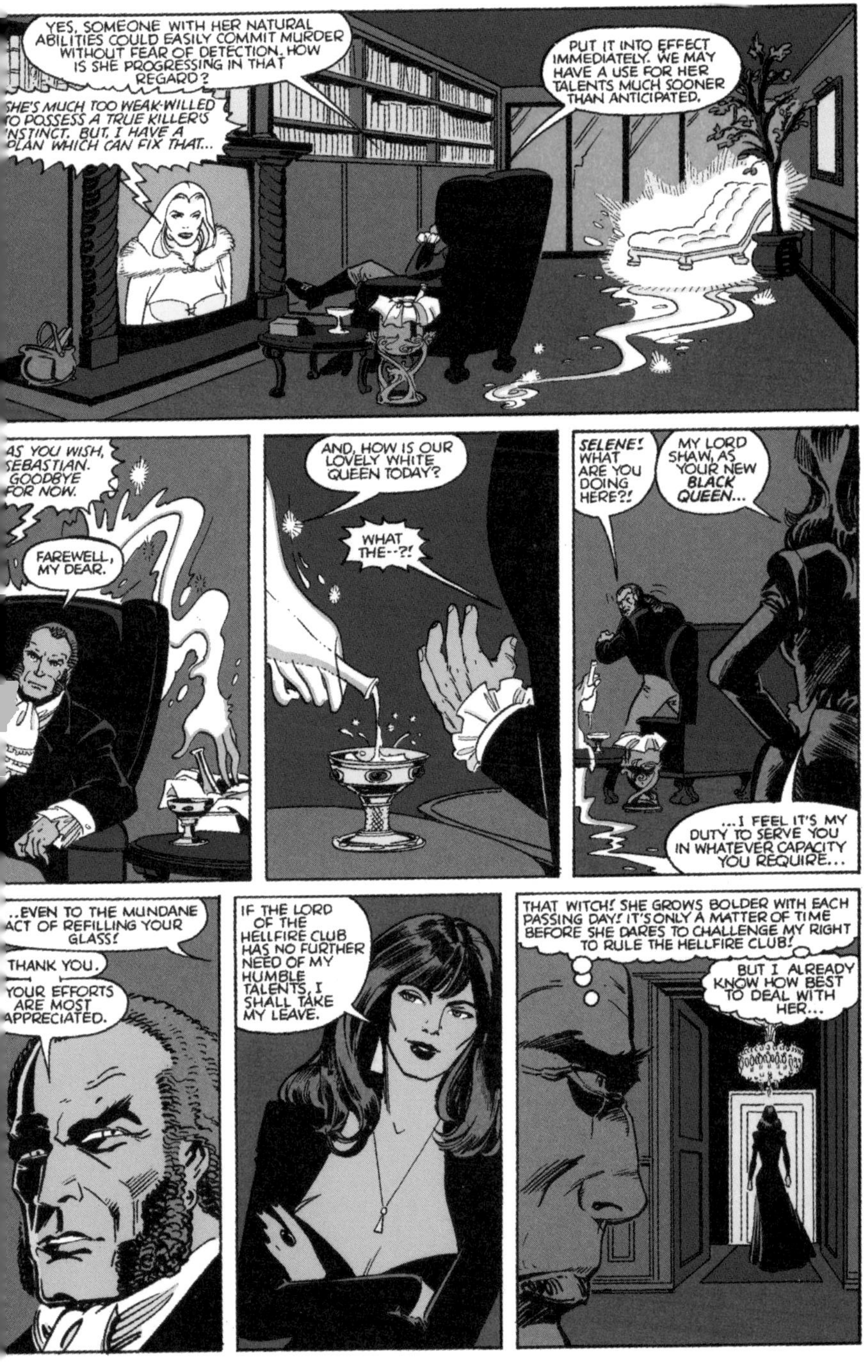
YES, SOMEONE WITH HER NATURAL ABILITIES COULD EASILY COMMIT MURDER WITHOUT FEAR OF DETECTION. HOW IS SHE PROGRESSING IN THAT REGARD?
SHE'S MUCH TOO WEAK-WILLED TO POSSESS A TRUE KILLER'S INSTINCT. BUT, I HAVE A PLAN WHICH CAN FIX THAT...
PUT IT INTO EFFECT IMMEDIATELY. WE MAY HAVE A USE FOR HER TALENTS MUCH SOONER THAN ANTICIPATED.
AS YOU WISH, SEBASTIAN. GOODBYE FOR NOW.
FAREWELL, MY DEAR.
AND, HOW IS OUR LOVELY WHITE QUEEN TODAY?
WHAT THE--?!
SELENE! WHAT ARE YOU DOING HERE?!
MY LORD SHAW, AS YOUR NEW BLACK QUEEN...
...I FEEL IT'S MY DUTY TO SERVE YOU IN WHATEVER CAPACITY YOU REQUIRE...
..EVEN TO THE MUNDANE ACT OF REFILLING YOUR GLASS!
THANK YOU.
YOUR EFFORTS ARE MOST APPRECIATED.
IF THE LORD OF THE HELLFIRE CLUB HAS NO FURTHER NEED OF MY HUMBLE TALENTS, I SHALL TAKE MY LEAVE.
THAT WITCH! SHE GROWS BOLDER WITH EACH PASSING DAY! IT'S ONLY A MATTER OF TIME BEFORE SHE DARES TO CHALLENGE MY RIGHT TO RULE THE HELLFIRE CLUB!
BUT I ALREADY KNOW HOW BEST TO DEAL WITH HER...

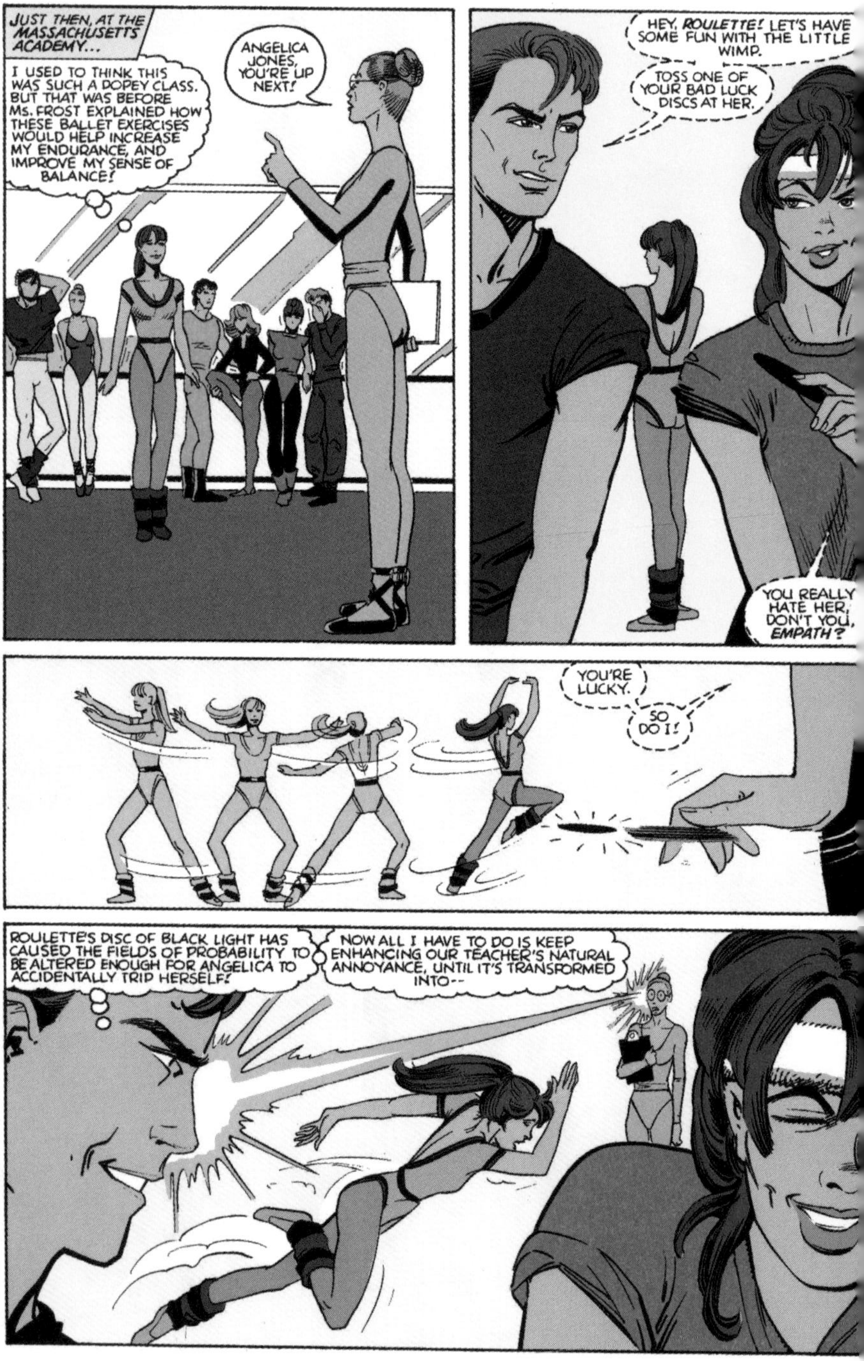
JUST THEN, AT THE MASSACHUSETTS ACADEMY...
I USED TO THINK THIS WAS SUCH A DOPEY CLASS. BUT THAT WAS BEFORE Ms. FROST EXPLAINED HOW THESE BALLET EXERCISES WOULD HELP INCREASE MY ENDURANCE, AND IMPROVE MY SENSE OF BALANCE!
ANGELICA JONES, YOU'RE UP NEXT!
HEY, ROULETTE! LET'S HAVE SOME FUN WITH THE LITTLE WIMP.
TOSS ONE OF YOUR BAD LUCK DISCS AT HER.
YOU REALLY HATE HER, DON'T YOU, EMPATH?
YOU'RE LUCKY.
SO DO I!
ROULETTE'S DISC OF BLACK LIGHT HAS CAUSED THE FIELDS OF PROBABILITY TO BE ALTERED ENOUGH FOR ANGELICA TO ACCIDENTALLY TRIP HERSELF!
NOW ALL I HAVE TO DO IS KEEP ENHANCING OUR TEACHER'S NATURAL ANNOYANCE, UNTIL IT'S TRANSFORMED INTO--

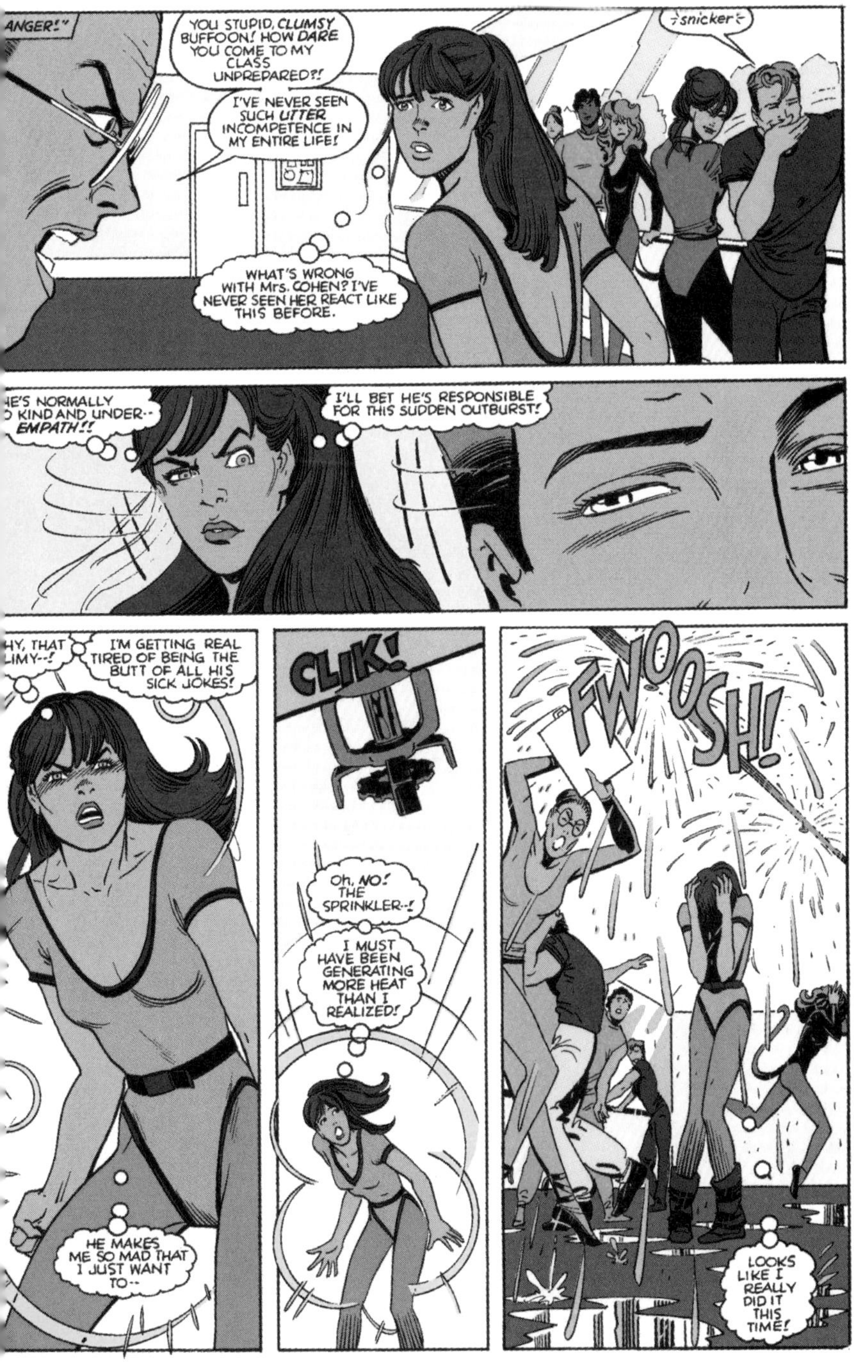
ANGER!"
YOU STUPID, CLUMSY BUFFOON! HOW DARE YOU COME TO MY CLASS UNPREPARED?!
I'VE NEVER SEEN SUCH UTTER INCOMPETENCE IN MY ENTIRE LIFE!
WHAT'S WRONG WITH Mrs. COHEN? I'VE NEVER SEEN HER REACT LIKE THIS BEFORE.
snicker
HE'S NORMALLY KIND AND UNDER-- EMPATH!!
I'LL BET HE'S RESPONSIBLE FOR THIS SUDDEN OUTBURST!
WHY, THAT SLIMY--!
I'M GETTING REAL TIRED OF BEING THE BUTT OF ALL HIS SICK JOKES!
HE MAKES ME SO MAD THAT I JUST WANT TO--
CLIK!
Oh, NO! THE SPRINKLER--!
I MUST HAVE BEEN GENERATING MORE HEAT THAN I REALIZED!
FWOOSH!
LOOKS LIKE I REALLY DID IT THIS TIME!

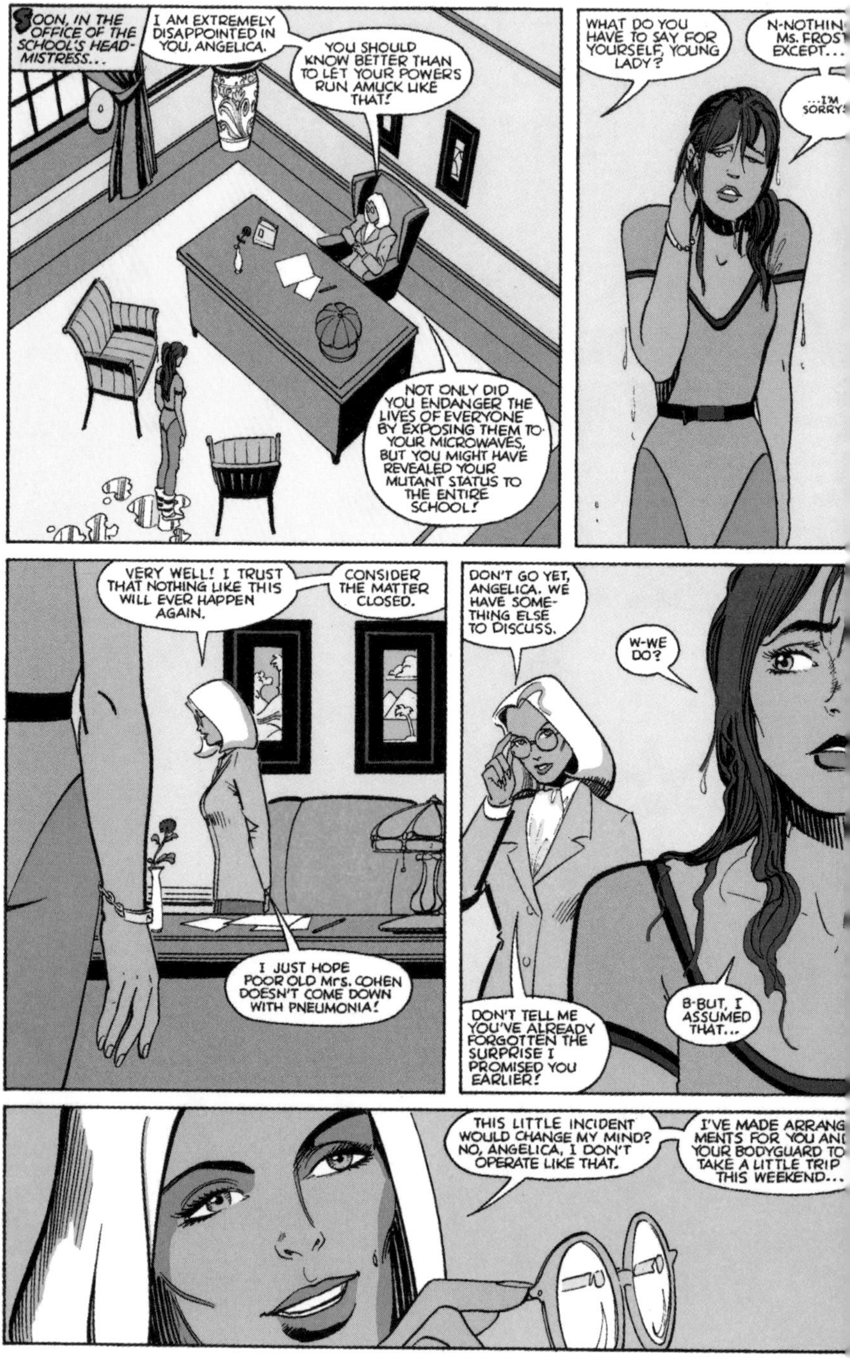
SOON, IN THE OFFICE OF THE SCHOOL'S HEAD-MISTRESS...
I AM EXTREMELY DISAPPOINTED IN YOU, ANGELICA.
YOU SHOULD KNOW BETTER THAN TO LET YOUR POWERS RUN AMUCK LIKE THAT!
NOT ONLY DID YOU ENDANGER THE LIVES OF EVERYONE BY EXPOSING THEM TO YOUR MICROWAVES, BUT YOU MIGHT HAVE REVEALED YOUR MUTANT STATUS TO THE ENTIRE SCHOOL!
WHAT DO YOU HAVE TO SAY FOR YOURSELF, YOUNG LADY?
N-NOTHIN MS. FROST EXCEPT...
...I'M SORRY!
VERY WELL! I TRUST THAT NOTHING LIKE THIS WILL EVER HAPPEN AGAIN.
CONSIDER THE MATTER CLOSED.
I JUST HOPE POOR OLD Mrs. COHEN DOESN'T COME DOWN WITH PNEUMONIA!
DON'T GO YET, ANGELICA. WE HAVE SOME-THING ELSE TO DISCUSS.
W-WE DO?
DON'T TELL ME YOU'VE ALREADY FORGOTTEN THE SURPRISE I PROMISED YOU EARLIER!
B-BUT, I ASSUMED THAT...
THIS LITTLE INCIDENT WOULD CHANGE MY MIND? NO, ANGELICA, I DON'T OPERATE LIKE THAT.
I'VE MADE ARRANG MENTS FOR YOU AN YOUR BODYGUARD TO TAKE A LITTLE TRIP THIS WEEKEND...

YOU'RE GOING *HOME*, ANGELICA! BACK TO WEST MORRIS, NEW JERSEY, TO VISIT YOUR FATHER!

Oh, MS. FROST! I... DON'T KNOW WHAT TO SAY OR HOW TO THANK YOU!

YOU JUST HAVE A GOOD TIME FOR YOURSELF--AND THAT WILL BE ENOUGH THANKS FOR ME.

I CAN'T WAIT TO TELL RANDALL THE GOOD NEWS!

NO SOONER DOES THE YOUNG GIRL LEAVE THE OFFICE, THAN...

KNOK KNOK

COME IN, MISTER STEIN.

HAVE YOU MADE ALL THE NECESSARY ARRANGEMENTS?

YES, MA'AM.

GOOD. THIS ASSIGNMENT IS OF THE UTMOST IMPORTANCE TO ME.

LATER, IN ANGELICA'S DORMITORY ROOM...

I'M SO EXCITED, RANDALL! THIS WILL BE MY FIRST TRIP HOME SINCE I ENROLLED IN THIS SCHOOL.

I CAN'T WAIT TO SEE MY FATHER AGAIN!

I'LL BET THAT'S WHY MS. FROST ARRANGED THIS TRIP. SHE'S ALWAYS THINKING OF OTHERS.

YEAH. SHE'S A REAL PRIZE, ALL RIGHT.

BUT WHAT'S HER ANGLE?!

65

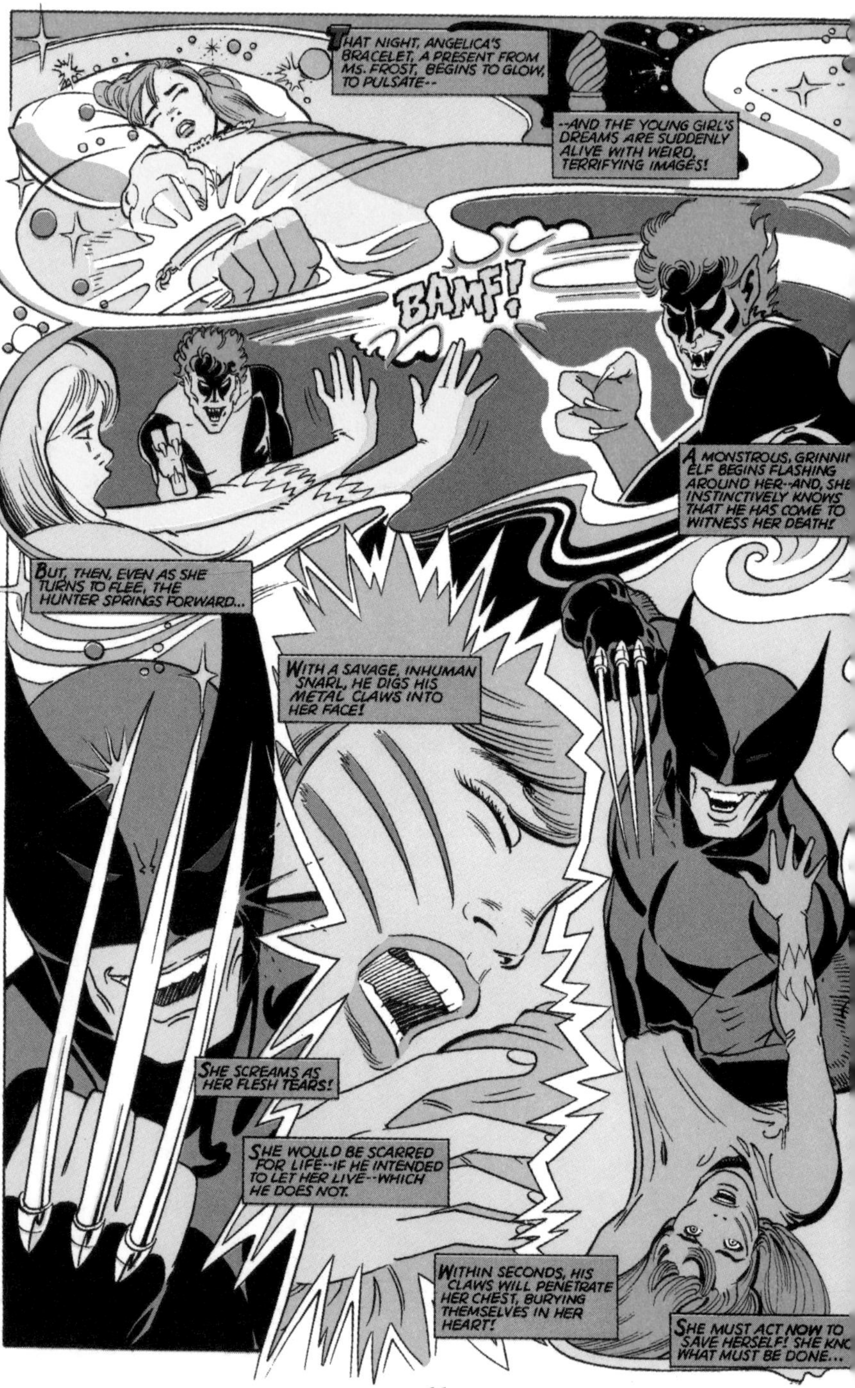
THAT NIGHT, ANGELICA'S BRACELET, A PRESENT FROM MS. FROST, BEGINS TO GLOW, TO PULSATE--
--AND THE YOUNG GIRL'S DREAMS ARE SUDDENLY ALIVE WITH WEIRD, TERRIFYING IMAGES!
BAMF!
A MONSTROUS, GRINNI ELF BEGINS FLASHING AROUND HER--AND, SHE INSTINCTIVELY KNOWS THAT HE HAS COME TO WITNESS HER DEATH!
BUT, THEN, EVEN AS SHE TURNS TO FLEE, THE HUNTER SPRINGS FORWARD...
WITH A SAVAGE, INHUMAN SNARL, HE DIGS HIS METAL CLAWS INTO HER FACE!
SHE SCREAMS AS HER FLESH TEARS!
SHE WOULD BE SCARRED FOR LIFE--IF HE INTENDED TO LET HER LIVE--WHICH HE DOES NOT.
WITHIN SECONDS, HIS CLAWS WILL PENETRATE HER CHEST, BURYING THEMSELVES IN HER HEART!
SHE MUST ACT NOW TO SAVE HERSELF! SHE KNO WHAT MUST BE DONE...

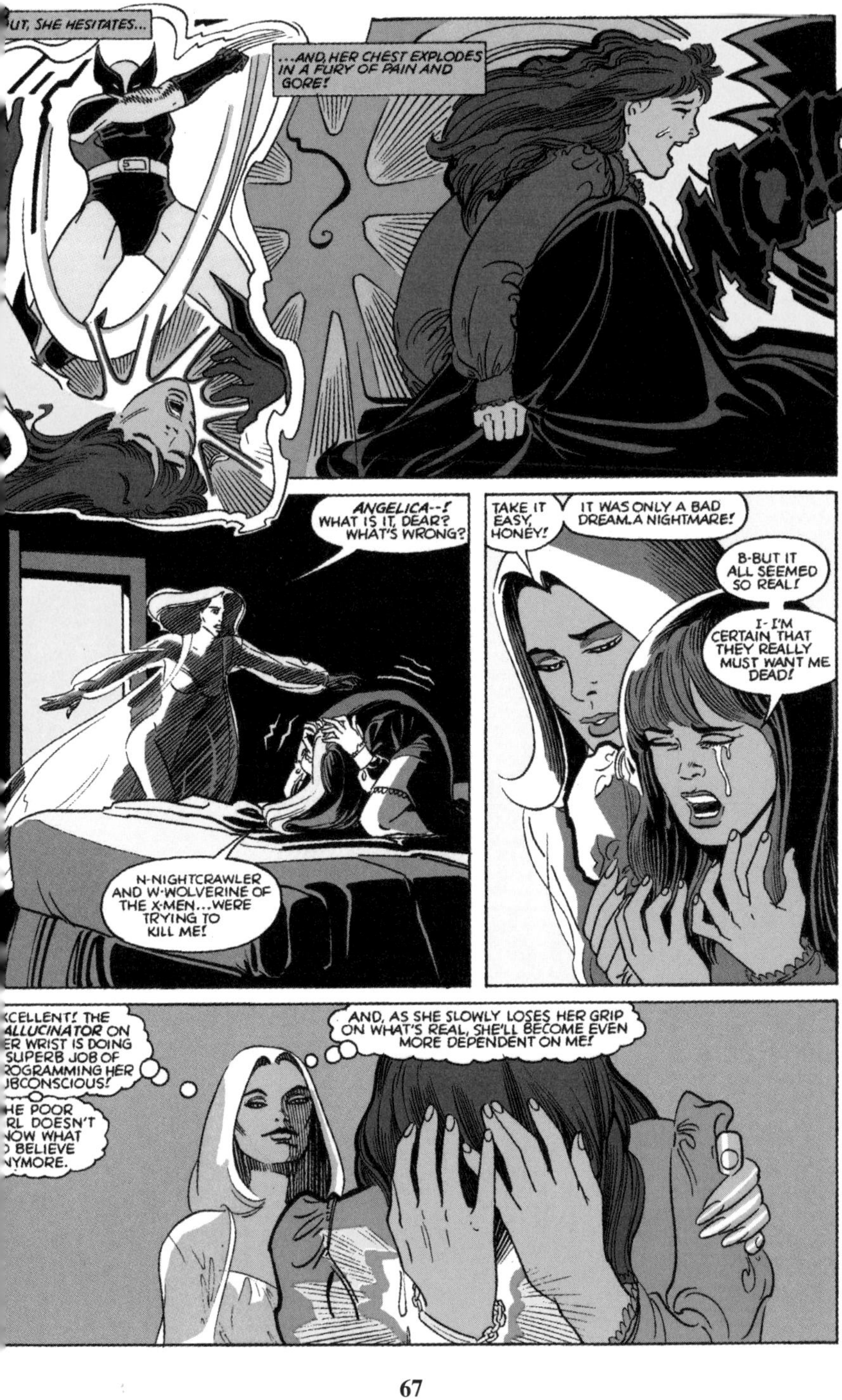
UT, SHE HESITATES...
...AND, HER CHEST EXPLODES IN A FURY OF PAIN AND GORE!
NO!!
ANGELICA--! WHAT IS IT, DEAR? WHAT'S WRONG?
N-NIGHTCRAWLER AND W-WOLVERINE OF THE X-MEN...WERE TRYING TO KILL ME!
TAKE IT EASY, HONEY!
IT WAS ONLY A BAD DREAM. A NIGHTMARE!
B-BUT IT ALL SEEMED SO REAL!
I- I'M CERTAIN THAT THEY REALLY MUST WANT ME DEAD!
XCELLENT! THE ALLUCINATOR ON ER WRIST IS DOING SUPERB JOB OF ROGRAMMING HER UBCONSCIOUS!
HE POOR RL DOESN'T NOW WHAT O BELIEVE NYMORE.
AND, AS SHE SLOWLY LOSES HER GRIP ON WHAT'S REAL, SHE'LL BECOME EVEN MORE DEPENDENT ON ME!

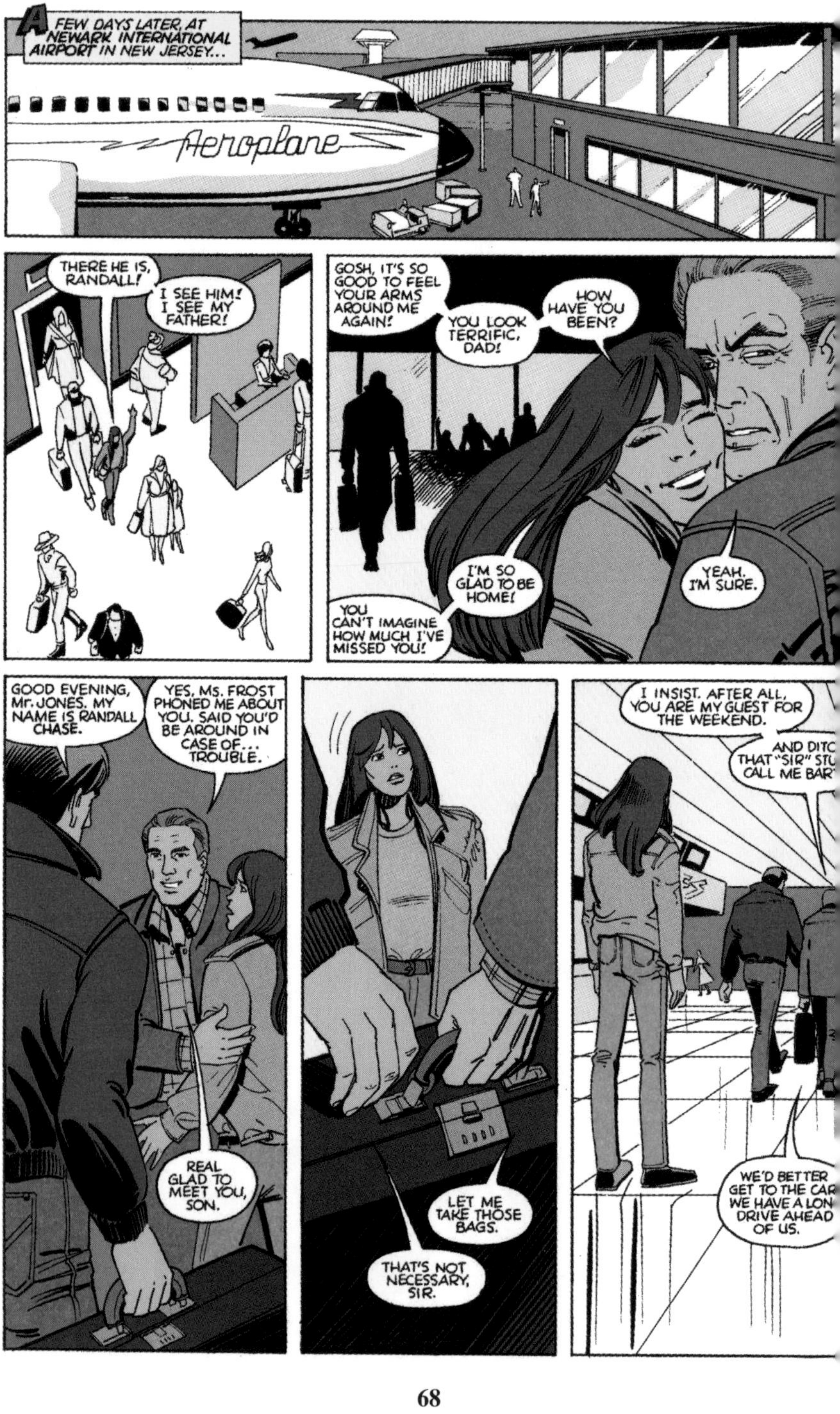
A FEW DAYS LATER, AT NEWARK INTERNATIONAL AIRPORT IN NEW JERSEY...
Aeroplane
THERE HE IS, RANDALL!
I SEE HIM! I SEE MY FATHER!
GOSH, IT'S SO GOOD TO FEEL YOUR ARMS AROUND ME AGAIN!
YOU LOOK TERRIFIC, DAD!
HOW HAVE YOU BEEN?
I'M SO GLAD TO BE HOME!
YOU CAN'T IMAGINE HOW MUCH I'VE MISSED YOU!
YEAH. I'M SURE.
GOOD EVENING, Mr. JONES. MY NAME IS RANDALL CHASE.
YES, Ms. FROST PHONED ME ABOUT YOU. SAID YOU'D BE AROUND IN CASE OF... TROUBLE.
REAL GLAD TO MEET YOU, SON.
LET ME TAKE THOSE BAGS.
THAT'S NOT NECESSARY, SIR.
I INSIST. AFTER ALL, YOU ARE MY GUEST FOR THE WEEKEND.
AND DITC THAT "SIR" STU CALL ME BAR
WE'D BETTER GET TO THE CAR WE HAVE A LON DRIVE AHEAD OF US.

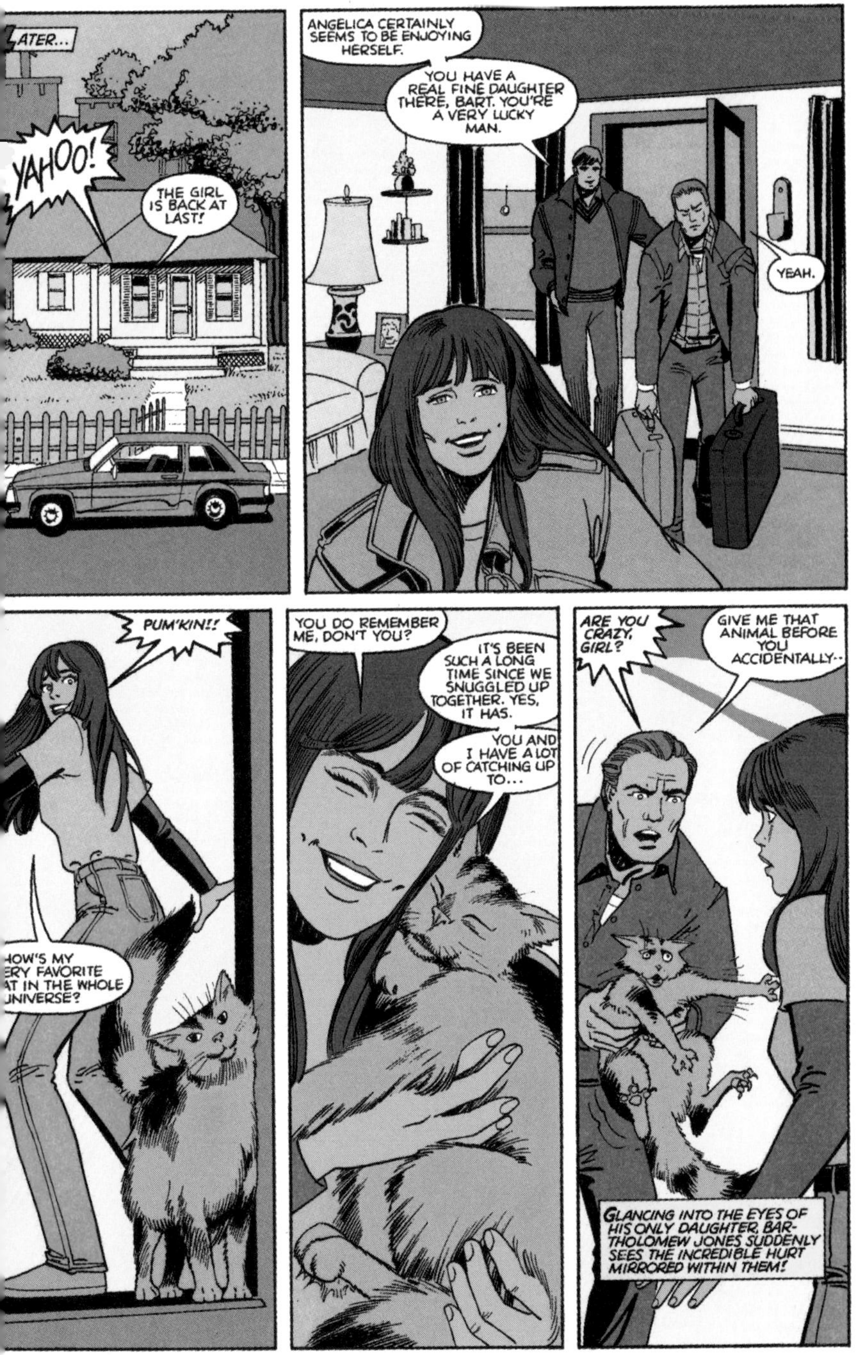

ATER...
YAHOO!
THE GIRL IS BACK AT LAST!
ANGELICA CERTAINLY SEEMS TO BE ENJOYING HERSELF.
YOU HAVE A REAL FINE DAUGHTER THERE, BART. YOU'RE A VERY LUCKY MAN.
YEAH.
PUM'KIN!!
HOW'S MY ERY FAVORITE AT IN THE WHOLE UNIVERSE?
YOU DO REMEMBER ME, DON'T YOU?
IT'S BEEN SUCH A LONG TIME SINCE WE SNUGGLED UP TOGETHER. YES, IT HAS.
YOU AND I HAVE A LOT OF CATCHING UP TO...
ARE YOU CRAZY, GIRL?
GIVE ME THAT ANIMAL BEFORE YOU ACCIDENTALLY--
GLANCING INTO THE EYES OF HIS ONLY DAUGHTER, BARTHOLOMEW JONES SUDDENLY SEES THE INCREDIBLE HURT MIRRORED WITHIN THEM!

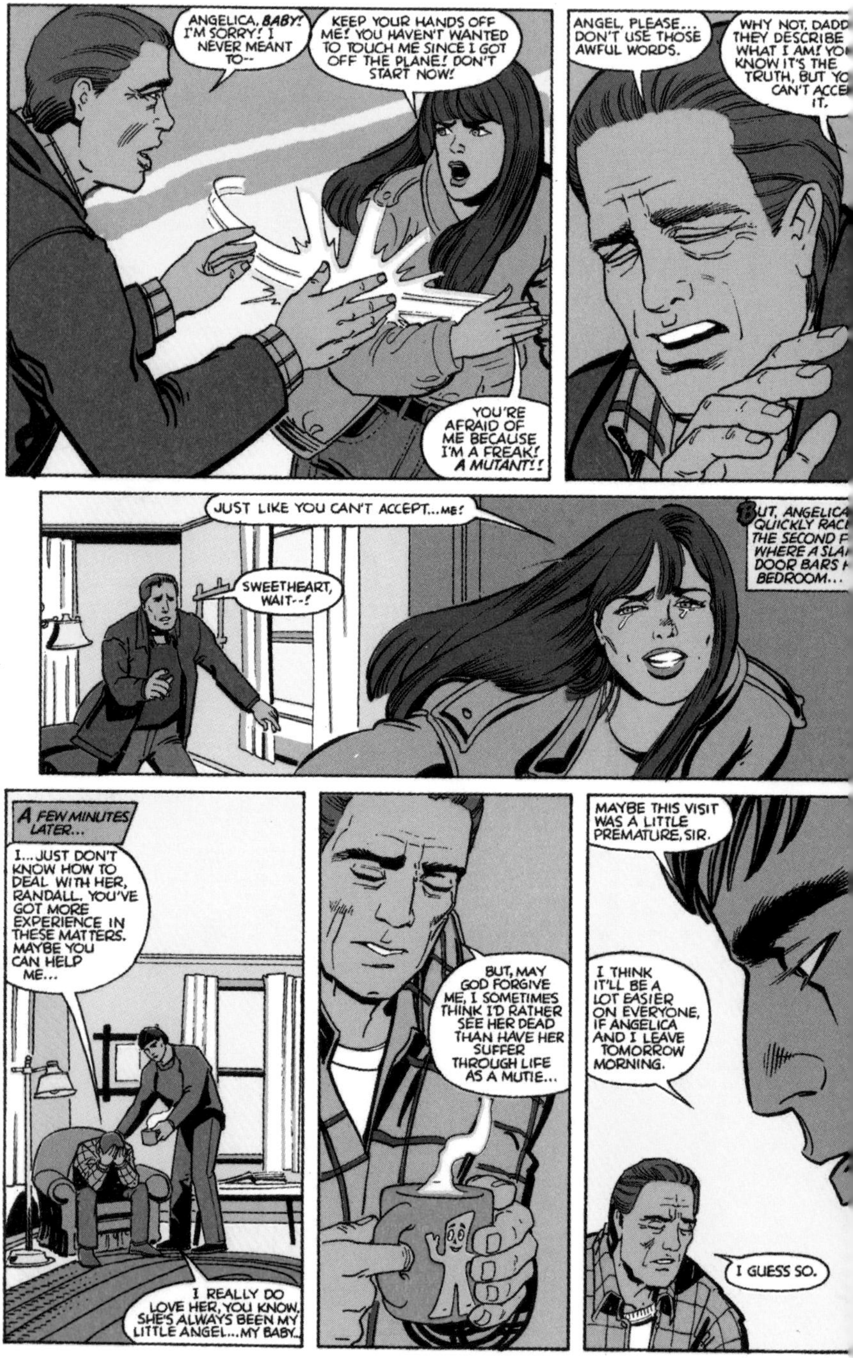
ANGELICA, BABY! I'M SORRY! I NEVER MEANT TO--
KEEP YOUR HANDS OFF ME! YOU HAVEN'T WANTED TO TOUCH ME SINCE I GOT OFF THE PLANE! DON'T START NOW!
YOU'RE AFRAID OF ME BECAUSE I'M A FREAK! A MUTANT!!
ANGEL, PLEASE... DON'T USE THOSE AWFUL WORDS.
WHY NOT, DADD THEY DESCRIBE WHAT I AM! YO KNOW IT'S THE TRUTH, BUT YO CAN'T ACCE IT.
JUST LIKE YOU CAN'T ACCEPT...ME!
SWEETHEART, WAIT--!
BUT, ANGELICA QUICKLY RAC THE SECOND F WHERE A SLA DOOR BARS BEDROOM...
A FEW MINUTES LATER...
I...JUST DON'T KNOW HOW TO DEAL WITH HER, RANDALL. YOU'VE GOT MORE EXPERIENCE IN THESE MATTERS. MAYBE YOU CAN HELP ME...
I REALLY DO LOVE HER, YOU KNOW. SHE'S ALWAYS BEEN MY LITTLE ANGEL...MY BABY...
BUT, MAY GOD FORGIVE ME, I SOMETIMES THINK I'D RATHER SEE HER DEAD THAN HAVE HER SUFFER THROUGH LIFE AS A MUTIE...
MAYBE THIS VISIT WAS A LITTLE PREMATURE, SIR.
I THINK IT'LL BE A LOT EASIER ON EVERYONE, IF ANGELICA AND I LEAVE TOMORROW MORNING.
I GUESS SO.

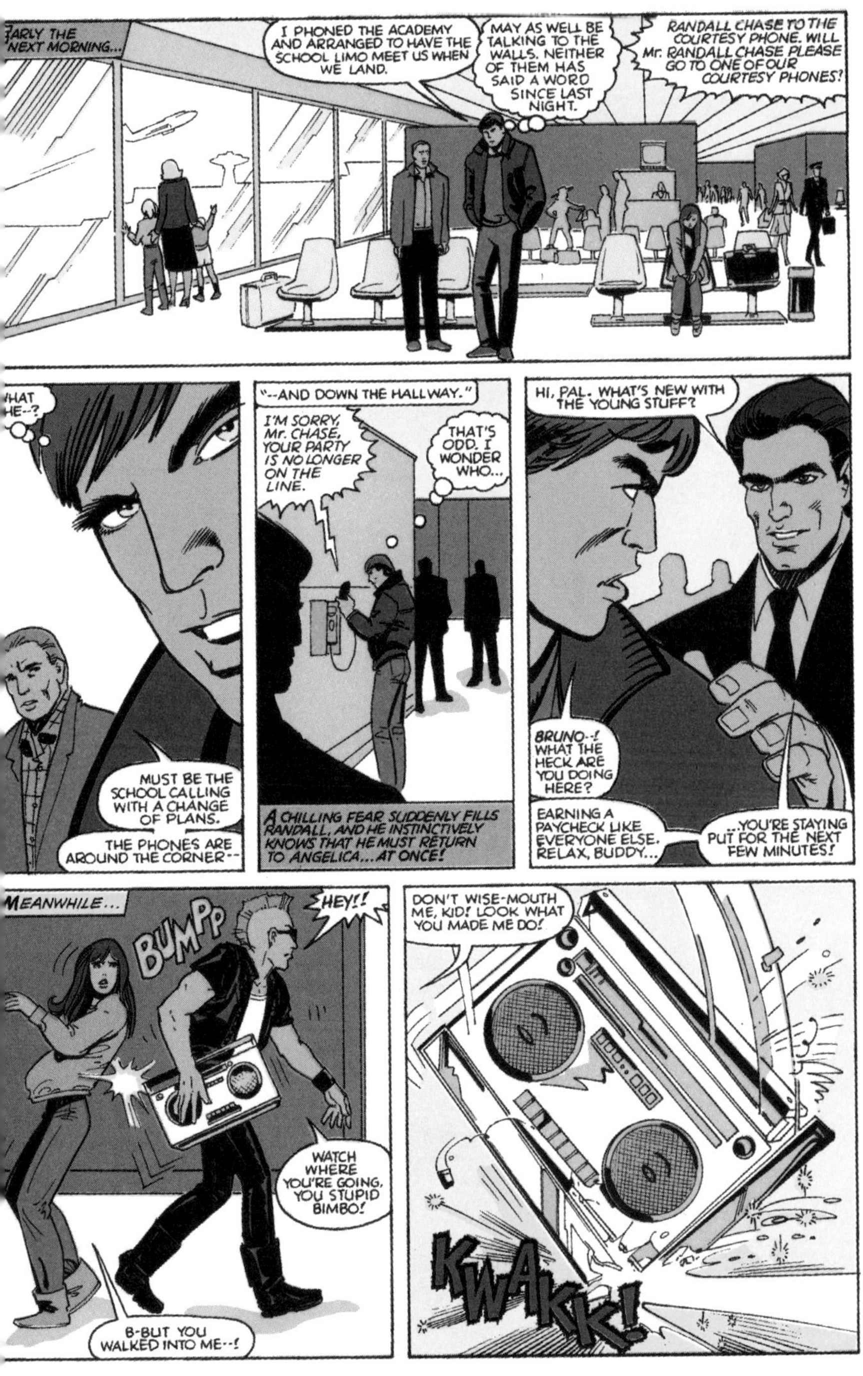
EARLY THE NEXT MORNING...
I PHONED THE ACADEMY AND ARRANGED TO HAVE THE SCHOOL LIMO MEET US WHEN WE LAND.
MAY AS WELL BE TALKING TO THE WALLS. NEITHER OF THEM HAS SAID A WORD SINCE LAST NIGHT.
RANDALL CHASE TO THE COURTESY PHONE. WILL Mr. RANDALL CHASE PLEASE GO TO ONE OF OUR COURTESY PHONES?
WHAT THE--?
MUST BE THE SCHOOL CALLING WITH A CHANGE OF PLANS.
THE PHONES ARE AROUND THE CORNER--
"--AND DOWN THE HALLWAY."
I'M SORRY, Mr. CHASE, YOUR PARTY IS NO LONGER ON THE LINE.
THAT'S ODD. I WONDER WHO...
A CHILLING FEAR SUDDENLY FILLS RANDALL, AND HE INSTINCTIVELY KNOWS THAT HE MUST RETURN TO ANGELICA... AT ONCE!
HI, PAL. WHAT'S NEW WITH THE YOUNG STUFF?
BRUNO--! WHAT THE HECK ARE YOU DOING HERE?
EARNING A PAYCHECK LIKE EVERYONE ELSE. RELAX, BUDDY...
...YOU'RE STAYING PUT FOR THE NEXT FEW MINUTES!
MEANWHILE...
BUMPP
HEY!!
WATCH WHERE YOU'RE GOING, YOU STUPID BIMBO!
B-BUT YOU WALKED INTO ME--!
DON'T WISE-MOUTH ME, KID! LOOK WHAT YOU MADE ME DO!
KWAKK!

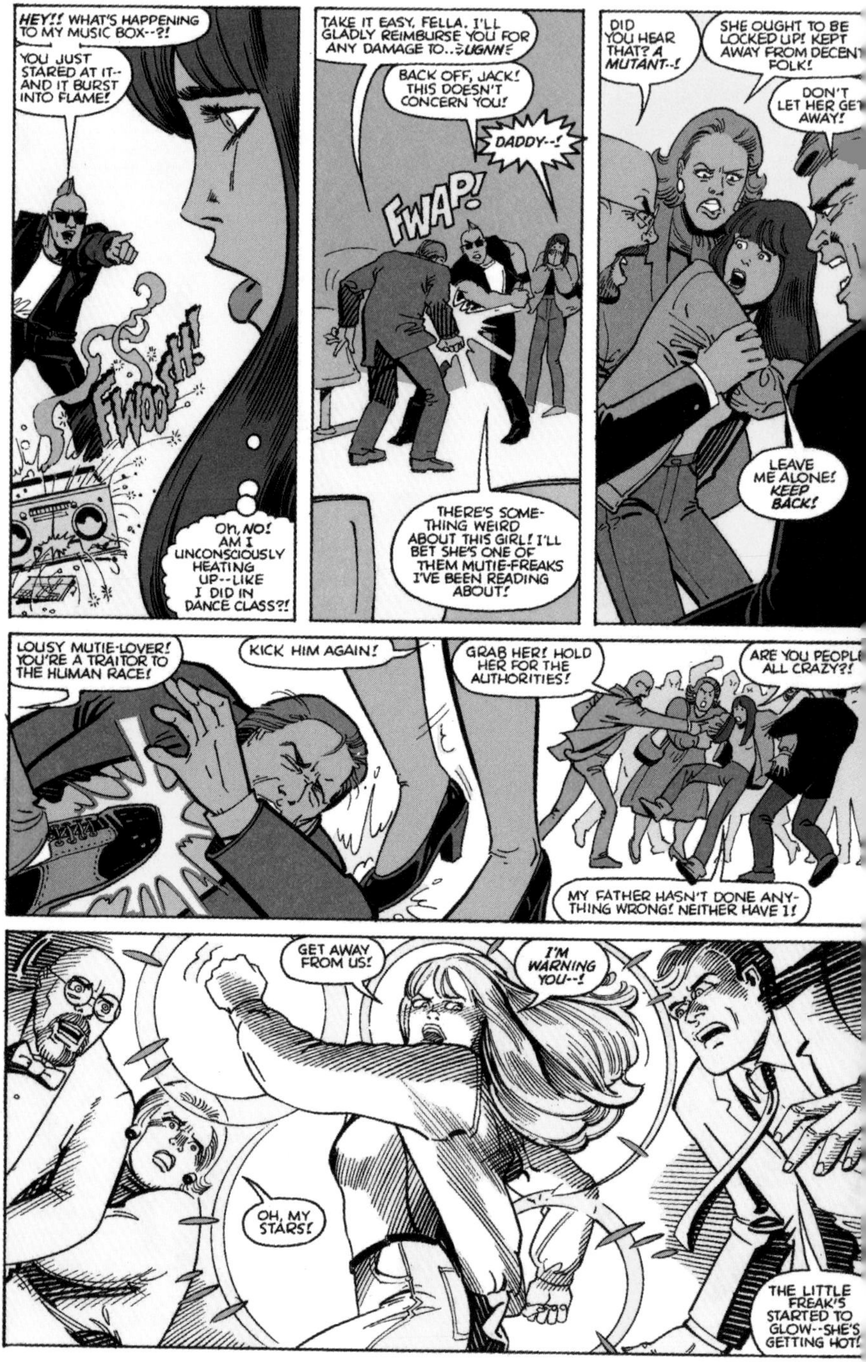

HEY!! WHAT'S HAPPENING TO MY MUSIC BOX--?!
YOU JUST STARED AT IT-- AND IT BURST INTO FLAME!
FWOOSH!
Oh, NO! AM I UNCONSCIOUSLY HEATING UP--LIKE I DID IN DANCE CLASS?!
TAKE IT EASY, FELLA. I'LL GLADLY REIMBURSE YOU FOR ANY DAMAGE TO...UGNN!
BACK OFF, JACK! THIS DOESN'T CONCERN YOU!
DADDY--!
FWAP!
THERE'S SOMETHING WEIRD ABOUT THIS GIRL! I'LL BET SHE'S ONE OF THEM MUTIE-FREAKS I'VE BEEN READING ABOUT!
DID YOU HEAR THAT? A MUTANT--!
SHE OUGHT TO BE LOCKED UP! KEPT AWAY FROM DECENT FOLK!
DON'T LET HER GET AWAY!
LEAVE ME ALONE! KEEP BACK!
LOUSY MUTIE-LOVER! YOU'RE A TRAITOR TO THE HUMAN RACE!
KICK HIM AGAIN!
GRAB HER! HOLD HER FOR THE AUTHORITIES!
ARE YOU PEOPLE ALL CRAZY?!
MY FATHER HASN'T DONE ANYTHING WRONG! NEITHER HAVE I!
GET AWAY FROM US!
I'M WARNING YOU--!
OH, MY STARS!
THE LITTLE FREAK'S STARTED TO GLOW--SHE'S GETTING HOT!

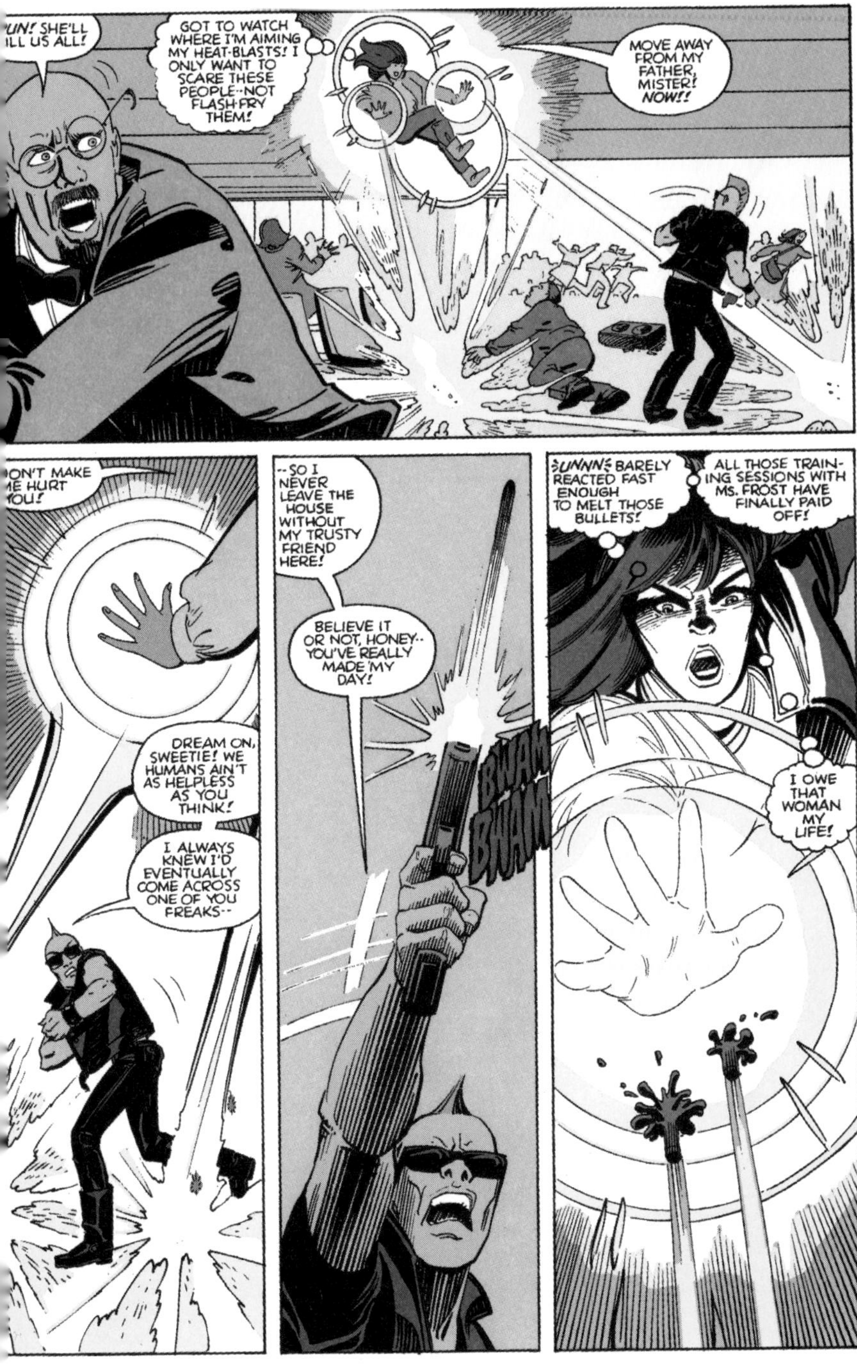

-UN! SHE'LL -ILL US ALL!
GOT TO WATCH WHERE I'M AIMING MY HEAT-BLASTS! I ONLY WANT TO SCARE THESE PEOPLE--NOT FLASH-FRY THEM!
MOVE AWAY FROM MY FATHER, MISTER! NOW!!
-ON'T MAKE -E HURT -OU!
DREAM ON, SWEETIE! WE HUMANS AIN'T AS HELPLESS AS YOU THINK!
I ALWAYS KNEW I'D EVENTUALLY COME ACROSS ONE OF YOU FREAKS--
--SO I NEVER LEAVE THE HOUSE WITHOUT MY TRUSTY FRIEND HERE!
BELIEVE IT OR NOT, HONEY-- YOU'VE REALLY MADE MY DAY!
BWAM
BWAM
UNNN! BARELY REACTED FAST ENOUGH TO MELT THOSE BULLETS!
ALL THOSE TRAINING SESSIONS WITH MS. FROST HAVE FINALLY PAID OFF!
I OWE THAT WOMAN MY LIFE!

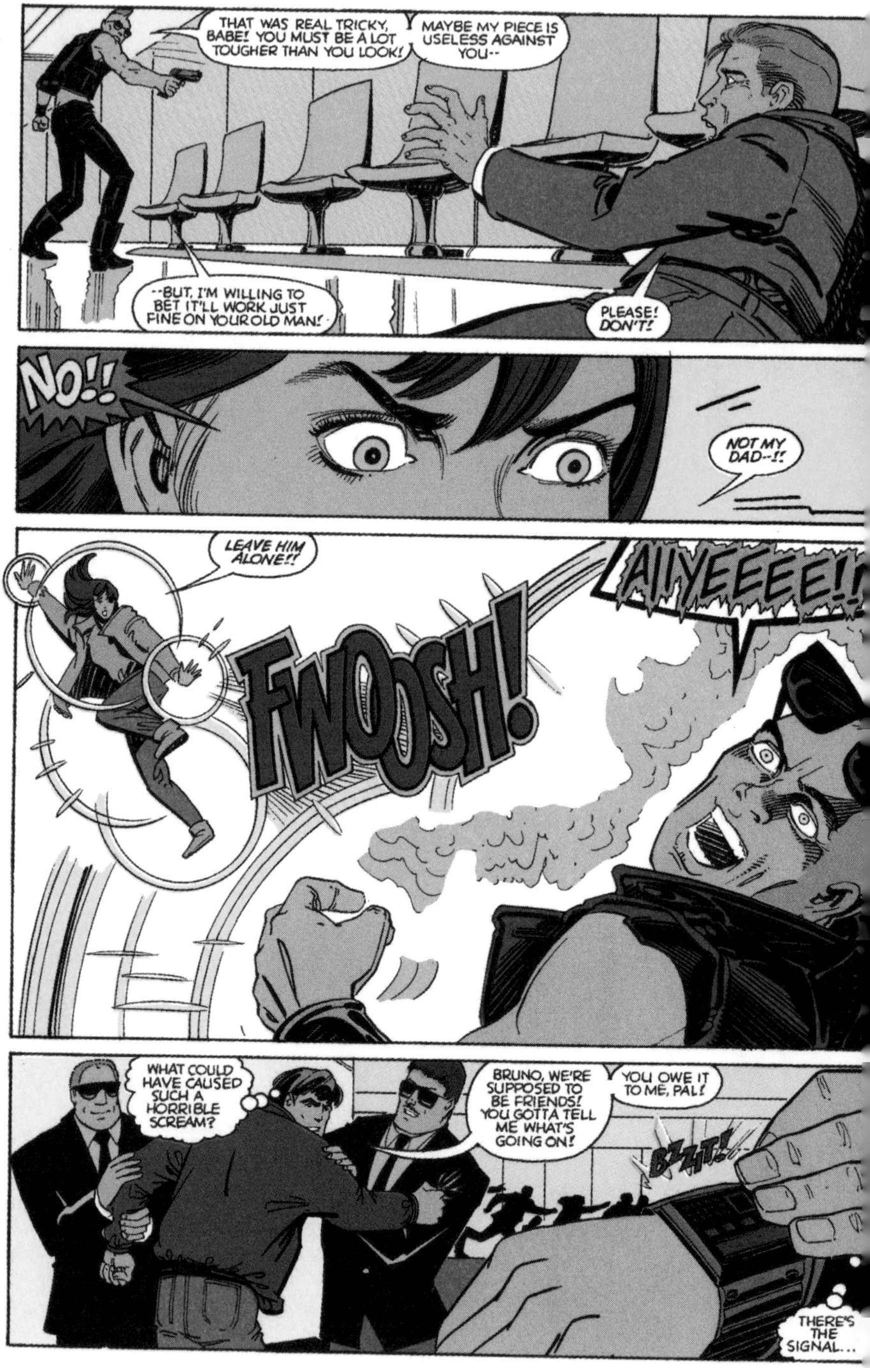
THAT WAS REAL TRICKY, BABE! YOU MUST BE A LOT TOUGHER THAN YOU LOOK!
MAYBE MY PIECE IS USELESS AGAINST YOU--
--BUT, I'M WILLING TO BET IT'LL WORK JUST FINE ON YOUR OLD MAN!
PLEASE! DON'T!
NO!!
NOT MY DAD--!!
LEAVE HIM ALONE!!
FWOOSH!
AIIYEEEE!!
WHAT COULD HAVE CAUSED SUCH A HORRIBLE SCREAM?
BRUNO, WE'RE SUPPOSED TO BE FRIENDS! YOU GOTTA TELL ME WHAT'S GOING ON!
YOU OWE IT TO ME, PAL!
BZZIT!
THERE'S THE SIGNAL...

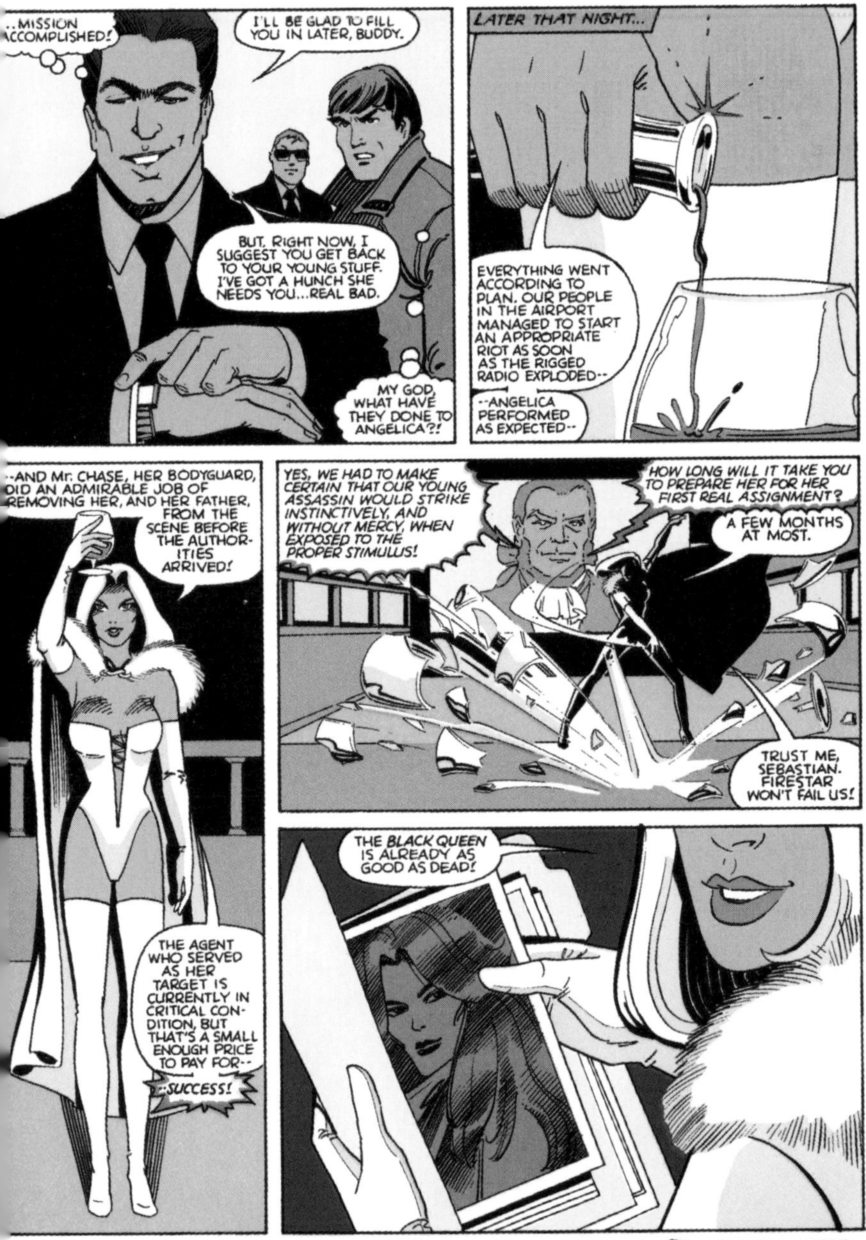
..MISSION ACCOMPLISHED!
I'LL BE GLAD TO FILL YOU IN LATER, BUDDY.
BUT, RIGHT NOW, I SUGGEST YOU GET BACK TO YOUR YOUNG STUFF. I'VE GOT A HUNCH SHE NEEDS YOU...REAL BAD.
MY GOD, WHAT HAVE THEY DONE TO ANGELICA?!
LATER THAT NIGHT...
EVERYTHING WENT ACCORDING TO PLAN. OUR PEOPLE IN THE AIRPORT MANAGED TO START AN APPROPRIATE RIOT AS SOON AS THE RIGGED RADIO EXPLODED--
--ANGELICA PERFORMED AS EXPECTED--
--AND Mr. CHASE, HER BODYGUARD, DID AN ADMIRABLE JOB OF REMOVING HER, AND HER FATHER, FROM THE SCENE BEFORE THE AUTHOR-ITIES ARRIVED!
THE AGENT WHO SERVED AS HER TARGET IS CURRENTLY IN CRITICAL CON-DITION, BUT THAT'S A SMALL ENOUGH PRICE TO PAY FOR--
--SUCCESS!
YES, WE HAD TO MAKE CERTAIN THAT OUR YOUNG ASSASSIN WOULD STRIKE INSTINCTIVELY, AND WITHOUT MERCY, WHEN EXPOSED TO THE PROPER STIMULUS!
HOW LONG WILL IT TAKE YOU TO PREPARE HER FOR HER FIRST REAL ASSIGNMENT?
A FEW MONTHS AT MOST.
TRUST ME, SEBASTIAN. FIRESTAR WON'T FAIL US!
THE BLACK QUEEN IS ALREADY AS GOOD AS DEAD!

BE HERE NEXT ISSUE FOR THE STARTLING CONCLUSION TO THE SAGA OF FIRESTAR! DON'T MISS ANGELICA JONE'S LAST YEAR IN...

NOW STRIKES THE ASSASSIN!

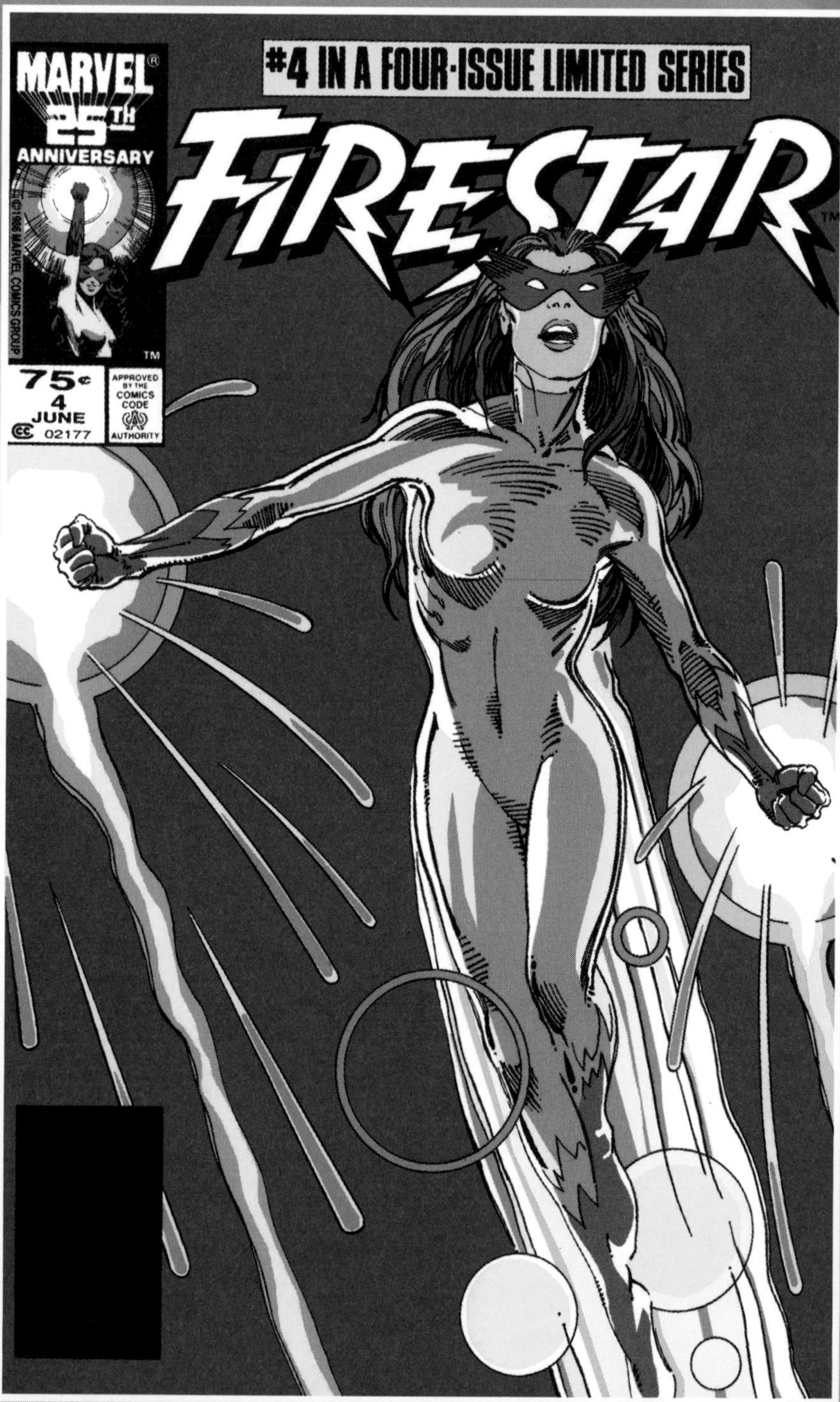
MARVEL®
25TH ANNIVERSARY
©1986 MARVEL COMICS GROUP
TM
#4 IN A FOUR-ISSUE LIMITED SERIES
FIRESTAR™
75¢
4
JUNE
02177
APPROVED BY THE COMICS CODE AUTHORITY

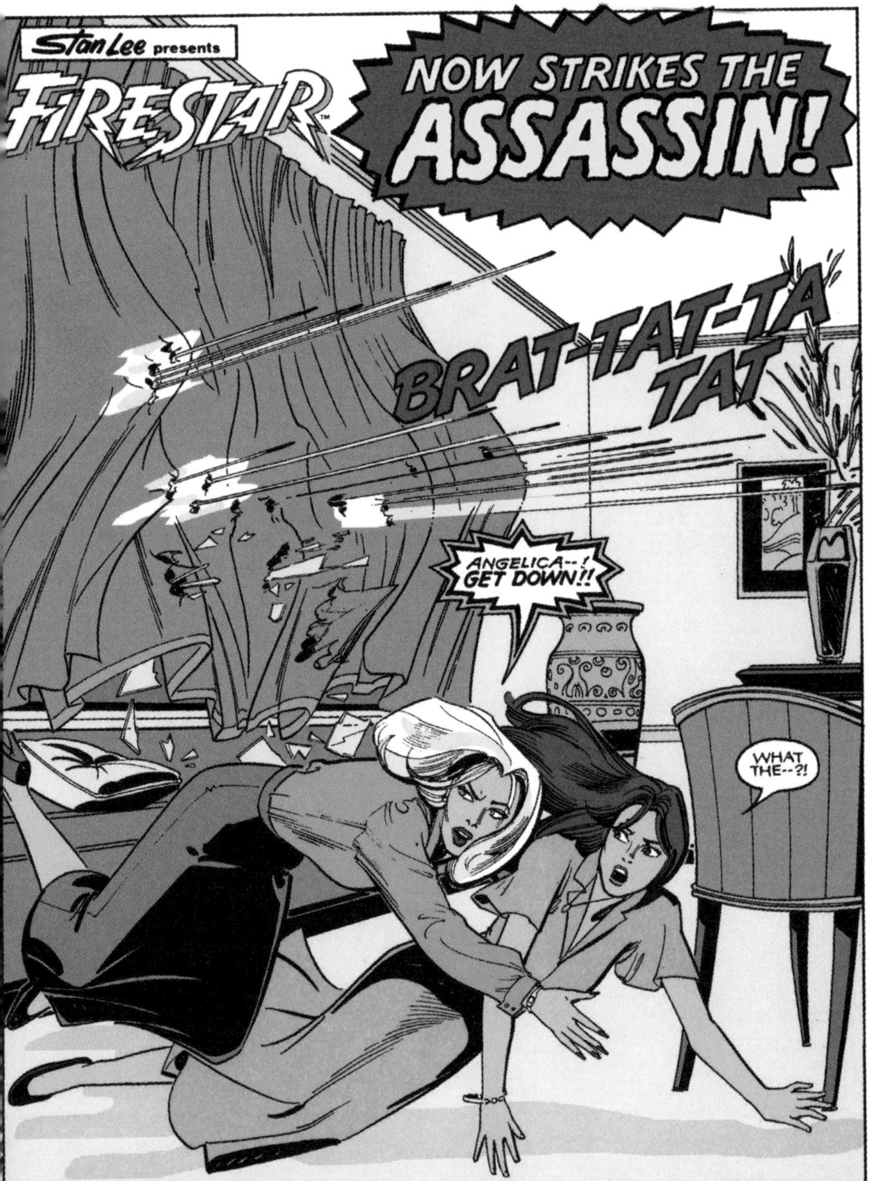
Stan Lee presents
FIRESTAR™
NOW STRIKES THE ASSASSIN!
BRAT-TAT-TA TAT
ANGELICA--! GET DOWN!!
WHAT THE--?!
TOM DeFALCO WRITER
MARY WILSHIRE PENCILER
STEVE LEIALOHA INKER
ORZECHOWSKI & BUHALIS LETTERERS
DAINA GRAZIUNUS COLORIST
ANN NOCENTI EDITOR
JIM SHOOTER EDITOR IN CHIEF

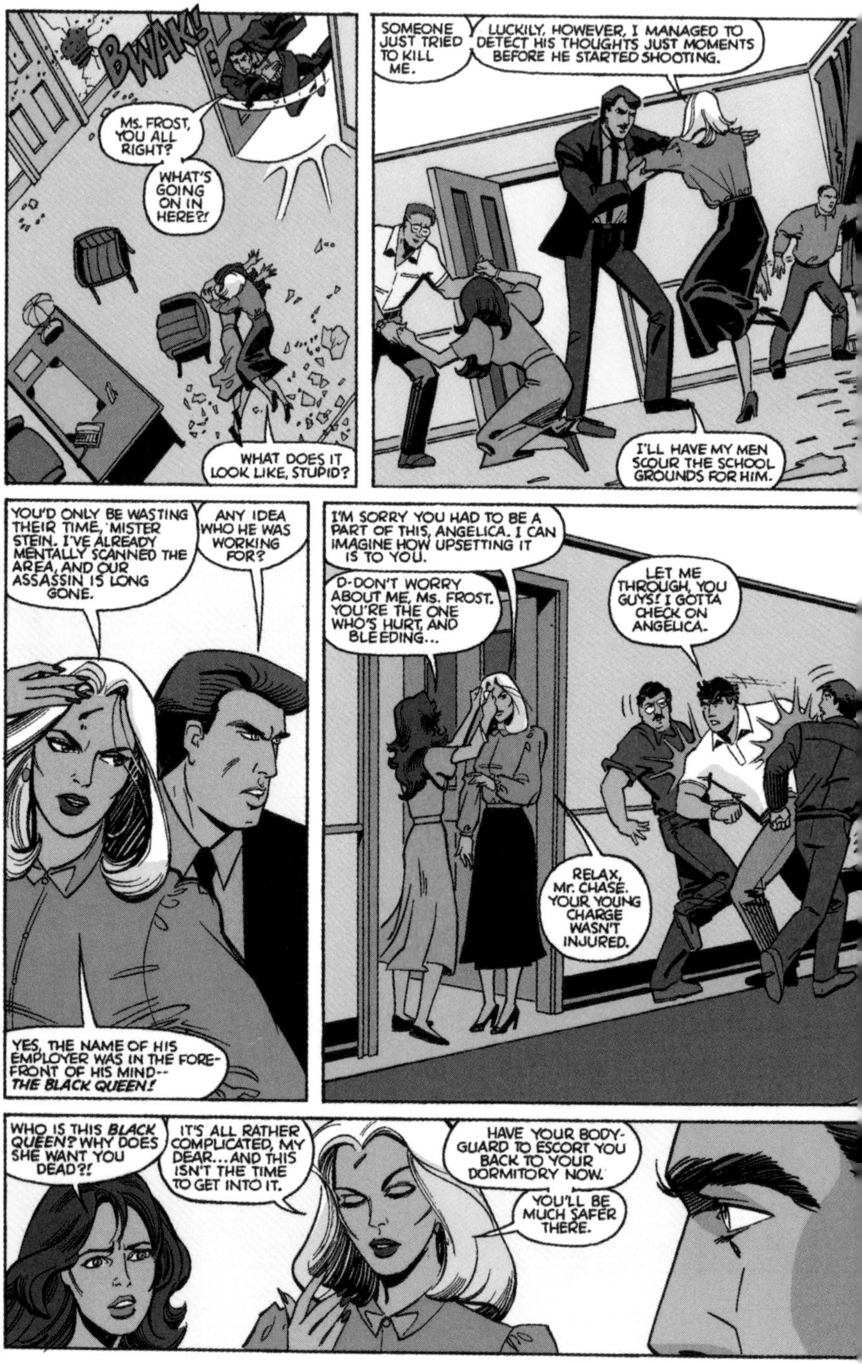
BWAK!
MS. FROST, YOU ALL RIGHT?
WHAT'S GOING ON IN HERE?!
WHAT DOES IT LOOK LIKE, STUPID?
SOMEONE JUST TRIED TO KILL ME.
LUCKILY, HOWEVER, I MANAGED TO DETECT HIS THOUGHTS JUST MOMENTS BEFORE HE STARTED SHOOTING.
I'LL HAVE MY MEN SCOUR THE SCHOOL GROUNDS FOR HIM.
YOU'D ONLY BE WASTING THEIR TIME, MISTER STEIN. I'VE ALREADY MENTALLY SCANNED THE AREA, AND OUR ASSASSIN IS LONG GONE.
ANY IDEA WHO HE WAS WORKING FOR?
YES, THE NAME OF HIS EMPLOYER WAS IN THE FORE-FRONT OF HIS MIND-- *THE BLACK QUEEN!*
I'M SORRY YOU HAD TO BE A PART OF THIS, ANGELICA. I CAN IMAGINE HOW UPSETTING IT IS TO YOU.
D-DON'T WORRY ABOUT ME, Ms. FROST. YOU'RE THE ONE WHO'S HURT, AND BLEEDING...
LET ME THROUGH, YOU GUYS! I GOTTA CHECK ON ANGELICA.
RELAX, Mr. CHASE. YOUR YOUNG CHARGE WASN'T INJURED.
WHO IS THIS *BLACK QUEEN*? WHY DOES SHE WANT YOU DEAD?!
IT'S ALL RATHER COMPLICATED, MY DEAR... AND THIS ISN'T THE TIME TO GET INTO IT.
HAVE YOUR BODY-GUARD TO ESCORT YOU BACK TO YOUR DORMITORY NOW.
YOU'LL BE MUCH SAFER THERE.

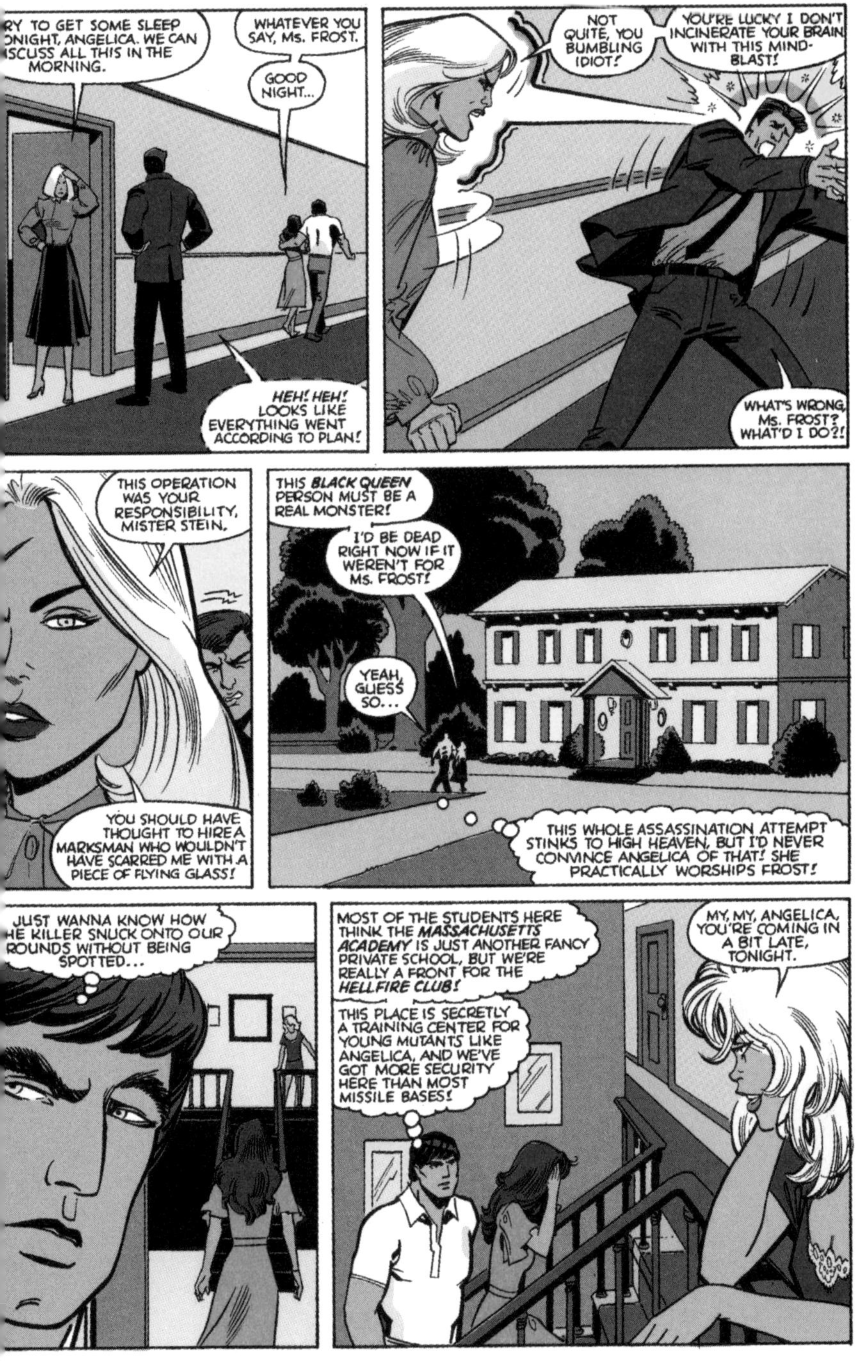
RY TO GET SOME SLEEP
ONIGHT, ANGELICA. WE CAN
ISCUSS ALL THIS IN THE
MORNING.
WHATEVER YOU SAY, Ms. FROST.
GOOD NIGHT...
HEH! HEH! LOOKS LIKE EVERYTHING WENT ACCORDING TO PLAN!
NOT QUITE, YOU BUMBLING IDIOT!
YOU'RE LUCKY I DON'T INCINERATE YOUR BRAIN WITH THIS MIND-BLAST!
WHAT'S WRONG, Ms. FROST? WHAT'D I DO?!
THIS OPERATION WAS YOUR RESPONSIBILITY, MISTER STEIN.
YOU SHOULD HAVE THOUGHT TO HIRE A MARKSMAN WHO WOULDN'T HAVE SCARRED ME WITH A PIECE OF FLYING GLASS!
THIS BLACK QUEEN PERSON MUST BE A REAL MONSTER!
I'D BE DEAD RIGHT NOW IF IT WEREN'T FOR Ms. FROST!
YEAH, GUESS SO...
THIS WHOLE ASSASSINATION ATTEMPT STINKS TO HIGH HEAVEN, BUT I'D NEVER CONVINCE ANGELICA OF THAT! SHE PRACTICALLY WORSHIPS FROST!
JUST WANNA KNOW HOW
HE KILLER SNUCK ONTO OUR
ROUNDS WITHOUT BEING
SPOTTED...
MOST OF THE STUDENTS HERE THINK THE MASSACHUSETTS ACADEMY IS JUST ANOTHER FANCY PRIVATE SCHOOL, BUT WE'RE REALLY A FRONT FOR THE HELLFIRE CLUB!
THIS PLACE IS SECRETLY A TRAINING CENTER FOR YOUNG MUTANTS LIKE ANGELICA, AND WE'VE GOT MORE SECURITY HERE THAN MOST MISSILE BASES!
MY, MY, ANGELICA, YOU'RE COMING IN A BIT LATE, TONIGHT.

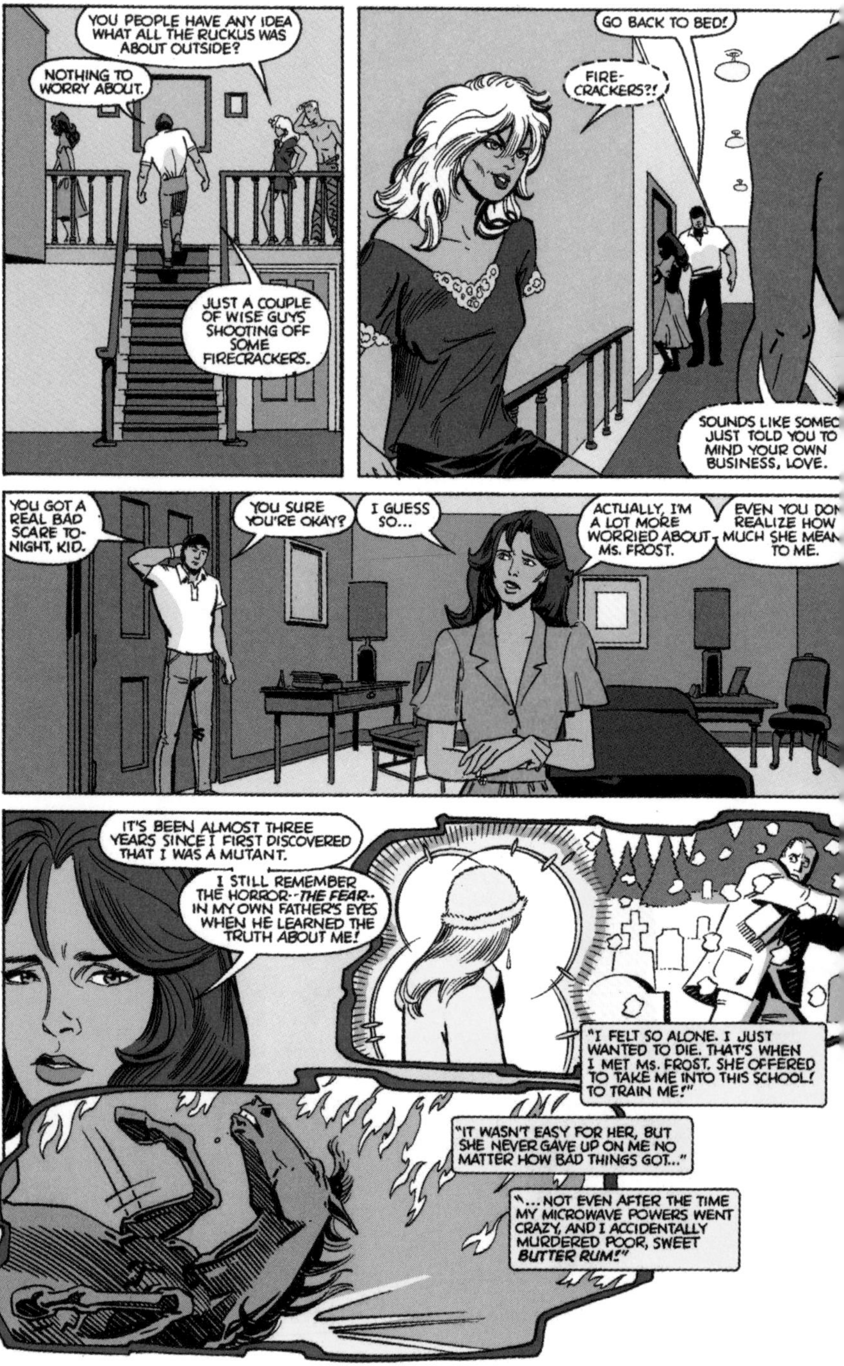
YOU PEOPLE HAVE ANY IDEA WHAT ALL THE RUCKUS WAS ABOUT OUTSIDE?
NOTHING TO WORRY ABOUT.
JUST A COUPLE OF WISE GUYS SHOOTING OFF SOME FIRECRACKERS.
GO BACK TO BED!
FIRE-CRACKERS?!
SOUNDS LIKE SOMEC JUST TOLD YOU TO MIND YOUR OWN BUSINESS, LOVE.
YOU GOT A REAL BAD SCARE TO-NIGHT, KID.
YOU SURE YOU'RE OKAY?
I GUESS SO...
ACTUALLY, I'M A LOT MORE WORRIED ABOUT MS. FROST.
EVEN YOU DON REALIZE HOW MUCH SHE MEAN TO ME.
IT'S BEEN ALMOST THREE YEARS SINCE I FIRST DISCOVERED THAT I WAS A MUTANT.
I STILL REMEMBER THE HORROR--THE FEAR-- IN MY OWN FATHER'S EYES WHEN HE LEARNED THE TRUTH ABOUT ME!
"I FELT SO ALONE. I JUST WANTED TO DIE. THAT'S WHEN I MET MS. FROST. SHE OFFERED TO TAKE ME INTO THIS SCHOOL! TO TRAIN ME!"
"IT WASN'T EASY FOR HER, BUT SHE NEVER GAVE UP ON ME NO MATTER HOW BAD THINGS GOT..."
"...NOT EVEN AFTER THE TIME MY MICROWAVE POWERS WENT CRAZY, AND I ACCIDENTALLY MURDERED POOR, SWEET BUTTER RUM!"

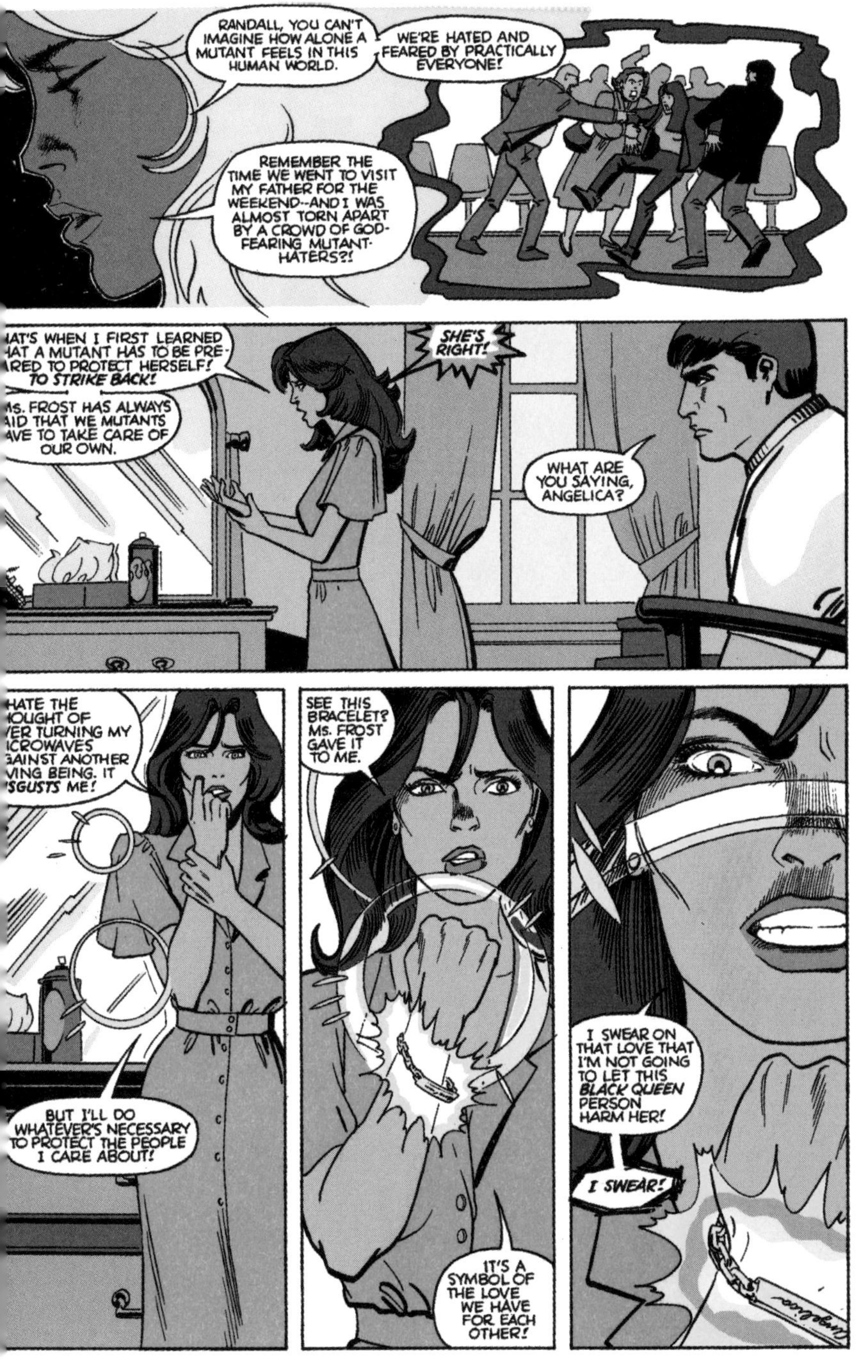
RANDALL, YOU CAN'T IMAGINE HOW ALONE A MUTANT FEELS IN THIS HUMAN WORLD.
WE'RE HATED AND FEARED BY PRACTICALLY EVERYONE!
REMEMBER THE TIME WE WENT TO VISIT MY FATHER FOR THE WEEKEND--AND I WAS ALMOST TORN APART BY A CROWD OF GOD-FEARING MUTANT-HATERS?!
AT'S WHEN I FIRST LEARNED AT A MUTANT HAS TO BE PRE-ARED TO PROTECT HERSELF! TO STRIKE BACK!
MS. FROST HAS ALWAYS AID THAT WE MUTANTS AVE TO TAKE CARE OF OUR OWN.
SHE'S RIGHT!
WHAT ARE YOU SAYING, ANGELICA?
HATE THE HOUGHT OF VER TURNING MY ICROWAVES GAINST ANOTHER VING BEING. IT SGUSTS ME!
BUT I'LL DO WHATEVER'S NECESSARY TO PROTECT THE PEOPLE I CARE ABOUT!
SEE THIS BRACELET? MS. FROST GAVE IT TO ME.
IT'S A SYMBOL OF THE LOVE WE HAVE FOR EACH OTHER!
I SWEAR ON THAT LOVE THAT I'M NOT GOING TO LET THIS BLACK QUEEN PERSON HARM HER!
I SWEAR!

SHA-BWOOM!

ANGELICA--!

EASY DOES IT, KID. YOU OUGHTA KNOW BETTER THAN TO GO TOSSING YOUR MICROWAVE BLASTS AROUND LIKE THAT!

JUST LOOK AT THAT MESS!

WHAT WOULD MS. FROST SAY?

PERFECT!

I'M GLAD TO SEE YOU SO PLEASED, EMMA.

YOU MUST ACTUALLY BELIEVE THAT YOUNG *FIRESTAR* HAS A CHANCE OF SUCCESSFULLY COMPLETING HER FIRST MISSION FOR US!

AN EXCELLENT ONE, SEBASTIAN!

THEN, WHAT'S TROUBLING YOU, MY DEAR?

...NEVER COULD HIDE ANYTHING FROM YOU, SEBASTIAN.

FIRESTAR STILL DOESN'T REALIZE THAT I'VE BEEN SECRETLY GROOMING HER TO SERVE AS THE HELLFIRE CLUB'S ASSASSIN EVER SINCE I FIRST BECAME AWARE OF HER BODY'S ABILITY TO STORE AND PROJECT MICROWAVES!

I KNEW SHE'D HAVE TO BE EXPENDABLE, SO I NEVER PERMITTED HER TO TRAIN, OR FORM BONDS WITH ANY OF MY OTHER MUTANT STUDENTS...

SO MUCH TIME AND EFFORT WENT INTO TRAINING HER...

...THAT I JUST WISH WE COULD GET A LITTLE MORE USE OUT OF HER BEFORE SENDING HER ON SUCH AN OBVIOUS SUICIDE ASSIGNMENT!

UNFORTUNATELY, THAT CAN'T BE HELPED, EMMA.

PERHAPS WE'LL HAVE BETTER LUCK WITH YOUR NEXT MUTANT FIND.

CLIKK

IF I DIDN'T KNOW BETTER, I'D ALMOST THINK EMMA ACTUALLY FELT SOMETHING FOR THAT GIRL.

IT DOESN'T MATTER. EMMA'S LOYALTY TO ME IS UNQUESTIONABLE. SHE'LL DO WHAT-EVER I REQUIRE.

AND, WHAT I REQUIRE MOST RIGHT NOW IS A DEADLY PAWN!

SHAW! WHAT A PLEASANT SURPRISE--!

DO YOU LIKE MY NEW GOWN?

I BOUGHT IT FOR OUR UPCOMING FANCY DRESS BALL!

IT'S STUNNING, SELENE... THOUGH IT PALES IN COMPARISON TO YOUR OWN GREAT BEAUTY!

THIS WITCH DOESN'T FOOL ME FOR A MOMENT. I KNOW SHE'S SECRETLY PLANNING TO SEIZE CONTROL OF THE INNER CIRCLE OF THE HELLFIRE CLUB FROM ME.

BUT, I'VE ALREADY PREPARED A SURPRISE FOR MY BLACK QUEEN. A RATHER UN-PLEASANT ONE!

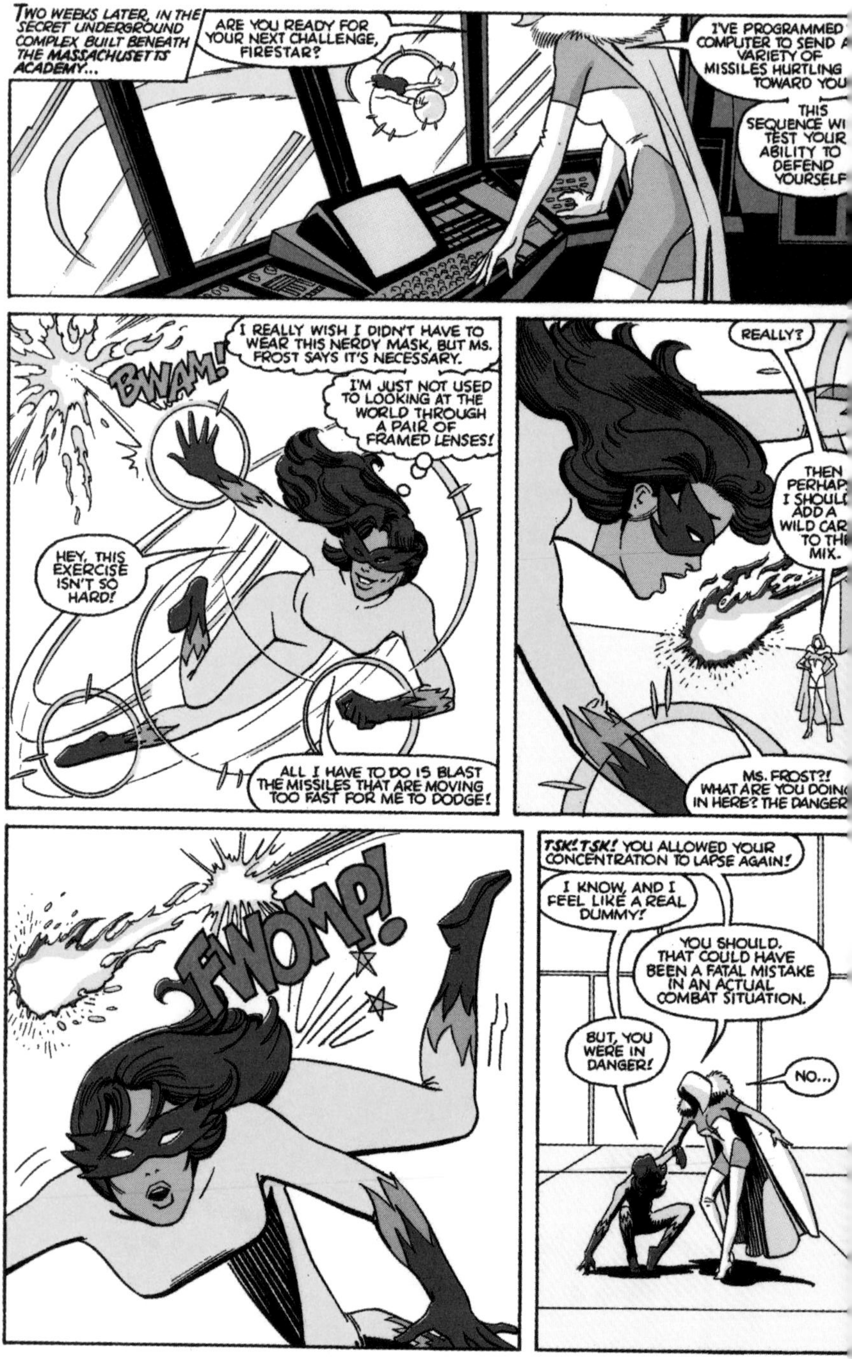
TWO WEEKS LATER, IN THE SECRET UNDERGROUND COMPLEX BUILT BENEATH THE MASSACHUSETTS ACADEMY...
ARE YOU READY FOR YOUR NEXT CHALLENGE, FIRESTAR?
I'VE PROGRAMMED COMPUTER TO SEND A VARIETY OF MISSILES HURTLING TOWARD YOU
THIS SEQUENCE WI TEST YOUR ABILITY TO DEFEND YOURSELF
BWAM!
I REALLY WISH I DIDN'T HAVE TO WEAR THIS NERDY MASK, BUT MS. FROST SAYS IT'S NECESSARY.
I'M JUST NOT USED TO LOOKING AT THE WORLD THROUGH A PAIR OF FRAMED LENSES!
HEY, THIS EXERCISE ISN'T SO HARD!
ALL I HAVE TO DO IS BLAST THE MISSILES THAT ARE MOVING TOO FAST FOR ME TO DODGE!
REALLY?
THEN PERHAP I SHOUL ADD A WILD CAR TO TH MIX.
MS. FROST?! WHAT ARE YOU DOIN IN HERE? THE DANGER
FWOMP!
TSK! TSK! YOU ALLOWED YOUR CONCENTRATION TO LAPSE AGAIN!
I KNOW, AND I FEEL LIKE A REAL DUMMY!
YOU SHOULD. THAT COULD HAVE BEEN A FATAL MISTAKE IN AN ACTUAL COMBAT SITUATION.
BUT, YOU WERE IN DANGER!
NO...

THIS TRAINING ROOM HAS BEEN PROGRAMMED TO IGNORE MY PRESENCE!

I'M COMPLETELY MASKED FROM ITS SENSORS!

BY THE WAY, ASIDE FROM THAT LAST LITTLE MISHAP, I'VE BEEN QUITE PLEASED WITH YOUR PROGRESS LATELY.

YOU'RE DOING VERY WELL. YOUR CONTROL OVER YOUR POWERS SEEMS TO BE IN- CREASING ON A DAILY BASIS.

YOU'RE OBVIOUSLY WORKING VERY HARD, AND I THINK YOU DESERVE A REWARD...

I'VE BEEN INVITED TO A FANCY DRESS BALL IN MANHATTAN NEXT WEEK.

WOULD YOU LIKE TO COME?

3 ADMINISTRA
2 ADMINISTRA
1 ADMINISTRA
B SECURITY
S1 LOCKERS
S2 CONTROL R
EBRIEFING
DANGER RO
S5 MAINTENANC
S6 ARSENAL
S7 PRIORITY AC
S8 PRIORITY AC

A FORMAL DANCE?

ARE YOU SERIOUS?!

RANDALL! Ms. FROST IS TAKING ME TO A FORMAL DANCE IN NEW YORK CITY NEXT WEEK.

YOU'RE... KIDDING.

IS IT REALLY WISE TO LEAVE THE PROTECTION OF THE SCHOOL SO SOON AFTER AN ASSASSINATION ATTEMPT?

ARE YOU QUESTIONING MY JUDGMENT, Mr. CHASE?

N-NO, MA'AM! I'D NEVER DO THAT!

GOOD! SEE THAT YOU DON'T!

I KNOW I SHOULD MIND MY OWN BUSINESS...

...BUT, HOW CAN I WHEN I'M CERTAIN THAT ANGELICA'S IN DANGER?!

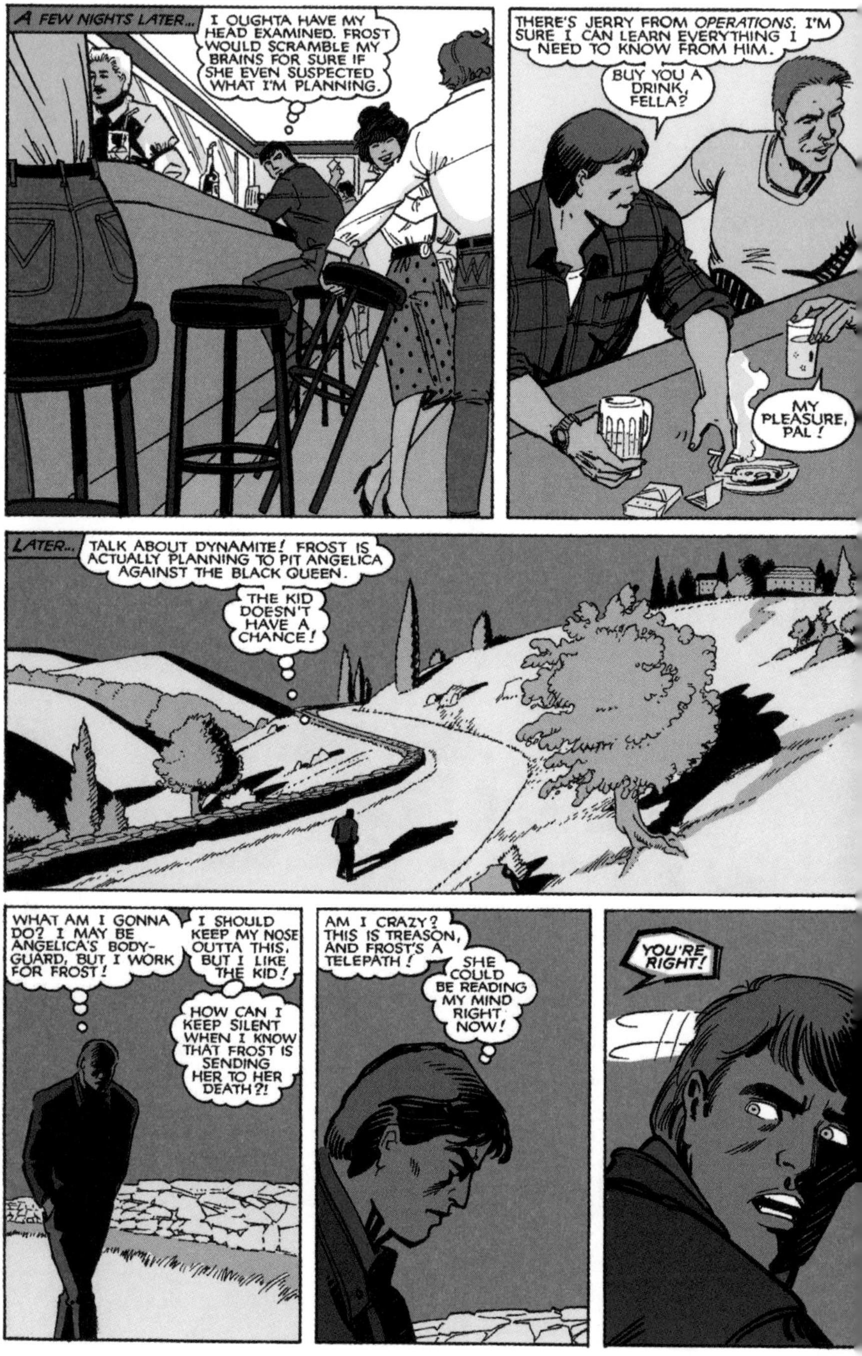
A FEW NIGHTS LATER...
I OUGHTA HAVE MY HEAD EXAMINED. FROST WOULD SCRAMBLE MY BRAINS FOR SURE IF SHE EVEN SUSPECTED WHAT I'M PLANNING.
THERE'S JERRY FROM *OPERATIONS*. I'M SURE I CAN LEARN EVERYTHING I NEED TO KNOW FROM HIM.
BUY YOU A DRINK, FELLA?
MY PLEASURE, PAL!
LATER...
TALK ABOUT DYNAMITE! FROST IS ACTUALLY PLANNING TO PIT ANGELICA AGAINST THE BLACK QUEEN.
THE KID DOESN'T HAVE A CHANCE!
WHAT AM I GONNA DO? I MAY BE ANGELICA'S BODY-GUARD, BUT I WORK FOR FROST!
I SHOULD KEEP MY NOSE OUTTA THIS, BUT I LIKE THE KID!
HOW CAN I KEEP SILENT WHEN I KNOW THAT FROST IS SENDING HER TO HER DEATH?!
AM I CRAZY? THIS IS TREASON, AND FROST'S A TELEPATH!
SHE COULD BE READING MY MIND RIGHT NOW!
YOU'RE RIGHT!

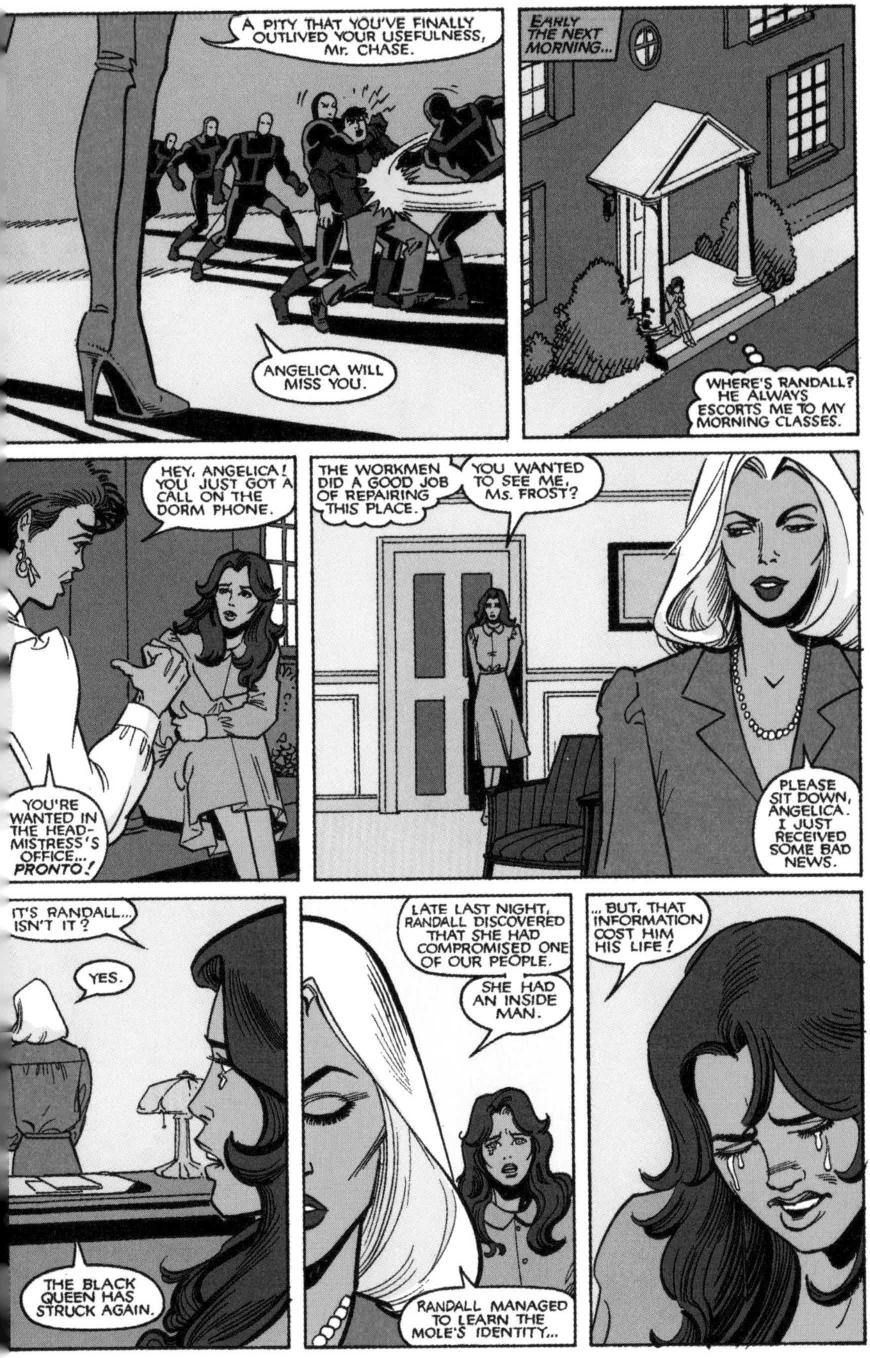
A PITY THAT YOU'VE FINALLY OUTLIVED YOUR USEFULNESS, Mr. CHASE.
ANGELICA WILL MISS YOU.
EARLY THE NEXT MORNING...
WHERE'S RANDALL? HE ALWAYS ESCORTS ME TO MY MORNING CLASSES.
HEY, ANGELICA! YOU JUST GOT A CALL ON THE DORM PHONE.
YOU'RE WANTED IN THE HEAD-MISTRESS'S OFFICE... PRONTO!
THE WORKMEN DID A GOOD JOB OF REPAIRING THIS PLACE.
YOU WANTED TO SEE ME, Ms. FROST?
PLEASE SIT DOWN, ANGELICA. I JUST RECEIVED SOME BAD NEWS.
IT'S RANDALL... ISN'T IT?
YES.
THE BLACK QUEEN HAS STRUCK AGAIN.
LATE LAST NIGHT, RANDALL DISCOVERED THAT SHE HAD COMPROMISED ONE OF OUR PEOPLE.
SHE HAD AN INSIDE MAN.
RANDALL MANAGED TO LEARN THE MOLE'S IDENTITY...
...BUT, THAT INFORMATION COST HIM HIS LIFE!

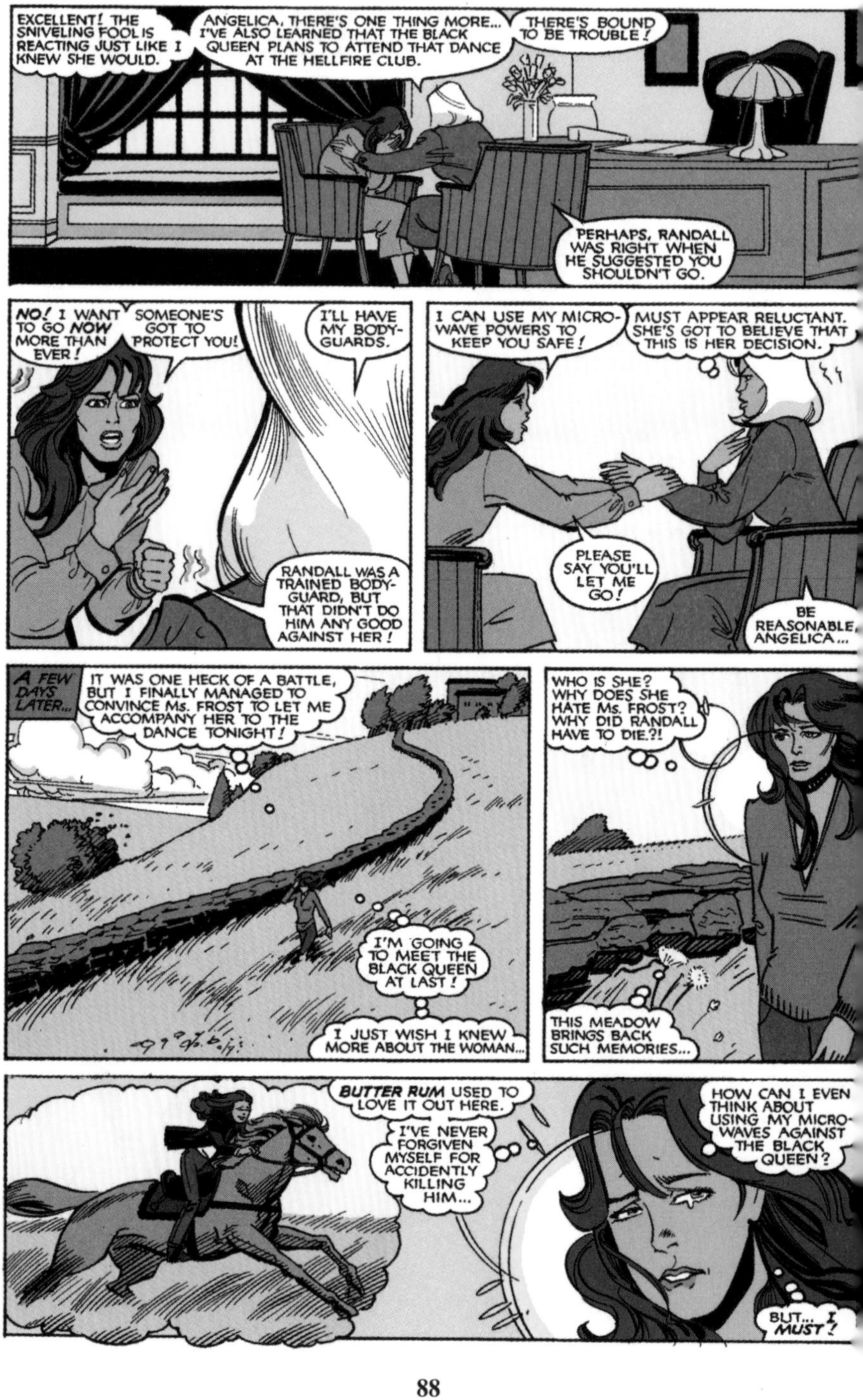

EXCELLENT! THE SNIVELING FOOL IS REACTING JUST LIKE I KNEW SHE WOULD.
ANGELICA, THERE'S ONE THING MORE... I'VE ALSO LEARNED THAT THE BLACK QUEEN PLANS TO ATTEND THAT DANCE AT THE HELLFIRE CLUB.
THERE'S BOUND TO BE TROUBLE!
PERHAPS, RANDALL WAS RIGHT WHEN HE SUGGESTED YOU SHOULDN'T GO.
NO! I WANT TO GO NOW MORE THAN EVER!
SOMEONE'S GOT TO PROTECT YOU!
I'LL HAVE MY BODY-GUARDS.
RANDALL WAS A TRAINED BODY-GUARD, BUT THAT DIDN'T DO HIM ANY GOOD AGAINST HER!
I CAN USE MY MICRO-WAVE POWERS TO KEEP YOU SAFE!
MUST APPEAR RELUCTANT. SHE'S GOT TO BELIEVE THAT THIS IS HER DECISION.
PLEASE SAY YOU'LL LET ME GO!
BE REASONABLE, ANGELICA...
A FEW DAYS LATER...
IT WAS ONE HECK OF A BATTLE, BUT I FINALLY MANAGED TO CONVINCE Ms. FROST TO LET ME ACCOMPANY HER TO THE DANCE TONIGHT!
I'M GOING TO MEET THE BLACK QUEEN AT LAST!
I JUST WISH I KNEW MORE ABOUT THE WOMAN...
WHO IS SHE? WHY DOES SHE HATE Ms. FROST? WHY DID RANDALL HAVE TO DIE.?!
THIS MEADOW BRINGS BACK SUCH MEMORIES...
BUTTER RUM USED TO LOVE IT OUT HERE.
I'VE NEVER FORGIVEN MYSELF FOR ACCIDENTLY KILLING HIM...
HOW CAN I EVEN THINK ABOUT USING MY MICRO-WAVES AGAINST THE BLACK QUEEN?
BUT... I MUST!

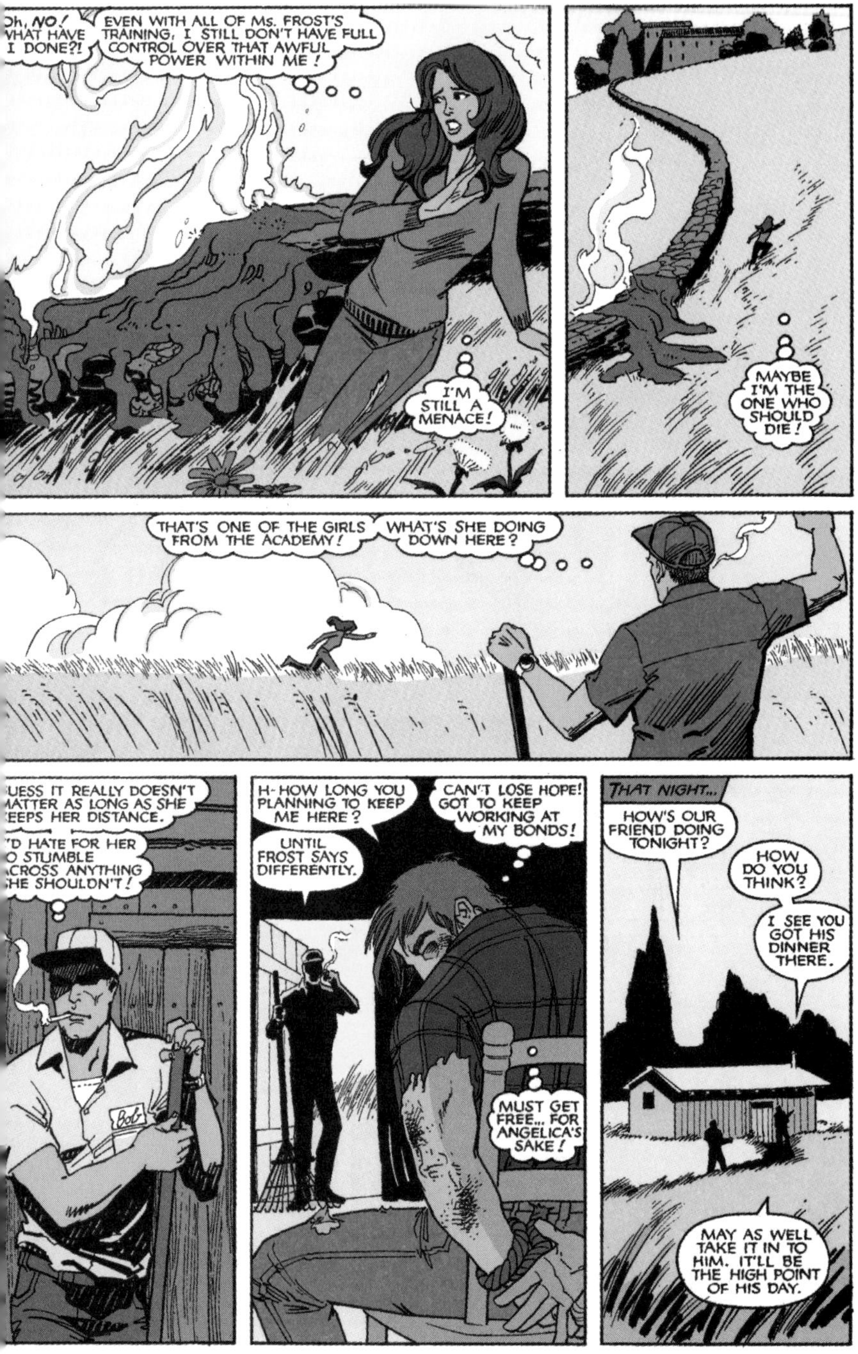
Oh, NO! WHAT HAVE I DONE?!
EVEN WITH ALL OF Ms. FROST'S TRAINING, I STILL DON'T HAVE FULL CONTROL OVER THAT AWFUL POWER WITHIN ME!
I'M STILL A MENACE!
MAYBE I'M THE ONE WHO SHOULD DIE!
THAT'S ONE OF THE GIRLS FROM THE ACADEMY!
WHAT'S SHE DOING DOWN HERE?
UESS IT REALLY DOESN'T ATTER AS LONG AS SHE EEPS HER DISTANCE.
'D HATE FOR HER O STUMBLE ACROSS ANYTHING HE SHOULDN'T!
Bob
H-HOW LONG YOU PLANNING TO KEEP ME HERE?
UNTIL FROST SAYS DIFFERENTLY.
CAN'T LOSE HOPE! GOT TO KEEP WORKING AT MY BONDS!
MUST GET FREE... FOR ANGELICA'S SAKE!
THAT NIGHT...
HOW'S OUR FRIEND DOING TONIGHT?
HOW DO YOU THINK?
I SEE YOU GOT HIS DINNER THERE.
MAY AS WELL TAKE IT IN TO HIM. IT'LL BE THE HIGH POINT OF HIS DAY.

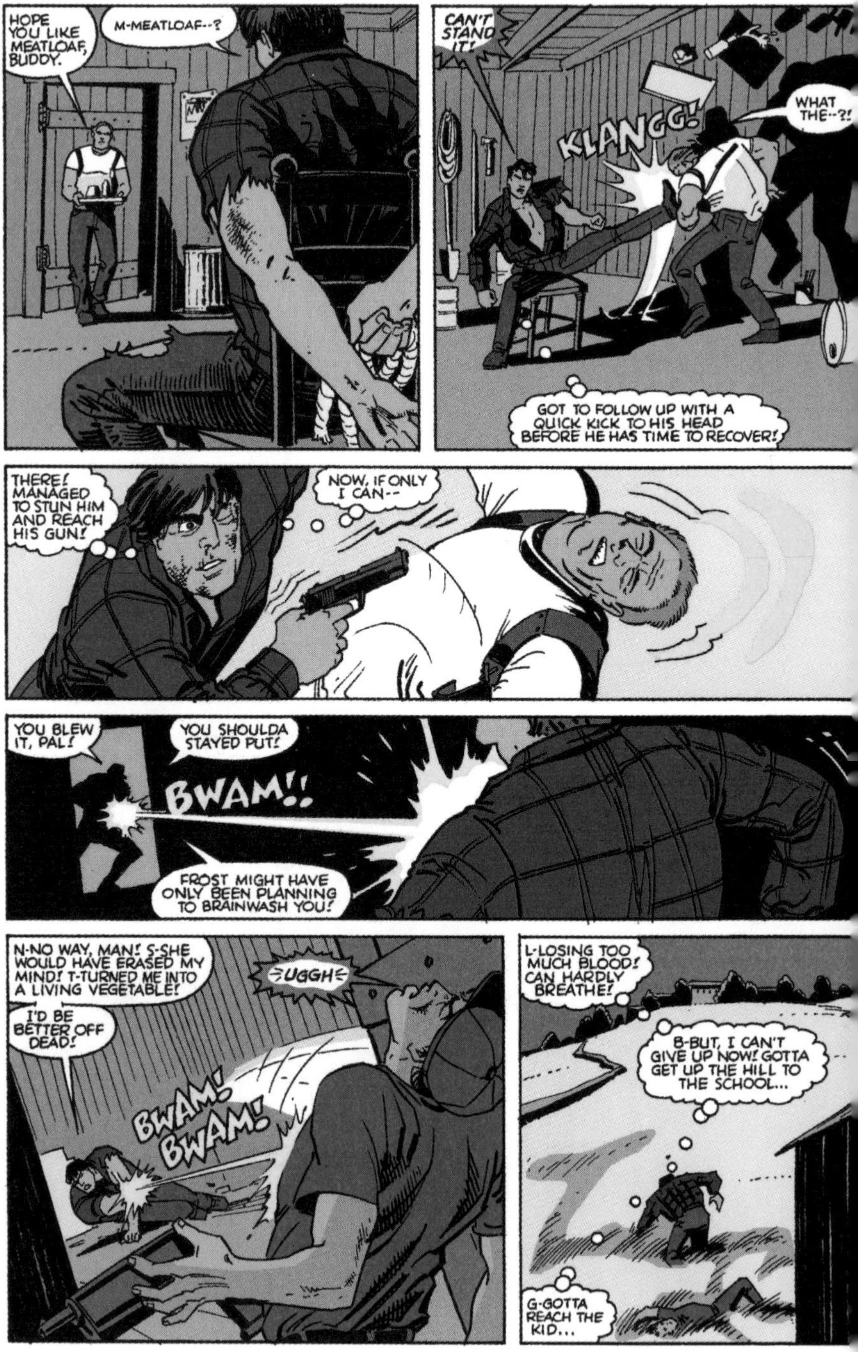
HOPE YOU LIKE MEATLOAF, BUDDY.
M-MEATLOAF--?
CAN'T STAND IT!
KLANGG!
WHAT THE--?!
GOT TO FOLLOW UP WITH A QUICK KICK TO HIS HEAD BEFORE HE HAS TIME TO RECOVER!
THERE! MANAGED TO STUN HIM AND REACH HIS GUN!
NOW, IF ONLY I CAN--
YOU BLEW IT, PAL!
YOU SHOULDA STAYED PUT!
BWAM!!
FROST MIGHT HAVE ONLY BEEN PLANNING TO BRAINWASH YOU!
N-NO WAY, MAN! S-SHE WOULD HAVE ERASED MY MIND! T-TURNED ME INTO A LIVING VEGETABLE!
UGGH
I'D BE BETTER OFF DEAD!
BWAM! BWAM!
L-LOSING TOO MUCH BLOOD! CAN HARDLY BREATHE!
B-BUT, I CAN'T GIVE UP NOW! GOTTA GET UP THE HILL TO THE SCHOOL...
G-GOTTA REACH THE KID...

...GOTTA WARN HER!"

MY FIRST FORMAL [D]ANCE! THIS IS SUP[P]OSED TO BE ONE [OF] THE HAPPIEST [D]AYS OF MY LIFE.

[B]IT COULD [V]ERY WELL BE [M]Y LAST.

[W]HO KNOWS [WH]AT'LL HAPPEN [WH]EN I FINALLY [M]EET THE [BL]ACK [QU]EEN?

MS. FROST IS PROBABLY WAITING FOR ME DOWN-STAIRS...

...BUT, THERE'S SOMETHING I'VE GOT TO DO BEFORE I LEAVE.

WOW! WHERE DO YOU THINK SHE'S HEADED?

GAME TONIGHT

I'D LAY ODDS THAT IT AIN'T TO THE GYM FOR THE BASKET-BALL GAME!

PLEASE MAKE HIM BE HOME··!

RRRING!!

DADDY? IT'S ANGELICA. LISTEN, I KNOW YOU'VE NEVER QUITE ACCEPTED THE FACT THAT I'M A MUTANT.

I KNOW YOU'RE STILL AFRAID OF ME, BUT...

...I STILL *LOVE* YOU, DADDY!

CLIKK

I NEVER STOPPED!

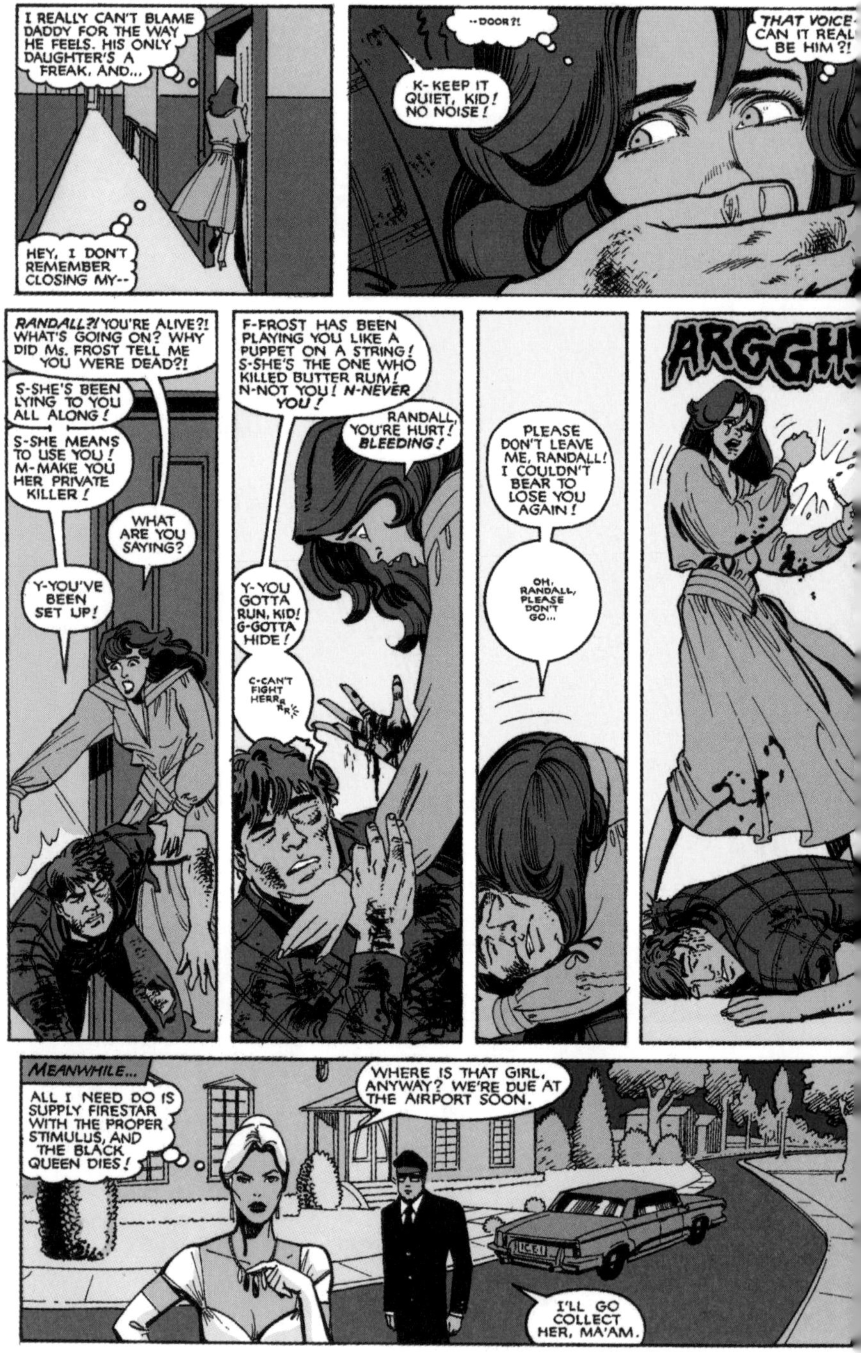

I REALLY CAN'T BLAME DADDY FOR THE WAY HE FEELS. HIS ONLY DAUGHTER'S A FREAK, AND...
HEY, I DON'T REMEMBER CLOSING MY--
--DOOR?!
K-KEEP IT QUIET, KID! NO NOISE!
THAT VOICE- CAN IT REAL BE HIM?!
RANDALL?! YOU'RE ALIVE?! WHAT'S GOING ON? WHY DID Ms. FROST TELL ME YOU WERE DEAD?!
S-SHE'S BEEN LYING TO YOU ALL ALONG!
S-SHE MEANS TO USE YOU! M-MAKE YOU HER PRIVATE KILLER!
WHAT ARE YOU SAYING?
Y-YOU'VE BEEN SET UP!
F-FROST HAS BEEN PLAYING YOU LIKE A PUPPET ON A STRING! S-SHE'S THE ONE WHO KILLED BUTTER RUM! N-NOT YOU! N-NEVER YOU!
RANDALL, YOU'RE HURT! BLEEDING!
Y-YOU GOTTA RUN, KID! G-GOTTA HIDE!
C-CAN'T FIGHT HERR RR
PLEASE DON'T LEAVE ME, RANDALL! I COULDN'T BEAR TO LOSE YOU AGAIN!
OH, RANDALL, PLEASE DON'T GO...
ARGGH!
MEANWHILE...
ALL I NEED DO IS SUPPLY FIRESTAR WITH THE PROPER STIMULUS, AND THE BLACK QUEEN DIES!
WHERE IS THAT GIRL, ANYWAY? WE'RE DUE AT THE AIRPORT SOON.
I'LL GO COLLECT HER, MA'AM.

...UT, BARELY THREE MINUTES LATER...

BAD NEWS, Ms. FROST! RANDAL'S ESCAPED--!

THAT AIN'T THE HALF OF IT!

I FOUND HIS BODY UP IN THE KID'S ROOM... WITH *THIS*!

ANGELICA'S GOWN... COVERED WITH BLOOD!

WHERE *IS* SHE?!

Oh, *NO!* THE CROWD AT THE BASKET-BALL GAME IS PROVIDING TOO MUCH OF A DISTRACTION FOR ME TO LOCATE HER TELEPATHICALLY.

GO TEAM

I'M CERTAIN THAT THE MUTANT SCANNER IN MY UNDERGROUND COMPLEX CAN FIND HER.

AND, WHEN IT DOES--!

...UT, HEN...

WHAT THE--? IT LOOKS LIKE AN ARMY'S BEEN THROUGH HERE!

I CAN TELEPATHICALLY SENSE THAT MY MEN ARE ALIVE, THOUGH UNCONSCIOUS. WHO COULD HAVE--

FIRESTAR!! SHE'S NEARBY, AND ABOUT TO--

SHA-BWOOM!

93

I SEE THAT YOU'VE DROPPED YOUR CLOAKING ILLUSION, FROST!

GOOD, IT'S TIME WE STRIPPED ALL THE ILLUSIONS AWAY!

ANGELICA, HAVE YOU GONE MAD?!

OF ALL THE BLASTED LUCK! I CAN SENSE THAT SHE KNOWS-- EVERYTHING!

I'D BETTER SUBDUE HER WITH A MIND-BLAST BEFORE SHE CAN STRIKE AGAIN!

UNNE NICE TRY, FROST, BUT YOU'VE TRAINED ME A LITTLE TOO WELL!

BESIDES, I HAVE SOME TRIC OF MY OWN

--LIKE USING MY MICROWAVES TO HEAT UP THE FLOOR YOU'RE LYING ON!

MEANWHILE, AT THE HELL-FIRE CLUB...

WHERE IS EMMA? IF ANYTHING'S GONE WRONG--!

YOU LOOK LIKE YOU'VE BEEN STOOD UP, SHAW. HAVE YOU BEEN WAITING FOR SOMEONE SPECIAL?

I HAVE, SELENE... YOU!

WILL YOU PERMIT ME THE HONOR OF ESCORTING YOU TO TONIGHT'S BALL?

I LIVE TO SERVE YOU, SIRE!

AND SO YOU SHALL YOU LYING WITCH!

ELSEWHERE...

MOVE IT!

I JUST G A MENTA SUMMON FROM ME FROST! S NEEDS

WE'RE RIGHT BEHIN YOU, STEIN

LOOK! IT'S THAT FIRESTAR KID!

SHE'S GONE CRAZY!

STOP HER!!

94

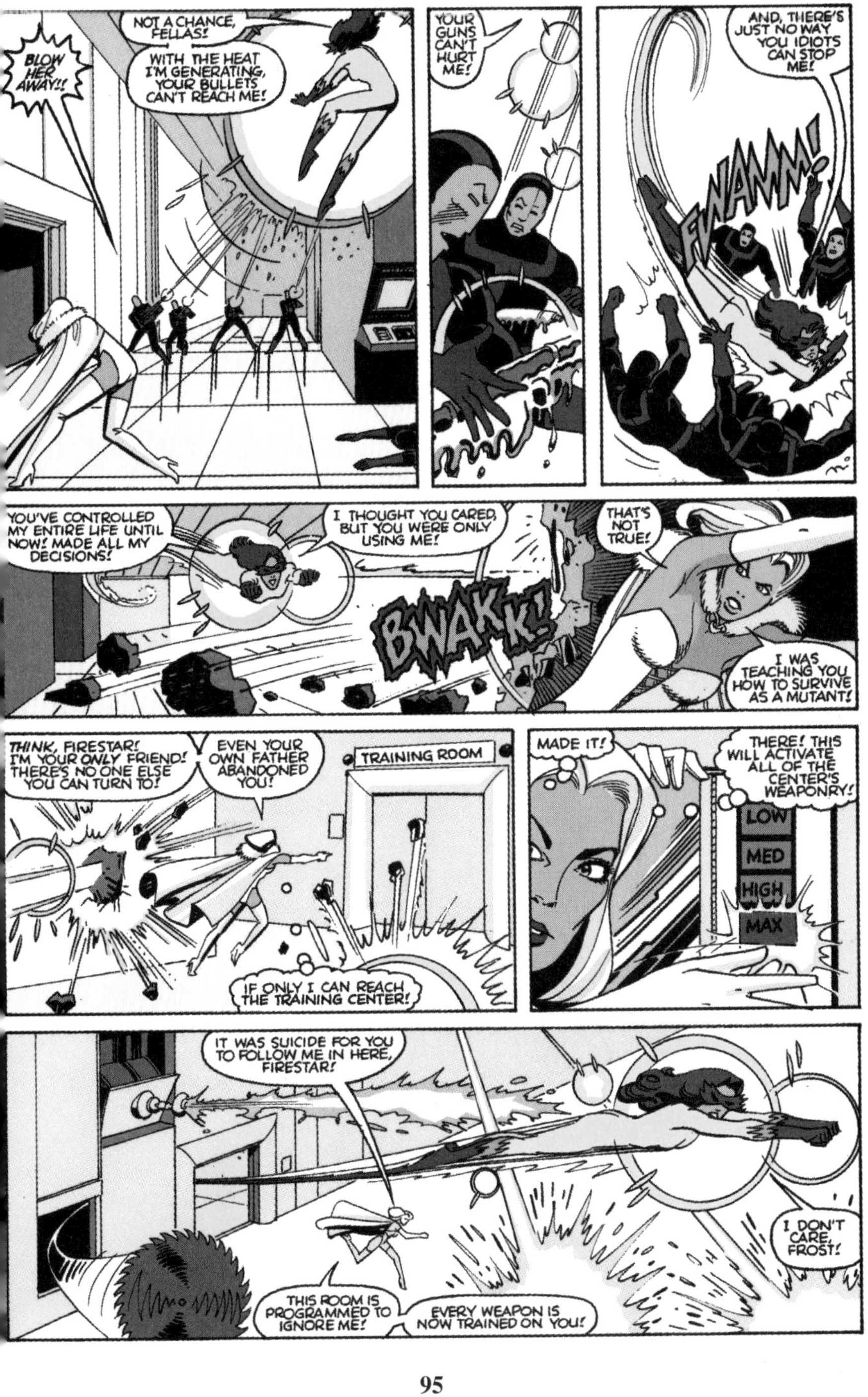
BLOW HER AWAY!!
NOT A CHANCE, FELLAS!
WITH THE HEAT I'M GENERATING, YOUR BULLETS CAN'T REACH ME!
YOUR GUNS CAN'T HURT ME!
AND, THERE'S JUST NO WAY YOU IDIOTS CAN STOP ME!
FWANM!
YOU'VE CONTROLLED MY ENTIRE LIFE UNTIL NOW! MADE ALL MY DECISIONS!
I THOUGHT YOU CARED, BUT YOU WERE ONLY USING ME!
BWAKK!
THAT'S NOT TRUE!
I WAS TEACHING YOU HOW TO SURVIVE AS A MUTANT!
THINK, FIRESTAR! I'M YOUR ONLY FRIEND! THERE'S NO ONE ELSE YOU CAN TURN TO!
EVEN YOUR OWN FATHER ABANDONED YOU!
TRAINING ROOM
IF ONLY I CAN REACH THE TRAINING CENTER!
MADE IT!
THERE! THIS WILL ACTIVATE ALL OF THE CENTER'S WEAPONRY!
LOW
MED
HIGH
MAX
IT WAS SUICIDE FOR YOU TO FOLLOW ME IN HERE, FIRESTAR!
I DON'T CARE, FROST!
THIS ROOM IS PROGRAMMED TO IGNORE ME!
EVERY WEAPON IS NOW TRAINED ON YOU!

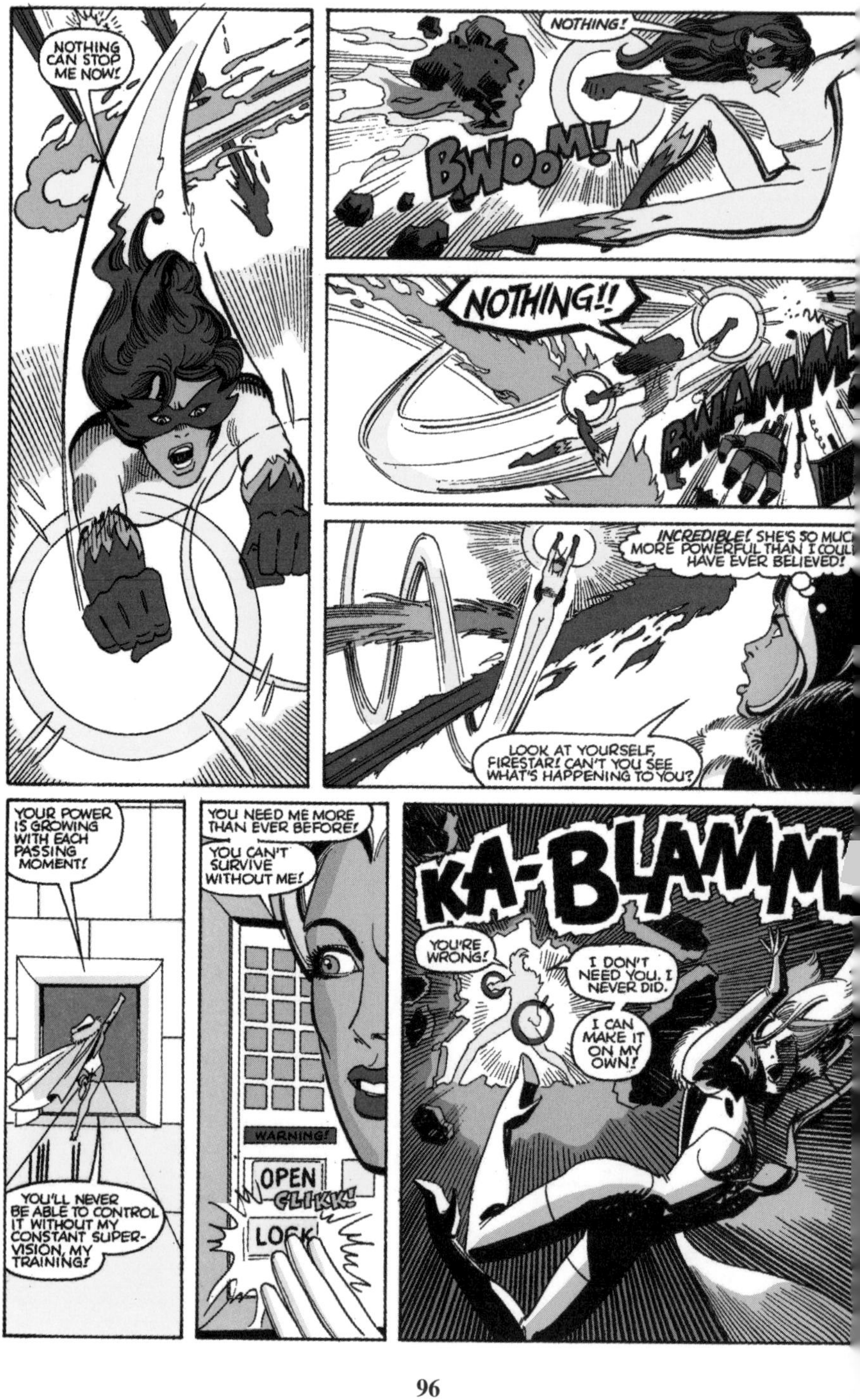
NOTHING CAN STOP ME NOW!
NOTHING!
BWOOM!
NOTHING!!
BWAMM
INCREDIBLE! SHE'S SO MUCH MORE POWERFUL THAN I COULD HAVE EVER BELIEVED!
LOOK AT YOURSELF, FIRESTAR! CAN'T YOU SEE WHAT'S HAPPENING TO YOU?
YOUR POWER IS GROWING WITH EACH PASSING MOMENT!
YOU'LL NEVER BE ABLE TO CONTROL IT WITHOUT MY CONSTANT SUPER-VISION, MY TRAINING!
YOU NEED ME MORE THAN EVER BEFORE!
YOU CAN'T SURVIVE WITHOUT ME!
WARNING!
OPEN
CLIKK!
LOCK
KA-BLAMM
YOU'RE WRONG!
I DON'T NEED YOU. I NEVER DID.
I CAN MAKE IT ON MY OWN!

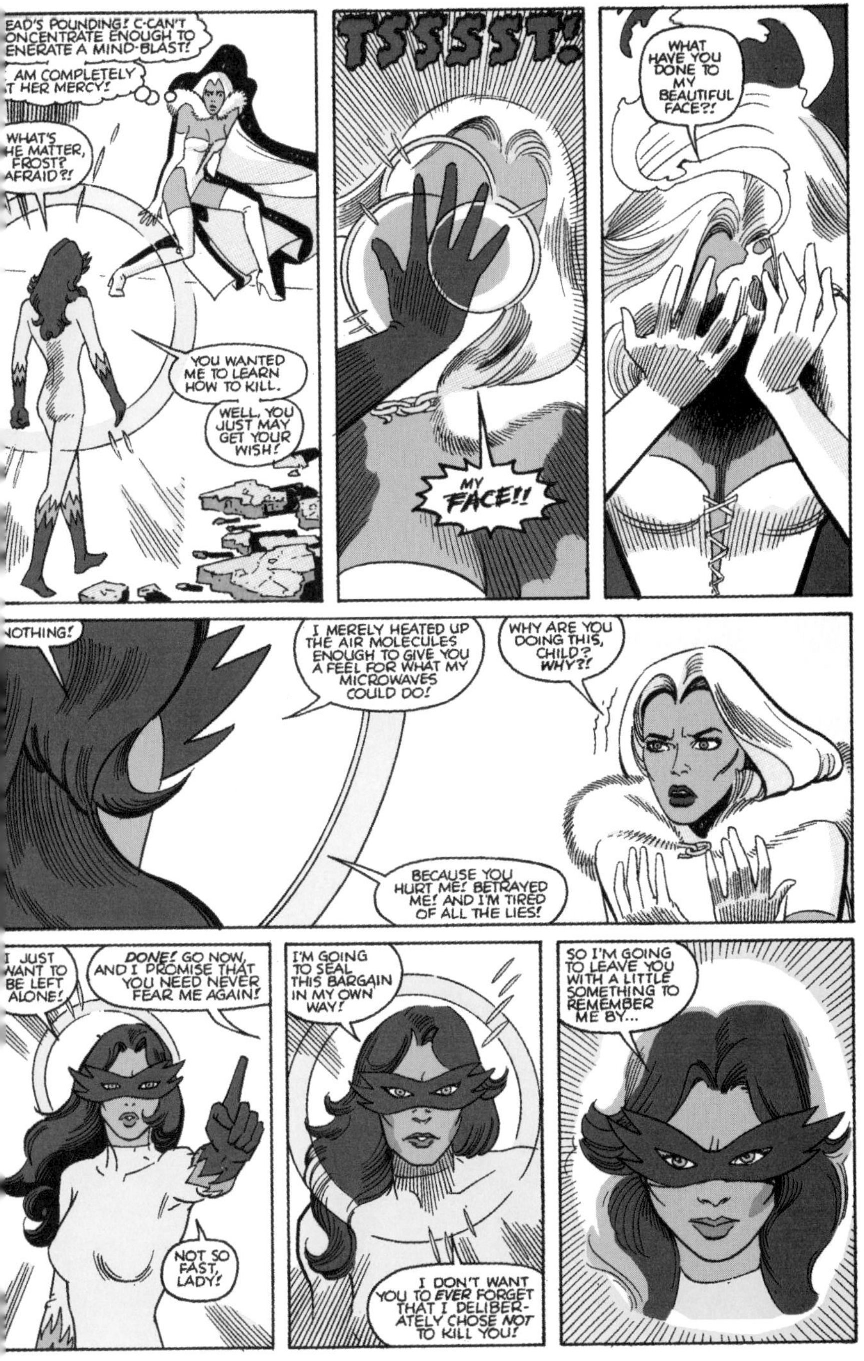
EAD'S POUNDING! C-CAN'T ONCENTRATE ENOUGH TO ENERATE A MIND-BLAST!
AM COMPLETELY T HER MERCY!
WHAT'S HE MATTER, FROST? AFRAID?!
YOU WANTED ME TO LEARN HOW TO KILL.
WELL, YOU JUST MAY GET YOUR WISH!
TSSSSST!
MY FACE!!
WHAT HAVE YOU DONE TO MY BEAUTIFUL FACE?!
NOTHING!
I MERELY HEATED UP THE AIR MOLECULES ENOUGH TO GIVE YOU A FEEL FOR WHAT MY MICROWAVES COULD DO!
WHY ARE YOU DOING THIS, CHILD? WHY?!
BECAUSE YOU HURT ME! BETRAYED ME! AND I'M TIRED OF ALL THE LIES!
I JUST WANT TO BE LEFT ALONE!
DONE! GO NOW, AND I PROMISE THAT YOU NEED NEVER FEAR ME AGAIN!
NOT SO FAST, LADY!
I'M GOING TO SEAL THIS BARGAIN IN MY OWN WAY!
I DON'T WANT YOU TO EVER FORGET THAT I DELIBER-ATELY CHOSE NOT TO KILL YOU!
SO I'M GOING TO LEAVE YOU WITH A LITTLE SOMETHING TO REMEMBER ME BY...

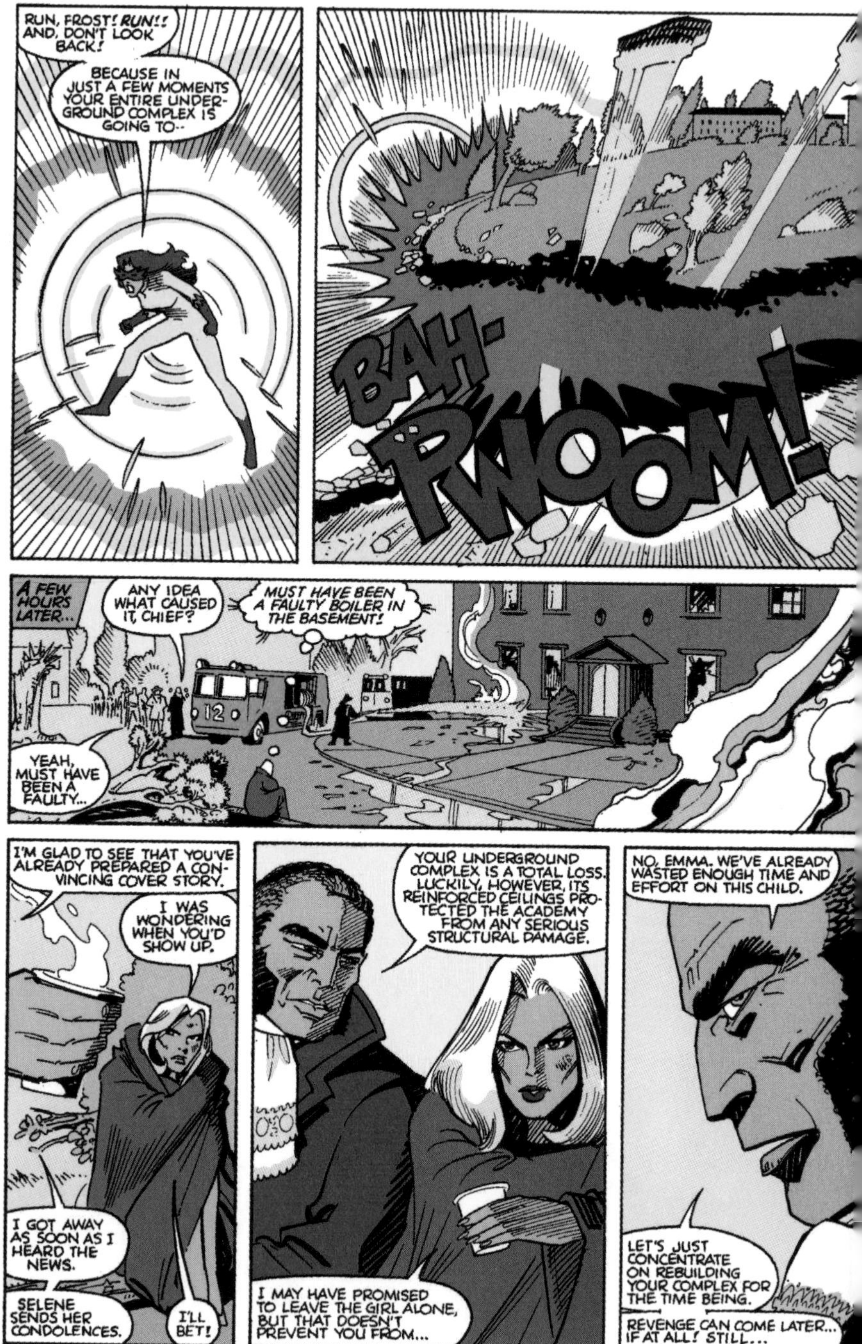
RUN, FROST! RUN!! AND, DON'T LOOK BACK!
BECAUSE IN JUST A FEW MOMENTS YOUR ENTIRE UNDERGROUND COMPLEX IS GOING TO--
BAH-RWOOM!
A FEW HOURS LATER...
ANY IDEA WHAT CAUSED IT, CHIEF?
MUST HAVE BEEN A FAULTY BOILER IN THE BASEMENT!
YEAH, MUST HAVE BEEN A FAULTY...
I'M GLAD TO SEE THAT YOU'VE ALREADY PREPARED A CONVINCING COVER STORY.
I WAS WONDERING WHEN YOU'D SHOW UP.
I GOT AWAY AS SOON AS I HEARD THE NEWS.
SELENE SENDS HER CONDOLENCES.
I'LL BET!
YOUR UNDERGROUND COMPLEX IS A TOTAL LOSS. LUCKILY, HOWEVER, ITS REINFORCED CEILINGS PROTECTED THE ACADEMY FROM ANY SERIOUS STRUCTURAL DAMAGE.
I MAY HAVE PROMISED TO LEAVE THE GIRL ALONE, BUT THAT DOESN'T PREVENT YOU FROM...
NO, EMMA. WE'VE ALREADY WASTED ENOUGH TIME AND EFFORT ON THIS CHILD.
LET'S JUST CONCENTRATE ON REBUILDING YOUR COMPLEX FOR THE TIME BEING.
REVENGE CAN COME LATER... IF AT ALL! STILL...

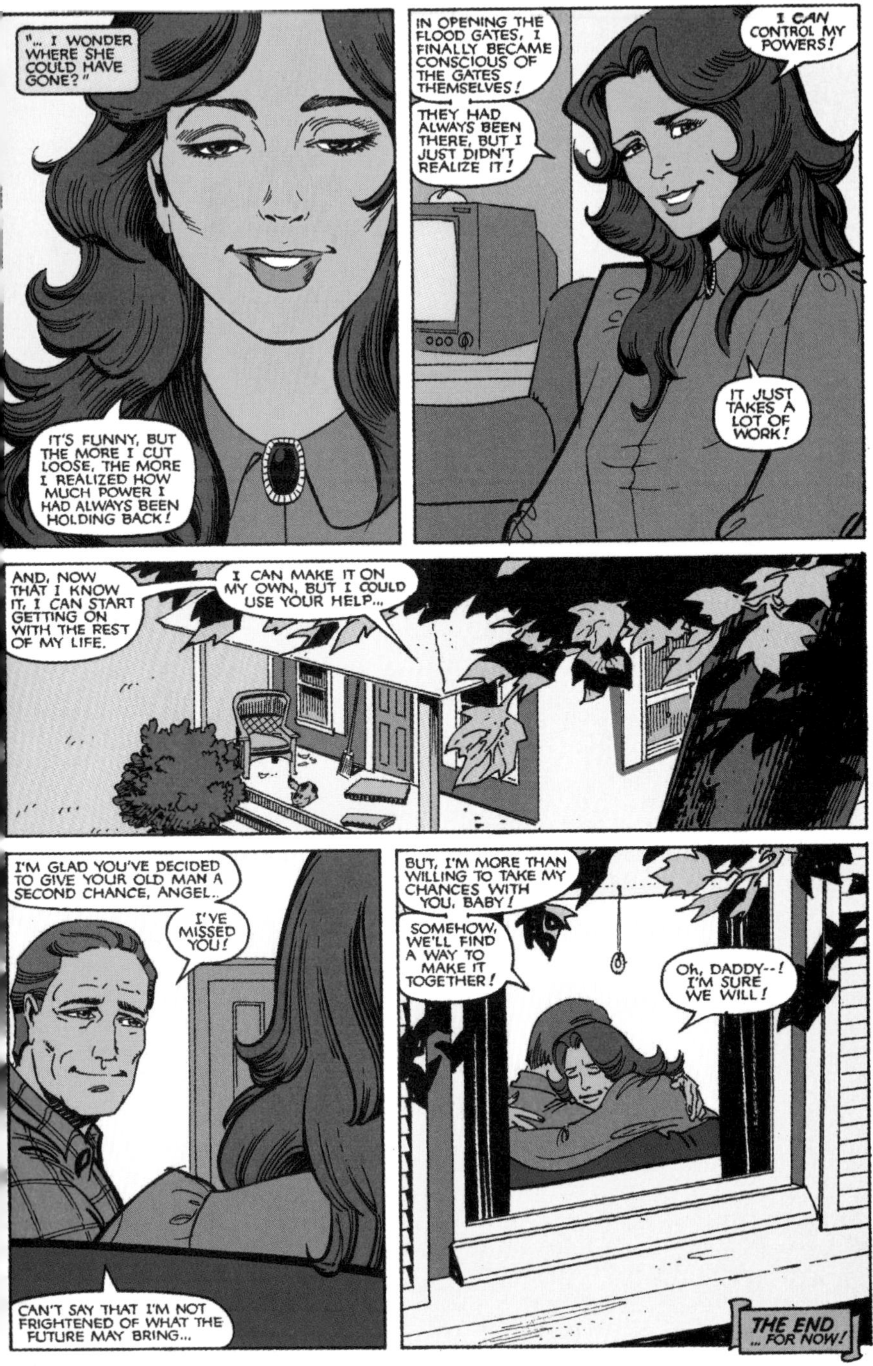
"... I WONDER WHERE SHE COULD HAVE GONE?"
IT'S FUNNY, BUT THE MORE I CUT LOOSE, THE MORE I REALIZED HOW MUCH POWER I HAD ALWAYS BEEN HOLDING BACK!
IN OPENING THE FLOOD GATES, I FINALLY BECAME CONSCIOUS OF THE GATES THEMSELVES!
THEY HAD ALWAYS BEEN THERE, BUT I JUST DIDN'T REALIZE IT!
I CAN CONTROL MY POWERS!
IT JUST TAKES A LOT OF WORK!
AND, NOW THAT I KNOW IT, I CAN START GETTING ON WITH THE REST OF MY LIFE.
I CAN MAKE IT ON MY OWN, BUT I COULD USE YOUR HELP...
I'M GLAD YOU'VE DECIDED TO GIVE YOUR OLD MAN A SECOND CHANCE, ANGEL..
I'VE MISSED YOU!
CAN'T SAY THAT I'M NOT FRIGHTENED OF WHAT THE FUTURE MAY BRING...
BUT, I'M MORE THAN WILLING TO TAKE MY CHANCES WITH YOU, BABY!
SOMEHOW, WE'LL FIND A WAY TO MAKE IT TOGETHER!
Oh, DADDY--! I'M SURE WE WILL!
THE END ... FOR NOW!

FIRESTAR

Real Name: Angelica Jones
Occupation: Student
Identity: Secret
Legal status: Citizen of the United States with no criminal record, still a minor
Place of birth: Unrevealed
Marital status: Single
Known relatives: Bartholomew (father)
Group affiliation: Student of the White Queen
Base of operations: Massachusetts Academy, Snow Valley, Massachusetts
First appearance: X-MEN #193
Origin: FIRESTAR #1–4

History: Angelica Jones was a thirteen-year-old high school student who fell victim to a series of misfortunes. She was badly treated by other girls at her school, her beloved grandmother died suddenly, and Angelica was frightened to discover that she herself was manifesting a strange superhuman power to generate great heat. With her grandmother gone, Angelica lived alone with her father, who was unable to cope with helping Angelica deal with her new power. Angelica was desperately confused, lonely, and miserable.

Angelica was in fact a mutant, and her newly emerging mutant ability caused her presence to be detected by Cerebro, a machine designed by Professor Charles Xavier, founder of the X-Men, for the purpose of locating superhumanly powerful mutants (see *Professor X, X-Men*). Cerebro functions by detecting the unusual waves of psionic energy emitted by all superhumanly powerful mutants. Angelica's presence was also registered by Mutivac, a similar machine employed by Emma Frost, the White Queen of the Inner Circle of the Hellfire Club (see *Hellfire Club, White Queen*). Xavier and the X-Men attempted to pinpoint the unknown mutant's location in order to recruit her for Xavier's school, where he trained mutants in using their powers. Meanwhile, Frost did the same, hoping to enlist the unknown mutant in her school, where she could train her to use her powers in order to serve the sinister purposes of the Inner Circle. Frost reached Angelica and her father only moments before the X-Men could. Frost, in her public role as headmistress of the Massachusetts Academy, a renowned private school, persuaded Angelica's father to send her there to receive the special help she needed.

A year later Angelica had made great progress in developing the use of her powers under the White Queen's guidance. Angelica remained an innocent, unaware of the true malevolent nature of the Hellfire Club and the White Queen. Angelica found some happiness at the Massachusetts Academy, and she was very grateful to Frost for the kindness she often showed her. Frost gave Angelica the code-name of Firestar.

Thunderbird, one of the Hellions, a team of adolescent mutants being trained by Frost, sought vengeance on Xavier and the X-Men for the death of his brother, the original Thunderbird, who had been killed in action while serving with the X-Men (see *Hellions, Deceased: Thunderbird I*). Two other Hellions, Empath and Roulette, decided to help Thunderbird against the X-Men despite his refusal of their assistance. Empath used his power to control the emotions of others to force Firestar to fall in love with him so deeply that she would do anything he asked. He thus forced her to participate in the three Hellions' attack on the X-Men, whom Frost had taught Angelica to regard as enemies, at the military base at Cheyenne Mountain, Colorado. However, the X-Men defeated Firestar, Empath, and Roulette, and Thunderbird realized he was wrong to want vengeance on Xavier and the X-Men.

Firestar, once free of Empath's control, felt despair and guilt over having helped the Hellions cause so much trouble at Cheyenne Mountain. She was pleased and touched, however, when Xavier offered to admit her into his school. She refused, though, out of loyalty to Frost, and returned to the Massachusetts Academy.

Whether Firestar stays at the Massachusetts Academy, however, remains to be seen.
Height: 5' 1"
Weight: 101 lbs.
Eyes: Green
Hair: Red

Strength level: Firestar possesses the normal human strength of a girl of her age, height, and build who engages in regular exercise.
Known superhuman powers: Firestar is a mutant who possesses the superhuman ability to project microwave energy, which she can utilize in different ways. Microwaves are comparatively short waves of electromagnetic energy. Firestar continually absorbs microwave energy from her environment, including microwave energy from the stars, and continually broadcasts it at low levels.

In order to use her microwave energy for specific purposes, Firestar must mentally concentrate, thus causing the microwaves to swirl about her body, creating a visible aura around her. In order to project the microwave energy towards a specific target, she must mentally "push" some of the energy swirling around her towards that target.

At present Firestar is still in the process of learning how to use her powers. Moreover, she is still quite young, and the strength of her powers will surely increase as she reaches adulthood. Hence, the full extent of Firestar's powers has yet to be determined.

Firestar can use her microwave energy to generate intense heat. At this point she can already melt a metal object the size of a cannon almost instantly. She has flown towards a thick wall of solid rock and melted through it so quickly that she could continue flying right through the hole she had melted without pausing.

By mentally "pushing" microwave energy behind or beneath herself for propulsion, Firestar can fly. Her maximum speed has yet to be established, but she can already fly quite swiftly and maneuver in flight quite well. She can generate enough propulsive force to carry considerable weights to great heights at high speed. For example, she has carried Colossus, in his metal-like form, which weighs 500 pounds, high into the air.

Although microwave energy can be lethal to ordinary humans, Firestar is apparently immune to its harmful effects. ∎

HELLFIRE CLUB

The Hellfire Club originated in England in the 1760s as a social organization for the elite of British society. The Club not only provided its members with pleasures, often of sorts that violated moral standards of the time, but also served as a means for the members to consolidate their influence over British economic and political matters.

A number of the Club's most important members, led by the wealthy trading company owner and former Member of Parliament Sir Patrick Clemens, and his mistress, the renowned actress Diana Knight, emigrated to the colony of New York in the 1770s, where they founded the new American Hellfire Club. Clemens and Knight served as its first leaders under their Club titles of Black King and Black Queen. The Club's headquarters was an abandoned church that stood on the site of the present day Hellfire Club mansion, located at what is now Fifth Avenue on Manhattan's East Side, only a few blocks away from the Avengers Mansion.

Today's Hellfire Club counts among its members the wealthy, the powerful, and the celebrated from virtually all over the world. Membership is by invitation only, but such invitations are rarely turned down, for membership in the Hellfire Club is universally regarded as the ultimate status symbol.

As far as the general public and, indeed, most of the Club's members are concerned, the Hellfire Club is a thoroughly respectable upper class social organization principally devoted to giving spectacular parties. It is also generally known that these parties serve as a means for members of the social, economic, and political elite to meet unofficially to discuss matters of mutual interest, and to strike political or business deals.

The Club's highest ranking members belong to its Inner Circle, who dress in late Eighteenth Century costumes for Circle meetings and other formal occasions involving the Club. Inner Circle members hold positions named after chess pieces: the leaders are King and Queens, followed by Bishops, Knights, Rooks, and Pawns. It is possible for there to be two Kings (a Black King and a White King) or two Queens (Black and White) in office simultaneously. However, such situations almost invariably lead to power struggles, and so there is usually only one King and one Queen at a time. If a member of one faction of the Inner Circle displaces a member of another faction as King or Queen, he or she usually names his rank after the opposite color to his predecessor's. Hence, when Sebastian Shaw deposed the most recent former leader, a White King, he became a Black King.

Unknown to most of the Club members, the Inner Circle members are engaged in a conspiracy to dominate the world through the accumulation of economic power and political influence. The Inner Circle commands great financial resources, highly advanced technology, and a large body of mercenaries (many of whom wear red and blue uniforms with masks), all of which they use in their subversive activities.

The previous leader of the Inner Circle, then known as the Council of the Chosen, was a White King who threw the Council's financial and technological support behind Dr. Stephen Lang's attempts to capture superhuman mutants with Sentinel robots (see *Sentinels*). Lang's endeavor ended in disaster, and Black Bishop Sebastian Shaw and White Queen Emma Frost seized the opportunity to turn the White King out of office. Shaw became the new Black King, leader of the Council, which he renamed the Inner Circle, and master of the entire Hellfire Club. As leader Shaw works closely with his ally Frost, the White Queen (see *Black King, White Queen*).

Shaw and Frost are both not only heads of major corporations but are also superhuman mutants. They have given other superhuman mutants positions of power within the Inner Circle. Moreover, Frost is also headmistress of the Massachusetts Academy, a private school in New England for which she recruits adolescent superhuman mutants as well as the sons and daughters of the elite so that she might bring them under the Inner Circle's influence. It is at the Academy that Frost trains a team of adolescent superhuman mutants known as the Hellions (see *Hellions, Massachusetts Academy*).

Shaw's corporation, Shaw Industries, has a secret contract to build Sentinels for the United States government's covert Project Wideawake, whose goal is to hunt down, capture, and study superhuman mutants (see *National Security Council*). Shaw hopes to use his position with the project for the Inner Circle's own ends. (None of the Inner Circle members are known to be mutants either by the United States government or by the general public.)

Some years ago, the mutant Jason Wyngarde, otherwise known as Mastermind, sought admission into the Inner Circle (see *Mastermind*). To prove his value, Wyngarde mesmerized the first member of the X-Men to be known as Phoenix into willingly becoming the Club's Black Queen. Although Wyngarde believed that Phoenix

BLACK KING
(Sebastian Shaw)

WHITE QUEEN
(Emma Frost)

BLACK QUEEN
(Selene)

BLACK BISHOP
(Harry Leland)

WHITE BISHOP
(Donald Pierce)

BLACK ROOK
(Friedrich von Roehm)

WHITE ROOK
(Emmanuel Da Costa)

TESSA
(Full name unrevealed)

BLACK QUEEN
(Phoenix)

MASTERMIND
(Jason Wyngarde)

was Jean Grey, also known as Marvel Girl, it now appears that Phoenix was actually an immensely powerful energy being who had taken on a human guise and persona patterned after Grey's (see *Marvel Girl, Phoenix*). Wyngarde's tampering with Phoenix's mind backfired by triggering her transformation into the satanic Dark Phoenix, who temporarily rendered him catatonic. The Inner Circle therefore withdrew its invitation to him to become a member.

Later Shaw survived an attempted challenge to his leadership of the Circle by its renegade White Bishop, Donald Pierce. Pierce kidnapped a young woman known only as Tessa, whose photographic memory has enabled her to function as a living storehouse of information about matters of importance to the Circle for Shaw. Professor Charles Xavier and the New Mutants defeated Pierce (see *New Mutants, Professor X*). Tessa returned to this day the Inner Circle, which expelled Pierce from the Club.

Still more recently Friedrich von Roehm, a member of the Inner Circle, sponsored the superhuman mutant and sorceress known as Selene for membership in the Circle. Selene has since become the Circle's Black Queen (see *Black Queen*). Hence there are now two women holding the rank of Queen within the Inner Circle.

In recent years the Hellfire Club's Inner Circle has clashed several times with the mutant X-Men, and the enmity between the two groups persists to this day (see *X-Men*).

The identities of most of the members of the Inner Circle have yet to be revealed. A number of the individuals who have been associated with the Inner Circle are described and depicted here.

First appearance: (as Council of the Chosen) X-MEN #100, (first mentioned under the name Hellfire Club) X-MEN #122, (first seen as the Hellfire Club) X-MEN #129.

BLACK KING
(Sebastian Shaw, chief executive officer, Shaw Industries)
Mutant with the power to absorb kinetic energy and convert it into physical strength.
First appeared in X-MEN #129
Status: Active, leader of Inner Circle, chairman of Hellfire Club

WHITE QUEEN
(Emma Frost, chief executive officer, Frost International, and head-mistress, Massachusetts Academy)
Mutant who possesses telepathic abilities
First appeared in X-MEN #129
Status: Active, member of Inner Circle

BLACK QUEEN
(Selene, self-styled goddess)
Mutant with telekinetic and psychic-vampiric abilities, sorceress
First appeared in NEW MUTANTS #9, joined in NEW MUTANTS #23
Status: Active, member of Inner Circle

BLACK BISHOP
(Harry Leland, corporate lawyer)
Mutant who can temporarily increase the mass of any person or object within 350 feet of him.
First appeared in X-MEN #132
Status: Active, member of Inner Circle

WHITE BISHOP
(Donald Pierce, mining magnate)
Cyborg with four artificial limbs possessing superhuman strength
First appeared in X-MEN #132
Status: Expelled from Hellfire Club

BLACK ROOK
(Friedrich von Roehm, jeweler)
First appeared in NEW MUTANTS #22
Status: Active, member of Inner Circle

WHITE ROOK
(Emmanuel Da Costa, business executive)
First appeared in MARVEL GRAPHIC NOVEL #4, joined Inner Circle in NEW MUTANTS #23
Status: Active, member of Inner Circle

TESSA
(full name unrevealed, no actual rank, assistant to Sebastian Shaw)
First appeared in X-MEN #132
Status: Employee of Inner Circle's current Black King

MASTERMIND
(Jason Wyngarde, professional criminal)
Mutant with the ability to cast illusions
First appeared in X-MEN #4
Status: Application for membership rejected

BLACK QUEEN
(Phoenix force imbued with spirit of Jean Grey, X-Man)
Extraterrestrial being taking the form of a mutant human with vast psionic powers
First appeared in X-MEN #101, became Black Queen in X-MEN #132
Status: No longer exists in form of Jean Grey

WHITE QUEEN

al name: Emma Frost

cupation: Chairperson of the Board and
ief Executive of Frost International, Chair-
son of the Board of Trustees of the Mas-
husetts Academy, Snow Valley, Mas-
chusetts.

ntity: Frost is known to be a leader of the
llfire Club, but her criminal activities are
public knowledge.

gal status: Citizen of the United States
h no criminal record

her status: None

ace of birth: Boston, Massachusetts

irital status: Single

own relatives: None

oup affiliation: The Inner Circle of the
llfire Club.

se of operations: Boston, Mas-
chusetts. Emma Frost also operates from
Massachusetts Academy, Snow Valley,
assachusetts, and the Hellfire Club man-
n in New York City. She maintains a town-
use in New York City, a home in the Berk-
re Mountains in Massachusetts (near the
assachusetts Academy), and places of re-
ence in various cities where Frost Interna-
nal has holdings, which include, besides
ston and New York City, Chicago, and
ashington, D.C.

st appearance: X-MEN #I32

igin: CLASSIC X-MEN #7

story: Emma Frost is a leading member
an old Boston mercantile family which
ived from England in the I600s. She inher-
d a good deal of wealth, but most of her
ge fortune is the result of her successes
business. She rose rapidly through the
rld of business thanks to her intelligence,
ve, personal charm, and her secret use of
r psionic abilities. She eventually became
e majority stockholder of a multi-billion dol-
multi-national conglomerate, which has
en renamed Frost International after her-
lf. Despite her youth, she is now chairper-
n of the board of Frost International and
chief executive officer. Frost International
principally involved in transportation (both
e building of ships and aircraft and their
e for freight and passenger transport) and
ectronics. Emma Frost has also become
airperson of the board of trustees of the
assachusetts Academy, a college pre-
ratory school for grades seven through
elve, located in the Berkshire Mountains
Snow Valley, Massachusetts. Frost serves
the Academy's headmistress, and
ends a great deal of her time there.

Emma Frost's beauty and talents brought
r an invitation to join the Hellfire Club, a
te social organization of the world's
ealthy and powerful figures (see *Hellfire
ub*). Frost became the ally of Sebastian
naw, who was a member of the Club's
uncil of the Chosen, which secretly con-
ires to achieve world domination through
onomic and political means (see *Black
ng*). Like Frost, Shaw was a superhuman
utant. The Leaders of the Club and Coun-
, its foremost Lords Cardinal, were the
hite King Edward Buckman and the White
ueen Paris Seville. (The Lords Cardinal
e given titles corresponding to the names
chess pieces.) Buckman threw the Coun-
's support behind Project Armageddon,
hich was scientist Steven Lang's program
build Sentinel robots and have them hunt
wn superhuman mutants (see *Sentinels*).
nowing Shaw was himself a mutant, Buck-
an told him that the Project was intended
capture superhuman mutants for use by
e council in seeking power. However,

Frost, through her psionic powers, learned that the Project was actually intended as a means of destroying all superhuman mutants. Together Shaw and Frost staged a coup that gave them control of the Council of the Chosen, which they renamed the Inner Circle. Shaw took the title of Black King and Frost became the new White Queen.

Under Shaw and Frost, the Inner Circle is now dominated by superhuman mutants. Frost has undertaken to recruit young superhuman mutants and train them in the use of their powers at her school so that might use those powers on the Inner Circle's behalf. Most of these mutant students are members of a team called the Hellions (see *Hellions*). Frost taught the young mutant Angelica Jones, alias Firestar, apart from the Hellions, but Firestar finally rebelled against Frost and left the school (see *Firestar*).

Frost first encountered the team of mutants called the X-Men when she attempted to recruit young mutant Katherine "Kitty" Pryde for her school and captured a number of X-Men (see *Shadowcat, X-Men*). Since then, Frost has crossed paths with the X-Men and their associates, the New Mutants, many times, often as their adversary (see *New Mutants*).

Height: 5' 10"
Weight: 125 lbs
Eyes: Blue
Hair: Ash blonde
Strength level: The White Queen possesses the normal human strength of a woman of her age, height, and build who engages in moderate regular exercise.
Known superhuman powers: The White Queen is a mutant with various telepathic abilities. She can read minds and project her thoughts into the minds of others. She can take psionic control of the minds of others. The White Queen can project psionic force bolts which have no physical effects but which can affect a victim's mind so as to cause the victim pain or unconsciousness. She can also induce mental pain merely by touching the brow of her victim. The White Queen can telepathically "sedate" her vic-

tims so that, if already rendered unconscious, they remain so for as long as she continues to "sedate" them. It is unknown how effective her "sedating" ability is on victims who are awake.

Abilities: The White Queen is highly skilled in electronic theory and electronics, and has learned how to build devices that can amplify psionic energy and utilize psionic energy for various effects. She devised the mechanism by which Mastermind projected his illusions directly into the mind of the Jean Gray version of Phoenix (see *Mastermind, Phoenix*).

The White Queen is an above average athlete and has had some training in hand-to-hand combat.

Weapons The White Queen has designed a gun-like device which she once used to exchange minds for a period of time with Storm of the X-Men (see *Storm*).